SCIENCE FICTION, FANTASY, AND HORROR WRITERS,

SCIENCE FICTION, FANTASY, AND HORROR WRITERS,

VOLUME 2 K-Z

Marie J. MacNee

An imprint of Gale Research Inc.,
an International Thomson Publishing Company

NEW YORK • LONDON • BONN • BOSTON • DETROIT • MADRID
MELBOURNE • MEXICO CITY • PARIS • SINGAPORE • TOKYO
TORONTO • WASHINGTON • ALBANY NY • BELMONT CA • CINCINNATI OH

Science Fiction, Fantasy, and Horror Writers
Marie J. MacNee

Staff

Kathleen L. Witman, U·X·L Assistant Developmental Editor
Carol DeKane Nagel, U·X·L Developmental Editor
Thomas L. Romig, U·X·L Publisher

Susan Brohman, *Permissions Associate (Pictures)*
Margaret A. Chamberlain, *Permissions Specialist (Pictures)*

Shanna Heilveil, *Production Assistant*
Evi Seoud, *Assistant Production Manager*
Mary Beth Trimper, *Production Director*

Mark Howell, *Art Director*
Philip A. Tan, *Cover Illustrator*
Cynthia Baldwin, *Product Design Manager*

A-R Editions Inc., *Typesetting*

Science fiction, fantasy, and horror writers / Marie J. MacNee, editor.
v. cm.
Includes bibliographical references and indexes.
Contents: v.1. A-J — v.2 K-Z.
ISBN 0-8103-9865-6 (set) : $38.00. — ISBN 0-8103-9866-4 (v. 1). —ISBN 0-8103-9867-2 (v. 2)
1. Science fiction—Bio-bibliography—Juvenile literature.
2. Fantastic fiction—Bio-bibliography—Juvenile literature.
3. Horror tales—Bio-bibliography—Juvenile literature.
4. Authors—Biography—Juvenile literature.
[1. Science fiction—Bio-bibliography. 2. Fantasy—Bio-bibliography. 3. Horror stories—Bio-bibliography.
4. Authors—Biography.] I. MacNee, Marie J.
Z5917.S36S2985 1995
[PN3448.S45]
016.813'0876208—dc20

94-32459
CIP
AC

This book is printed on acid-free paper that meets the minimum requirements of American National Standard for information Sciences—Permanence Paper for Printed Library Materials, ANSI Z39.48-1984.

Printed in the United States of America

Published simultaneously in the United Kingdom by Gale Research International Limited
(An affiliated company of Gale Research, Inc.)

I(T)P™ U·X·L is an imprint of Gale Research Inc., an International Thompson Publishing Company.
ITP logo is a trademark under license.

Advisory Board

Contents

Biographical Listings

Preface

veryone's familiar with the names of Stephen King, Mary Higgins Clark, and Isaac Asimov. But how many know how they got started in writing, who their favorite authors were, or what inspired their stories? *Science Fiction, Fantasy, and Horror Writers* provides a wealth of information on favorite authors—some of it common knowledge, some not—from the science fiction, fantasy, and horror genres. Did you know that Stephen King was always the last to be picked to play baseball in school? That Christopher Pike is a pseudonym taken from an early *Star Trek* episode? That André Norton created science fiction's first heroine? Or that William Golding's *Lord of the Flies* was rejected by 21 publishers before it was finally published?

What You'll Find Inside

In two volumes, *Science Fiction, Fantasy, and Horror Writers* contains 80 biographical entries covering the best-known, highest-praised, scariest, funniest, and most-promising author's of tales of future worlds, alternate universes, psychological spine-tinglers, and more. The authors range from Mary Wollstonecraft Shelley—whose nineteenth-century "hideous progeny," Frankenstein, is still a hot product—to contemporary award winners, celebrity authors, and even some newcomers.

The entries, listed alphabetically by author, follow an easy-to-use format:

Vital Information—the date and place of the author's birth and death.
Photos—a portait of the author and either a book jacket or movie still.
Biographical Sketch—a succinct yet comprehensive portrait of the author's life and creative work.
Best Bets—a short list, arranged chronologically, of some of the author's best works, with a brief description to help the interested reader decide what to read next.
Sources—suggested sources for further reading.

Some of the entries also include:

Reel Life—information on movie adaptations of the author's work.

Authors' and Critics' Quotes—brief quotes from literary critics about the authors or the authors' work, or notable quotable words from the authors themselves.

Science Fiction, Fantasy, and Horror Writers contains more than 150 photos including portraits of the authors, book jackets, and movie stills. An appendix lists the winners of the Hugo and Nebula awards and a handy index allows readers to look up individual titles, subjects, awards, and much more.

Whether the reader is writing a school report, is looking for ideas about what to read next, or just wants to dazzle friends with little-known facts about favorite authors, *Science Fiction, Fantasy, and Horror Writers* is chock full of interesting information.

Acknowledgments

The editor would like to thank Polly Vedder and Tom Ligotti for their assistance in selecting authors.

Comments and Suggestions

We welcome comments on this work as well as suggestions for authors to be featured in future editions of *Science Fiction, Fantasy, and Horror Writers*. Please write: Editor, *Science Fiction, Fantasy, and Horror Writers*, U•X•L, 835 Penobscot Building, Detroit, Michigan 48226-4094; call toll-free 1-800 877-4253; fax 313-961-6348.

Picture Credits

ADAMS, DOUGLAS
Jacket of *Hitchhiker's Guide to the Galaxy*, by Douglas Adams. Copyright © 1979 by Pan Books Ltd. Reprinted by permission of Pan Books Ltd./Photograph, Archive Photos/ SAGA/Frank Capri.

ADAMS, RICHARD
Photograph of Richard Adams posing with cover of *Watership Down*, AP/Wide World Photos./Photograph of Richard Adams, Archive Photos/Nordisk Pressfoto.

AIKEN, JOAN
Cover of *The Wolves of Willoughby Chase*, by Joan Aiken. Copyright © 1989 by Joan Aiken. Reprinted by permission of Doubleday, a division of Bantam Doubleday Dell Publishing Group, Inc./Photograph Jerry Bauer.

ALEXANDER, LLOYD
Jacket of *The Illyrian Adventure*, by Lloyd Alexander. Copyright © 1986 Dutton Books. Used by permission of New American Library, a division of Penguin Books USA Inc./ Photograph AP/Wide World Photos.

ANTHONY, PIERS
Jacket of *Wielding a Red Sword*, by Piers Anthony. Copyright © 1986 by Piers Anthony Jacob. Reprinted by permission of Ballantine Books, a division of Random House, Inc./ Photograph by Steve Zay.

ASIMOV, ISAAC
Cover of *Magical Wishes*, by Isaac Asimov. Copyright © 1986 by Nightfall, Inc., Martin Greenberg, and Charles G. Waugh. Reprinted by permission of New American Library, a division of Penguin Books USA Inc./Photograph, AP/Wide World Photos.

BABBITT, NATALIE
Cover of *Tuck Everlasting*, by Natalie Babbitt. Cornerstone Books, 1987. Copyright © 1975 by Natalie Babbitt. Cover illustration Jody Chapel, Cover to Cover Design. Reprinted by permission of Cover to Cover Design./Photograph by Steve Adams Photography.

BARKER, CLIVE
Photograph of Clive Barker with Books of Blood series, AP/Wide World Photos./ Photograph of Clive Barker by Geoff Shields.

BAUM, L. FRANK
Photograph, The Granger Collection.

BELLAIRS, JOHN
Cover of *The House with the Clock in its Walls*, by John Bellairs. Copyright © 1973 by John Bellairs. Reprinted by permission of Dell Books, a division of Bantam Doubleday Dell Publishing Group, Inc.

BLOCH, ROBERT
Photograph, Archive Photos/SAGA/Nancy Rica Schiff.

BRADBURY, RAY
Illustration from *The Halloween Tree*, by Ray Bradbury. Illustrated by Joseph Mugnaini. Reprinted by permission of Random House, Inc./ Photograph, Archive Photos/SAGA/ Nancy Rica Schiff.

BURROUGHS, EDGAR
Photograph, The Bettmann Archive.

BUTLER, OCTAVIA
Cover of *Kindred*, by Octavia Butler. Copyright © 1979 By Octavia E. Butler. Reprinted by permission of Beacon Press.

CAMERON, ELEANOR
Illustration from *The Wonderful Flight to the Mushroom Planet*, by Eleanor Cameron. Copyright © 1954, by Eleanor Cameron. Illustration by Robert Henneberger. Reprinted by permission of Little, Brown and Company.

CARROLL, LEWIS
Photograph, The Granger Collection.

CHRISTOPHER, JOHN
Cover of *The Sword of the Spirits*, by John Christopher. Copyright © 1972 by Macmillan Publishing Company. Illustration by Emanuel Schongut. Reprinted by permission of Macmillan Publishing Company.

CLARK, MARY HIGGINS
Cover of *The Anastasia Syndrome*, by Mary Higgins Clark. Copyright © 1989 by Mary Higgins Clark. Reprinted by permission of Pocket Books, a division of Simon & Schuster, Inc./ Photograph,Archive Photos/SAGA/Frank Capri.

CLARKE, ARTHUR C.
Movie still of *2001: A Space Odyssey*, by Movie Star News Photo, Copyright © 1968 by Metro Goldwyn Mayer Inc.

COONEY, CAROLINE
Movie still of *Rearview Mirror*, courtesy of Warner Bros.

COOPER, SUSAN
Cover of *The Grey King*, by Susan Cooper. Text copyright © 1975 by Susan Cooper. Reprinted by permission of Macmillan Publishing Company./ Photograph by Birgit Blyth, courtesy of Susan Cooper.

CRICHTON, MICHAEL
Cover of *Jurassic Park*, by Michael Crichton. Copyright © 1990 by Michael Crichton. Cover illustration by Chip Kidd. Reprinted by permission of Ballantine Books, a division of Random House, Inc./ Photograph by Joyce Ravid.

DAHL, ROALD
Movie still from *Willy Wonka and the Chocolate Factory*, copyright © Wolper Pictures Ltd. and the Quaker Oats Co./ Photograph, Archive Photos/Horst Tappe.

DICKINSON, PETER
Jacket of *The Flight of Dragons*, by Peter Dickinson. Copyright © illustrations by Wayne Anderson 1979. Reprinted by permission of HarperCollins Publishers Inc./ Photograph Jerry Bauer.

DOYLE, SIR ARTHUR CONAN
Jacket of *The Adventures of Sherlock Holmes*, by Sir Arthur Conan Doyle. Illustrations 1992 by Pennyroyal Press. Jacket illustration 1992 by Barry Moser. Reprinted by permission of William Morrow & Company, Inc./ Photograph, UPI/Bettmann.

DUNCAN, LOIS
Cover of *Stranger with My Face*, by Lois Duncan. Little Brown and Company, 1981. Copyright © 1981 by Lois Duncan. Illustration by Gary Watson. Reprinted by permission of Little Brown and Company.

ENGDAHL, SYLVIA
Illustration from *Enchantress of the Stars*, by Sylvia Louise Engdahl. Copyright © 1970 by Sylvia Louise Engdahl. Illustration by Rodney Shackell. Reprinted with the permission of Scribner, a division of Simon & Schuster Publishing Group.

GARDEN, NANCY
Illustration from *Witches*, by Nancy Garden. Copyright © 1975 by Nancy Garden. Reprinted by permission of HarperCollins Publishers, Inc./ Photograph Tim Morse 1982.

GARNER, ALAN
Cover of *Elidor*, by Alan Garner. Copyright © 1965 by Alan Garner. Cover illustration by George Barr. Reprinted by permission of HarperCollins Publishers Inc./ Photograph courtesy of William Collins & Sons Co., Ltd.

GIBSON, WILLIAM
Cover of *Mona Lisa Overdrive*, by William Gibson. Cover art copyright © 1989 by Will Cormier. Reprinted by permission of Bantam Books, a division of Bantam Doubleday Dell Publishing Group, Inc./ Photograph, Archive Photos.

GOLDING, WILLIAM
Movie still of *Lord of the Flies*, copyright © 1990 Columbia Pictures./ Photograph by AP/Wide World Photos.

HARRISON, HARRY
Cover illustration by Harry Harrison from his *The Stainless Steel Rat's Revenge*. Reprinted by permission of the author./ Photograph Jerry Bauer.

HEINLEIN, ROBERT
Jacket of *Stranger in a Strange Land*, by Robert A. Heinlein. Jacket design copyright © 1990 by One Plus One Studio. Reprinted by permission of G. P. Putnam, a division of The Putnam & Grosset Publishing Group./ Photograph, AP/Wide World Photos.

HERBERT, FRANK
Movie still from *Dune*, Copyright © 1983 by Universal City Studios, Inc./ Photograph, AP/Wide World Photos.

HOOVER, H. M.
Cover of *The Shepherd Moon: A Novel of the Future*, by H. M. Hoover. Copyright © 1984 by Viking Penguin, Inc. Jacket illustration by Derek James. Reprinted by permission of Viking Penguin, a division of Penguin Books USA Inc./ Photograph by Karen Katon.

HUGHES, MONICA
Jacket of *Beyond the Dark River*, by Monica Hughes. Atheneum, 1981. Copyright © 1979 by Monica Hughes. Jacket painting by Toni Morris. Reprinted by permission of Hamish Hamilton, Ltd./ Photograph by Russ Hughes, courtesy of Monica Hughes.

JACKSON, SHIRLEY
Cover of *We Have Always Lived in the Castle*, by Shirley Jackson. Copyright © Shirley Jackson, 1962. Cover design by Neil Stuart. Cover illustration by Jeffrey Smith. Reprinted by permission of Viking Penguin, a division of Penguin Books USA Inc.

JACQUES, BRIAN
Jacket of *Mattimeo*, by Brian Jacques. Copyright © 1990 by Brian Jacques. Reprinted by permission of Philomel Books, a division of The Putnam & Grosset Publishing Group.

JONES, DIANA WYNNE
Cover of *Charmed Life*, by Diana Wynne Jones. Alfred A. Knopf, 1989. Copyright © 1977 by Diana Wynne Jones. Cover art copyright © 1989 by Greg Winters. Reprinted by permission of Alfred A. Knopf, Inc.

JUSTER, NORTON
Movie still of *The Phantom Tollbooth*, Copyright © 1973 by Metro-Goldwyn Mayer./ Photograph by James Gipe Photography.

KING, STEPHEN
Movie still of *The Shining*, courtesy of Warner Bros.

KIPLING, RUDYARD
Movie still of *The Jungle Book*, copyright © MCMLXV Walt Disney Productions./ Photograph, Archive Photos.

KOONTZ, DEAN R.
Cover of *Lightning*, by Dean R. Koontz. Copyright © 1988 by Nkui, Inc. Reprinted by permission of Berkley Books./ Photograph, AP/Wide World Photos.

KOTZWINKLE, WILLIAM
Jacket of *Great World Circus*, by William Kotzwinkle. Illustrations copyright © 1983 by Joe Servello. Reprinted by permission of G. P. Putnam's Sons, a division of The Putnam & Grosset Publishing Group./ Photograph Joe Servello.

L'ENGLE, MADELEINE
Cover of *A Wrinkle in Time* by Madeleine L'Engle. Copyright © 1962 and renewal copyright © 1990 by Crosswicks Ltd. Illustration copyright © 1979 by Leo and Diane Dillon. Reprinted with the permission of Scribner, a division of Simon & Schuster Publishing Group.

LeGUIN, URSULA K.
Cover of *Tehanu*, by Ursula K. LeGuin. Border cover art copyright © 1991 by Ian Miller. Spot cover art copyright © 1991 by John Jude Palencar. Reprinted by permission of Bantam Books, a division of Bantam Doubleday Dell Publishing Group, Inc./ Photograph by Marian Wood Kolisch, courtesy of Ursula K. LeGuin.

LEWIS, C. S.
Jacket of *Prince Caspian*, by C. S. Lewis. Copyright © 1951 C. S. Lewis Pte. Ltd. Jacket illustration by Roger Hane. Reprinted by permission of Macmillan Publishing Company.

LOVECRAFT, H. P.
Cover of *At the Mountains of Madness*, by H. P. Lovecraft. Copyright © 1964 by August Derleth. Cover art by Michael Whelan. Reprinted by permission of Ballantine Books, a division of Random House, Inc./ Title page illustration from *Lovecraft: A Study in the Fantastic*, by Maurice Levy. ***Lovecraft ou du fantastique*** copyright © 1985 by Christian Bourgois Editeur. English translation copyright © 1988 by Wayne State University Press, Detroit, Michigan 48202. Cover design and illustration by Jason Eckhardt. Reprinted by permission of the Wayne State University Press.

MacDONALD, GEORGE
Cover of *At the Back of the North Wind*, by George MacDonald. Illustrations The Nonesuch Press Limited 1963. Cover design by Ted Bernstein. Reprinted by permission of Random House, Inc./ Photograph, The Granger Collection.

MAHY, MARGARET
Jacket of *Memory*, by Margaret Mahy. Copyright © by Margaret Mahy 1987. Jacket painting 1987 by Alan Hood. Reprinted with the permission of Margaret K. McElderry, a division of Macmillan Publishing Company.

McCAFFREY, ANNE
Jacket of *Dragonsong*, by Anne McCaffrey. Copyright © 1976 by Fred Marcellino. Reprinted by permission of Fred Marcellino./ Photograph by Edmund Ross, Dublin, courtesy of Anne McCaffrey.

McKILLIP, PATRICIA A.
Jacket of *Heir of Sea and Fire*, by Patricia A. McKillip. Jacket painting by Michael Mariano. Reprinted by permission of Scribner, a division of Simon & Schuster Publishing Group./ Photograph by Carol McKillip.

McKINLEY, ROBIN
Cover of *Beauty* by Robin McKinley. Reprinted by permission of HarperCollins Publishers, Inc./ Photograph 1985 Helen Marcus.

MOORCOCK, MICHAEL
Jacket of *The Nomad of Time*, by Michael Moorcock. Jacket painting by Fred Labitzke. Reprinted by permission of Doubleday, a division of Bantam Doubleday Dell Publishing Group, Inc.

NIXON, JOAN
Illustration from *Danger in Dinosaur Valley*, by Joan Nixon. Copyright © 1978 by Marc Simont. Illustration by Marc Simont. Reprinted by permission of the Putnam Publishing Group, Inc.

NORTON, ANDRÉ
Jacket of *Wraiths of Time*, by André Norton. Copyright © 1976 by André Norton. Illustration by Jack Gaughan. Reprinted by permission of Scribner, a division of Simon & Schuster./ Photograph copyright © by Jay Kay Klein.

ORWELL, GEORGE
Cover of *Animal Farm*, by George Orwell. Copyright, 1946, by Harcourt Brace Jovanovich, Inc. Reprinted by permission of Harcourt Brace and Company./ Photograph, AP/Wide World Photos.

PIERCE, MEREDITH ANN
Cover of *The Woman Who Loved Reindeer*, by Meredith Ann Pierce. Copyright © 1985 by Meredith Ann Pierce. Cover art by Dennis Nolan. Reprinted by permission of Tom Doherty Associates, Inc./ Photograph by Jo Ann Bell Pierce.

PIKE, CHRISTOPHER
Cover of *Remember Me*, by Christopher Pike. Copyright © 1989 by Christopher Pike. Cover art Copyright © 1989 by Brian Kotzky. Reprinted by permission of Pocket Books, a division of Simon & Schuster, Inc./ Photograph by Michael C. McFadden.

PINKWATER, DANIEL
Jacket illustration by Daniel Pinkwater from his *The Snarkout Boys & The Baconbury Horror*. Copyright © 1984 by Daniel Pinkwater. Reprinted by permission of Lothrop Lee & Shepard Books, a division of William Morrow and Company, Inc.

POE, EDGAR ALLAN
Illustration from *The Fall of the House of Usher*, by Edgar Allan Poe. Copyright, 1944, by Random House, Inc. Wood engravings by Fritz Eichenberg. Reprinted by permission of Random House, Inc./ Photograph, The Bettmann Archive.

PRATCHETT, TERRY
Jacket of *Wyrd Sisters*, by Terry Pratchett. Copyright © 1988 by Terry and Lyn Pratchett. Jacket art by Tom Kidd. Reprinted by permission of Penguin Books USA Inc./ Photograph 1990 Workman Publishing Company, Inc.

RICE, ANNE
Cover of *The Mummy*, by Anne Rice. Copyright © 1989 by Anne O'Brien Rice. Reprinted by permission of Ballantine Books, a division of Random House, Inc./ Photograph by AP/Wide World Photos.

SHELLEY, MARY
Movie still from *Bride of Frankenstein*, copyright © 1935 by Universal Pictures Corp./ Photograph, The Granger Collection.

SILVERBERG, ROBERT
Jacket of *The New Springtime*, by Robert Silverberg. Copyright © 1990 by Robert Silverberg. Jacket illustration by Michael Whelan. Jacket design by Don Puckey. Reprinted by permission of Warner Books, a division of Warner Communications Company.

SLEATOR, WILLIAM
Jacket of *The Duplicate*, by William Sleator. Copyright © 1988 by William Sleator. Reprinted by permission of New American Library, a division of Penguin Books USA Inc.

STEVENSON, ROBERT LOUIS
Jacket of *Treasure Island*, by Robert Louis Stevenson. Charles Scribner's Sons, 1911. Copyright renewed © 1939 by N. C. Wyeth. Illustration by N. C. Wyeth. Reprinted by permission of Charles Scribner's Sons, a division of Simon & Schuster, Inc./ Photograph, The Granger Collection.

STINE, R. L.
Cover of *The Betrayal*, by R. L. Stine. Reprinted by permission of Pocket Books, a division of Simon & Schuster, Inc./ Photograph courtesy of R. L. Stine.

STOKER, BRAM
Movie still from *Dracula*, copyright © 1931 by Universal Pictures Corp./ Photograph, The Granger Collection.

TOLKEIN, J. R. R.
Illustration from *The Return of the King*, by J. R. R. Tolkein. Copyright © 1978 by Michael Whelan. Reprinted by permission of of Ballantine Books, a division of Random House, Inc./ Photograph, AP/Wide World Photos.

VERNE, JULES
Illustration from *Twenty Thousand Leagues Under the Sea*, by Jules Verne. Copyright © 1992, 1950 by Rand McNally and Company. Illustration by Milo Winter. Reprinted by permission of Checkerboard Press, a Division of Macmillan, Inc./ Photograph by The Granger Collection.

VONNEGUT, KURT, JR.
Movie still from *Slaughterhouse Five*, courtesy of Universal Film./ Photograph by Archive Photos/SAGA/Frank Capri.

Stephen King

Born: September 21, 1947, Portland, Maine

Stephen King is perhaps the most commercially successful popular writer in history. His name is almost synonymous with late twentieth-century American horror, both in print and on film; at last count around 100 million copies of his works had been published worldwide. Books by King stay for months on the best-seller lists; in fact, he made the record for being the first writer to have more than two titles on the *New York Times* best-seller lists at the same time, and then he broke his own record by having more than three—and then more than four. His proven popularity led his publisher to break a record for the largest first-run edition of a book in hardcover, confident that a printing of 1.5 million copies of 1989's *The Dark Half* would sell quickly. Works by King have been adapted for film, television, and drama, recorded on video and audio, and spun off into calendars and gimmicks. He has gained the kind of celebrity status seldom achieved by writers—something beyond what most actors and even rock stars can hope for.

Photo copyright © 1987 by Thomas Victor

The author of Carrie *and* Misery *is just a regular guy who wants to scare people.*

A Regular Guy

King thinks of himself as a regular guy. Aside from the amount of money he makes, living in a Victorian mansion, and owning his own rock 'n' roll AM radio station and publishing company, he's a mainstream American, grateful for his wholesome family and in touch with everyday reality. His favorite pastimes include putting together jigsaw puzzles, bowling, and going to the

Best Bets

1976 *Carrie*
Shunned by her classmates, a teenager discovers that she has mysterious powers.

1977 *The Shining*
A young boy is forced to face his psychotic father, who happens to be the caretaker of a haunted hotel.

1983 *Christine*
An evil spirit possesses an automobile.

1983 *Pet Sematary*
A family moves into a house near an old Native American burial ground where the buried return to life somewhat altered.

1986 *It*
Seven teens battle an evil alien in a city's sewers.

1987 *Misery*
A demented fan holds a writer hostage so that he will resurrect her favorite character in a new book.

1994 *Insomnia*
A sleepy Maine town becomes a hospice for evil.

movies. The author—who used to be in a rock band—still likes to strum a few chords on his rhythm guitar; he believes, however, that he's not very good at it and tries not to bore anyone else with his playing. King is a hard worker: Every day after a long walk in the morning, he spends three hours on new material, and another three hours on rewriting or unusual writing projects.

King's roots are as ordinary as the image he tries to project of himself. He was the second son born into a blue-collar family in Portland, Maine. When King was two years old, his father, a merchant sailor, went out for a pack of cigarettes one night and never came back. The family moved around, finally resettling in Maine, where they could provide help for King's ailing grandparents out of their meager resources. Although King had friends, he was overweight and uncoordinated, and often felt like an outsider. "When I played baseball I was always the kid who got picked last," he told Mel Allen in *Yankee*. "'Ha, ha, you got King' the others would say."

The Village Vomit and the Art of Not Working

King began writing early, putting together his first story at the age of seven. At one point he discovered that his father loved horror and science fiction pulp magazines and that he had submitted stories for publication, with no luck. At the age of 12, Stephen submitted his own tales, with no success; when he was 18, however, his first story was accepted. In high school he went into publishing, producing a one-man newspaper—*The Village Vomit*—which contained satire and vicious insults aimed at his teachers. Thanks to a guidance counselor, King was offered a job writing sports news for a small local newspaper. The young author learned an important lesson from the editor of that paper: If you can write for a living you don't have to work for a living.

After high school, King and his brother—both of whom had won scholarships—attended the University of Maine. King continued to pursue

Jack Nicholson starred in the film adaptation of Stephen King's *The Shining*.

Reel Life

Carrie, 1976.

Sissy Spacek and John Travolta star in coming-of-age tale gone awry directed by Brian (*Raising Cain*) DePalma.

Cat's Eye, 1985.

Stray cat wanders through three King short stories. Stars Drew Barrymore and James Wood.

Children of the Corn, 1984.

Linda Hamilton stars in tale in which children sacrifice adults to appease malevolent demon. *Children of the Corn 2: The Final Sacrifice,* however, is not based on anything Stephen King wrote.

Christine, 1984.

John (*Halloween*) Carpenter directs cast of teens and four-wheeled vehicles.

Creepshow, 1982.

George (*Dawn of the Dead*) Romero directs Ted Danson, Hal Holbrock, and a cast of cockroaches. Author King plays dim-witted farmer.

Creepshow 2, 1987.

More Romero scare fare, this time with author King in the role of a truck driver.

Cujo, 1983.

Rabid canine dogs mother and child. Stars Dee Wallace Stone and Ed Lauter.

The Dark Half, 1991.

George Romero directs Timothy Hutton and ... Timothy Hutton in good-twin/evil-twin saga.

journalism, penning a column in the college paper. After working in a laundry and pumping gas, he eventually got a job teaching high school English; with a wife and two children, however, he felt he needed to increase his earnings. During these years he wrote fiction with little success. *Carrie,* which would be his first published novel, was actually the fifth novel he wrote. King had abandoned the story after writing only four pages of it, but his wife Tabitha retrieved the pages from the trash and encouraged him to continue. He did. A year later, in 1973, King was in the teacher's lounge at the Hampden Academy, preparing a class on American literature, when his wife called: A major publisher had accepted *Carrie* and the $2,500 advance was on its way. King's runaway success had begun and nothing has been able to stop it since.

> *I'll try to terrify you first, and if that doesn't work, I'll try to horrify you, and if I can't make it there, I'll try to gross you out. I'm not proud."*
>
> —Stephen King

Outsiders, Monsters, Parasites, and Fans

Carrie features an alienated teenager who gets revenge on her cruel and hostile peers through her powers of telekinesis (the apparent ability to move objects without contact). Although King has been criticized for his portrayals of vengeful women, *Carrie* nonetheless captures the anguish of being a teenage outsider. After *Carrie,* the author unleashed a parade of tales of terror. *Christine,* published nine years later, features a car haunted by a female spirit that takes control of a teenage boy.

In *The Shining* an alcoholic caretaker of an obscure resort motel—driven by evil spirits—tries to murder his wife and child.

The anxieties that accompany adulthood dominate *It,* in which a childhood monster kills children as a sacrifice for the sins of adults. In *Misery,* an author is imprisoned and tortured by his "number one fan"; King creates a nightmare out of the writer's anxieties while portraying the alienation people can face in becoming the object of desire. The author explores split identity in *The Dark Half:* The protagonist suffers from an alter ego in the form of an incompletely reabsorbed twin brother, living as a parasite in his brain. The rest of King's work is a patchwork of everyday fears, commonplace anxieties, and inevitable worries, worked into fast-paced, white-knuckled tales of terror.

Fear and Loathing and Popular Fiction

How does King come up with these nightmares-in-print? The process, as he describes it, is much like a real nightmare. The author begins with his own fears—and he's got plenty: elevators, closed-in places, the dark, sewers, funerals, being buried alive (an old staple of horror fiction dating back to the works of nineteenth-century author Edgar Allan Poe), cancer, heart attacks, being squashed, motorcycle crashes, choking, bugs, airplanes, and crowds are all fears to which the author has confessed in various interviews. King, who throws salt over his shoulder and avoids walking under ladders, confided to Susin Shapiro of the *New York Daily News:* "Whatever is the worst thing that could happen in a situation is what crosses my mind."

More Reel Life

Dead Zone, 1983.

David (*The Fly*) Cronenberg directs Christopher Walken as psychic accident victim.

Firestarter, 1984.

Drew Barrymore ignites special effect-laden tale also starring George C. Scott and Heather Locklear.

Graveyard Shift, 1990.

King and John Esposito-authored yarn about vampire cabdriver on the loose in the Big Apple. A.k.a. *Stephen King's Graveyard Shift.*

The Lawnmower Man, 1992.

Pierce Brosnan and Jeff Fahey star in vir-tual-reality tale based on King short story.

Maximum Overdrive, 1986.

Author King directs Emelio Estevez with the tuneful accompaniment of AC/DC. Adapted from King's "Trucks."

Misery, 1990.

Rob (*A Few Good Men*) Reiner directs Kathy Bates to 1990 Oscar ceremonies in tale of woman obsessed with writer.

Pet Sematary, 1989.

Fred Gwynne, Dale Midkiff star in tale of rejuvenated dead folk. King, by the way, had nothing to do with *Pet Sematary 2.*

Return to Salem's Lot, 1987.

Larry (*It's Alive*) Cohen directs Michael Moriarty in camp sequel to *Salem's Lot.*

Even More Reel Life

The Running Man, 1987.

Arnold Schwarzenegger jogs on the big screen with Richard Dawson and Maria Conchita Alonso.

Salem's Lot, 1979.

James Mason and David Soul star in vampire tale; also known as *Blood Thirst.*

The Shining, 1980.

Jack Nicholson plays a writer-gone-off-the-deep-end in loosely adapted King tale directed by Stanley (*2001: A Space Odyssey*) Kubrick.

Silver Bullet, 1985.

Corey Haim and Gary Busey star in adaptation of King's "Cycle of the Werewolf."

Sleepwalkers, 1992.

King wrote the screenplay for this tale of catlike vampire creatures. Look for Clive Barker—and other stars in the galaxy of horror—in cameo roles.

Stand By Me, 1986.

Rob Reiner directs River Phoenix, Corey Feldman, and Kiefer Sutherland in adaptation of King novella "The Body."

Stephen King's It, 1990.

Tommy Lee (*Halloween 3*) Wallace directs Tim Curry, Richard Thomas, and John Ritter in tale of mysterious serial child murders. King wrote screenplay based on his best-selling novel.

Tales from the Darkside: The Movie, 1990.

King shares the spotlight with Sir Arthur Conan Doyle and Michael McDowell. Stars Deborah Harry, Christian Slater, and Rae Dawn Chong.

King often creates his characters from people he knows in real life. Carrie and her mother were based on people he recalled from high school. "The Body," which was the basis of the film *Stand By Me,* is autobiographical, as is *Thinner,* a title King wrote under the pen name Richard Bachman. King writes intuitively, without rigid planning or outlines—discovering where each story will go as he writes it, as each step in a dream leads into the unknown. He virtually lives through the story as he writes, imagining something like a movie, only more vivid.

Although King devotes most of his attention to the darker side, his make-believe story-world consists of both Good and Evil. The important struggles in King's tales of terror do not arise from outside forces of evil; rather, the heroes in his stories must triumph over their own flaws and weaknesses. King counsels aspiring writers to look inward as well. Don't write for publication, he remarks in *Writer,* "Write it for yourself. It's the only way you can come out of one of the world's most grueling proj-ects still able to face rejection with equanimity [an even mind]."

Sources

Allen, Mel, "The Man Who Writes Nightmares," *Yankee,* March 1979.

Goldstein, Bill, "King of Horror: His Books Make Millions, But the Prolific Author Would Prefer to Be Recognized as Having Changed a Genre," *Publishers Weekly,* January 24, 1991, p. 6.

King, Stephen, article in *Writer,* June 1975.

Shapiro, Susin, "One Picture is Worth a Million Words," *New York Daily News,* July 13, 1986.

Marvel, Mark, interview with Stephen King, *Interview,* October 1991, p. 75.

Stroby, W. C., "Digging Up Stories with Stephen King" (interview), *Writer's Digest,* March 1992, p. 22.

Rudyard Kipling

Born: December 30, 1865, Bombay, India
Died: January 18, 1936, London, England

Rudyard Kipling, one of the best-known late Victorian poets and storytellers, was awarded the Nobel Prize for literature in 1907. However, the unpopular political views he held during his lifetime caused his works to be neglected by the public shortly after his death. But critics have continued to recognize the power of Kipling's work. "His unrelenting craftsmanship, his determination to be 'master of the bricks and mortar of his trade,' William Blackburn writes in *Writers for Children,* "and his genius as a storyteller, and especially as a teller of stories for children, will surely prove stronger than the murky and sordid vicissitudes of politics."

Kipling wrote exotic tales of adventure that are still classics more than 100 years after they were first published.

Hell and the House of Desolation

Kipling spent the first years of his life in India. In 1871, however, his parents sent him and his sister Beatrice—called "Trix"—to England, partly to avoid health problems, but also so that the children could begin their schooling. Kipling and his sister were placed with the widow of an old navy captain named Holloway at a boarding house called Lorne Lodge in Southsea, a suburb of Portsmouth. Kipling and Trix spent the better part of the next six years in that place, which they came to call the "House of Desolation."

The years from 1871 until 1877 became, for Kipling, years of misery. "I had never heard of Hell," Kipling recalls in his autobiography, "so I was

Best Bets

1894 *The Jungle Book*
The story of a boy, Mowgli, who is raised wild among the animals.

1906 *Puck of Pook's Hill*
Dan and Una learn the history of their land from the last remaining Old Thing in England.

introduced to it in all its terrors." Eventually, young Kipling suffered a sort of nervous breakdown. He did manage to have some happy times during those years, however: Kipling and his sister spent each December with his mother's sister, Lady Burne-Jones, at The Grange, a meeting-place frequented by the artistic friends of their uncle, the Pre-Raphaelite painter Sir Edward Coley Burne-Jones.

A Born-again Byron

In 1878 Kipling was sent off to school in Devon, in the west of England, where he attended the United Services College, a relatively new school aimed to educate the sons of army officers. Since his parents could not afford to send him to one of the major English universities, Kipling left the school in 1882, bound for India to rejoin his family and to begin a career as a journalist. For five years he was the assistant editor of the *Civil and Military Gazette* at Lahore. During those years he also published the stories that became *Plain Tales from the Hills,* works based on British lives in the resort town of Simla, and *Departmental Ditties,* his first major collection of poems.

In 1888 the young journalist moved south to join the Allahabad *Pioneer,* a much larger publication. At the same time, his works had begun to be published in cheap editions intended for sale in railroad terminals, and he began to earn a strong popular following with collections such as *The Phantom Rickshaw and Other Tales, The Story of the Gadsbys, Soldiers Three, Under the Deodars,* and *"Wee Willie Winkie" and Other Child Stories.* In March 1889 Kipling left India to return to England, determined to pursue his future as a writer there.

Married Life and Rikki-Tikki-Tavi

Kipling's soaring literary life in London around 1880 brought him to the attention of many people. One of them was a young American publisher named Wolcott Balestier, with whom Kipling collaborated on a novel, *The Naulahka.* The book was not a success, but Kipling benefitted in other ways from his friendship with the American: The young author married Balestier's sister, Caroline, in January 1892, and the couple settled near their family home in Brattleboro, Vermont.

A scene from Walt Disney's animated version of *The Jungle Book*.

The Kiplings lived in America for several years, in a house they built for themselves and called "Naulahka." Kipling developed a close friendship with then-undersecretary of the navy Theodore Roosevelt and often discussed politics and culture with him. Both of Kipling's daughters were born in Vermont, where the author composed *The Jungle Book*, which ranks among his best work. The jungle adventures of Mowgli, the foundling child raised by wolves in the Seeonee Hills of India, are "the cornerstones of Kipling's reputation as a children's writer," declared Blackburn, "and still among the most popular of all his works." The Mowgli stories and other, unrelated works from the collection—such as "Rikki-Tikki-Tavi" and "The White Seal"—have often been filmed and adapted for other media.

Courageous Captains and Kaleidoscopic *Kim*

The Kiplings left Vermont in 1896 after a fierce quarrel with Beatty Balestier, Kipling's surviving brother-in-law. The writer's retiring nature and

Reel Life

Since well before talkies hit the silver screen, Hollywood has had a field day with Rudyard Kipling's imaginative tales. A number of well-known adventure films— including *Captains Courageous, Wee Willie Winkie, Gunga Din, Kim,* and *The Man Who Would Be King*—are all adaptations of Kipling stories.

unwillingness to be interviewed made him unpopular with the American press, and he was savagely ridiculed when the facts of the family dispute became public. Rather than remain in America, Kipling and his wife returned to England, settling for a time in Rottingdean, Sussex, near the home of Kipling's parents. Drawing on his knowledge of New England life, the writer soon published another novel: *Captains Courageous,* the story of Harvey Cheney, a spoiled young man who is washed overboard while on his way to Europe and is rescued by fishermen. Cheney spends the summer learning about human nature and self-discipline: "After the ship has docked in Gloucester and Harvey's parents have come to take him home," explained Mary O'Toole, "his father, a self-made man, is pleased to see that his son has grown from a snobbish boy to a self-reliant young man who has learned how to make his own way through hard work and to judge people by their own merits rather than by their bank balances."

In 1899 Kipling's entire family came down with pneumonia, and his eldest daughter, Josephine, died. Devastated by the loss, Kipling sought solace in his work. In 1901 he published what many critics believe is his finest novel: *Kim,* the story of an orphaned Irish boy who grows up in the streets of Lahore, India. Educated at the expense of his father's old army regiment, Kim enters into "the Great Game," the "cold war" of espionage and counter-espionage on the borders of India between Great Britain and Russia in the late nineteenth century. "The glory of *Kim,*" O'Toole explained, "lies not in its plot nor in its characters but in its evocation of the complex Indian scene. The great diversity of the land—its castes; its sects; its geographical, linguistic, and religious divisions; its numberless superstitions; its kaleidoscopic sights, sounds, colors, and smells—are brilliantly and lovingly evoked."

In 1967 Disney studios released *The Jungle Book,* an animated version of the story of Mowgli, a young boy raised by wolves in the jungles of India, who must choose between his jungle friends and human "civilization."

Artifacts, History, and *Just So Stories*

In 1902 the Kiplings settled in their permanent home, a seventeenth-century house called "Bateman's" in Surrey. The *Just So Stories,* perhaps Kipling's best-remembered and best-loved work, resulted from his experimentation with new subjects and technique. Written for his own children and intended to be read aloud, the stories deal with the beginnings of things. The collection includes "How the Camel Got His Hump," "The Elephant's Child," "The Sing-Song of Old Man Kangaroo," "The Cat That Walked by Himself," and many others. In these works Kipling painted vivid word-pictures that honor—and at the same time parody—the language of traditional Eastern stories such as the ancient Jataka tales and the stories that comprise *The Arabian Nights*. "Kipling loved language (and children) too much to fall into the vulgar error that the resilience and beauty of the English language must be beaten into something dull and uniform to be appropriate for young readers," Blackburn declared.

*I made my own experiments in the weights, colours, perfumes, and attributes of words as read aloud so that they may hold the ear....
There is no line of my verse or prose which has not been mouthed till the tongue has made all smooth."*

—Rudyard Kipling

The area around Bateman's, rich in English history, inspired Kipling's last works for young readers, *Puck of Pook's Hill,* and its sequel, *Rewards and Fairies.* The main sources of their inspiration, Kipling explained in *Something of Myself,* came from artifacts discovered in a well they were drilling on the property: "When we stopped at twenty-five feet, we had found a Jacobean tobacco-pipe, a worn Cromwellian [seventeenth-century] latten spoon and, at the bottom of all, the bronze cheek of a Roman horse-bit." At the bottom of a drained pond, they "dredged two intact Elizabethan 'sealed quarts' ... all pearly with the patina of centuries. Its deepest mud yielded us a perfectly polished Neolithic axe-head with but one chip on its still-venomous edge." From these artifacts Kipling created a series of related stories of how Dan and Una come to meet Puck, the last remaining Old Thing in England, and from whom they learn the history of their land.

Kipling wrote many other works in addition to his classics for young readers. Actively involved in the Boer War in South Africa through his position as a war correspondent, he was assigned the post of "Honorary Literary Advisor" to the Imperial War Graves Commission in 1917—the same year that his son John, who had been missing in action for two years, was confirmed dead. In his final years, O'Toole explained, the author became even more withdrawn and bitter, losing much of his audience because of his unpopular political views—such as compulsory military service—and a "cruelty and desire for vengeance [in his writings] that his detractors detested." Modern critical opinions, O'Toole continued, "are contradictory because Kipling was a man of contradictions. He had enormous sympathy for the lower classes ... yet distrusted all forms of democratic government." The author—who declined awards offered him by his own government, yet accepted others from foreign nations—died following an intestinal hemorrhage early in 1936.

Sources

Blackburn, William, "Rudyard Kipling," *Writers for Children: Critical Studies of Major Authors since the Seventeenth Century,* edited by Jane H. Bingham, Scribners, 1988, pp. 329–336.

Cantalupo, Charles, "Rudyard Kipling," *Dictionary of Literary Biography,* Volume 19: *British Poets, 1840–1914,* Gale, 1983, pp. 247–273.

Kipling, Rudyard, *Something of Myself for My Friends Known and Unknown,* Doubleday, Doran, 1937.

O'Toole, Mary A., "Rudyard Kipling," *Dictionary of Literary Biography,* Volume 34: *British Novelists, 1890–1929: Traditionalists,* Gale, 1985, pp. 208–220.

Dean Koontz

Born: July 9, 1945, Everett, Pennsylvania

A prolific author who has produced nearly 70 books in less than 25 years, Dean Koontz regales his readers with inventive tales that blend elements of science fiction, horror, and suspense. His stories are marked by ordinary— and ultimately heroic—characters, ingenious and frightening plots, and logical, yet positive conclusions. The author's formula has proved popular with reading audiences; beginning in the mid-1980s, Koontz churned out a string of bestsellers, including *Watchers, Cold Fire, The Bad Place, Lightning,* and *Midnight*. Success has hardly slowed his frenetic writing pace.

Escape from a Violent Childhood

Koontz grew up the only child in a working-class family in Pennsylvania. Youth, however, was not a carefree time for the author. He once explained, "I began writing when I was a child, for both reading and writing provided much needed escape from the poverty in which we lived and from my father's frequent fits of alcohol-induced violence." In a *Los Angeles Times Magazine* profile by Sean Mitchell, Koontz expanded on the terrifying episodes he witnessed. "Most of my childhood memories are of him smashing furniture or carrying on one of his rages.... He was always in one sort of trouble or another. He could never hold a job. There were times when I was afraid he was going to kill us."

The Hugo Award-nominated author of Watchers *writes chilling tales about ordinary people.*

Best Bets

1987 ***Watchers***
Super-intelligent genetically altered dogs escape from the Banodyne Laboratories, threatening the human population.

1988 ***Lightning***
An orphan's mysterious "guardian angel" turns out to be a time traveler pursued by a Nazi stormtrooper.

1989 ***Midnight***
A mad scientist wants to turn the residents of a small town into a super-human race that experiences no emotions other than fear—which controls them.

1990 ***The Bad Place***
When amnesiac Frank Pollard finds himself mysteriously drenched in blood with bags of money next to his bed, he hires two detectives to help him find out what he's up to after the lights go out.

1992 ***Hideaway***
After drowning victim Hatch is revived, he senses that his recovery enabled an evil presence to return from the afterworld.

Fleeing from his unhappy home life, Koontz enrolled at Shippensburg State College. While still an undergraduate, he won an *Atlantic Monthly* fiction contest. He was more impressed, however, when he sold the same story for $50. Working several jobs after graduating from college, Koontz continued to write on the side. He sold a number of stories and several novels, but the prospect of taking the leap to be a full-time writer was daunting. Eventually, the struggling author's wife agreed to support him for five years while he concentrated solely on publishing books. Receiving relatively small advances, Koontz realized he would have to produce several novels a year in order to make a respectable living. Because he planned to experiment in various genres, he decided to write under a different name (or pseudonym) for every type of work he did, to avoid confusing his readers.

A Motley Group of Pseudonyms

Koontz published a great many books under various pseudonyms. *Chase,* written under the name K. R. Dwyer, focuses on the effects of a Vietnam veteran's war experiences. Writing under the name Owen West, Koontz produced *The Mask*—which earned a *Publishers Weekly* reviewer's praise as a "polished chiller." But Koontz's various pen names were doing nothing to further his reputation as a writer. Writing under yet another pseudonym, the author was unable to take credit for his first best-seller, *The Key to Midnight;* Koontz found it difficult to convince people that he was, in fact, best-selling author Leigh Nichols. "I began to realize that all these books that were being well-reviewed under pen names were doing absolutely nothing to build *my* name," Koontz remarked in an interview with Stanley Wiater in *Writer's Digest.* "Nobody knew those writers were me. If ... those good reviews had reflected upon me—not upon a motley group of pseudonyms—the reading public would have been aware of me far sooner."

Early in his career, Koontz wrote several science fiction works under his own name, but the thought of being categorized or limited to writing a certain type of book unnerved him. He revealed to Wiater, "When I began, I thought I'd be comfortable as a straight genre writer. I just kept switching genres as my interests grew. I've since been fortunate that—with a great deal of effort—I've been able to break the chains of genre labeling, and do larger and more complex books." In the 1980s Koontz developed a form of dark suspense, blending elements of science fiction and horror with the framework of a mainstream suspense novel. "From horror I borrowed mood more than anything—that cold sense of foreboding, eeriness, ineffable but frightening presences at the periphery of vision," he explained to Wiater. "From the suspense genre I took a contemporary setting—my books all take place in the present or past, never the far future."

Koontz also includes ingredients not often found in suspense and horror novels—such as romance, humor, and spiritualism. "There will always be a love story in my books because the most interesting way to bring out human relationships is through love," the author remarked in a *People* interview. His inclusion of spiritual elements, on the other hand, reflects his personal philosophy. "I think we're here for a purpose," Koontz explained to Mitchell. "That's why I could never write cynical books or the classic hard-boiled book where it's all despair and we all die and it's meaningless." And despite the gravity of the situations in his novels, Koontz periodically breaks the tension by slipping humor into his narratives. In a *Publishers Weekly* interview with Lisa See he reasoned, "Life is very hard and cruel, but let's try to look at it with black humor."

Whispers and *Watchers*

Publishing several books a year, Koontz perfected his craft and gained loyal readers; but he didn't enjoy widespread popularity. The author has noted that his breakthrough—in terms of sales—came in 1980 with the book *Whispers*. In this work, protagonist Hilary Thomas—who has overcome an unhappy childhood with two violent, alcoholic parents to become an Academy Award-nominated screenwriter—fatally stabs a would-be rapist. The deceased man reappears, however, and—already guilty of some twenty-odd murders—

What's in a name?

Koontz—whose novels have been translated into 16 languages—has written books under an assortment of pseudonyms, including David Axton, Deanna Dwyer, K. R. Dwyer, John Hill, Leigh Nichols, Anthony North, Richard Paige, and Owen West.

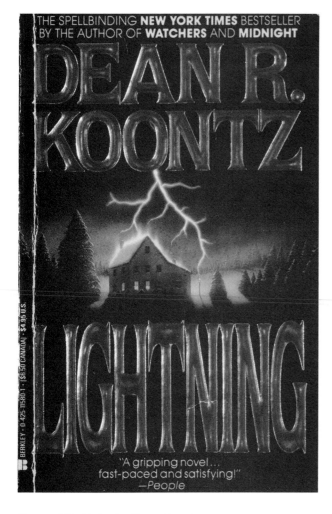

THE SPELLBINDING **NEW YORK TIMES** BESTSELLER BY THE AUTHOR OF **WATCHERS** AND **MIDNIGHT**

DEAN R. KOONTZ

LIGHTNING

"A gripping novel... fast-paced and satisfying!"
—People

BERKLEY • 0-425-11580-1 • ($6.50 CANADA) • $4.95 U.S.

Cover of *Lightning* by Dean Koontz.

believes he must off Hilary to survive. Critics considered *Whispers* an intense psychological thriller. Writing in *Library Journal*, Rex E. Klett called the work a "slick tale of horror," while *Punch* contributor Denis Pitts deemed *Whispers* a "superior crime read."

In his 1987 publication *Watchers,* Koontz outlines the frightening possibilities of misused scientific knowledge as he details a government lab experiment gone wrong. A defense project based at Banodyne Laboratories involves animals that have been genetically altered for use in war. Researchers endow a golden retriever with human intelligence to serve as a spy and produce the Outsider, a mutant (part dog and ape) fearless and ruthless killer. Their creators underestimate the beasts' intelligence, however, and the two animals escape from the lab. Federal agents, meanwhile, want to find both animals to cover up the government's role in the botched experiment. Mark Donovan, writing in *People,* stressed that *Watchers* contains "an ingenuity and depth of feeling that transcend the genre."

From One Best-seller to the Next

About Koontz's next book, *Lightning,* Michele Slung wrote in the *New York Times Book Review* that the author would "win ... new fans and please old ones." After overcoming a childhood filled with adversity, Laura Shane becomes a happily married, best-selling author. Involved in life-threatening situations at various junctures in her life, Laura has survived each trial thanks to a mysterious blond stranger who reveals himself only as her guardian. But the guardian brings trouble as well: A time traveler, he is being pursued by killers from his own era—killers who endanger Laura's life. Despite the outlandish plot twists in *Lightning, Los Angeles Times Book Review* contributor Dick Lochte deemed Koontz "particularly skilled at setting up believable characters and situations.

Koontz's 1989 best-seller, *Midnight,* again outlines the perils of misguided technology. The action takes place in the city of Moonlight Cove, where four characters join forces to combat "New People"—townsfolk who have been altered to incorporate the best aspects of machines and are able to experience only one emotion: fear. Koontz followed *Midnight* with *The Bad Place,* another best-seller published in 1990. Suffering from amnesic episodes after he apparently falls asleep, protagonist Frank Pollard awakens in the morning with physical evidence that he was doing something during the nighttime hours; for example, one morning he finds himself drenched in blood with money-filled bags next to his bed, while another day he discovers a rare insect and black sand in his possession. Hired to solve the mystery of Pollard's twilight excursions, husband-and-wife detective team Bobby and Julie Dakota eventually realize that their client is desperately trying to foil a mysterious potential murderer. Writing in the *Los Angeles Times Book Review,* Don G. Campbell deemed *The Bad Place* "as close to actual physical terror as the printed word can deliver."

Hideaway and Hope for the Future

Koontz continued to thrill his readers with 1992's *Hideaway.* In this work, Lindsey and Hatch Harrison—still trying to recover from the loss of their five-year-old son, Jimmy, to cancer four years earlier—are involved in a car accident in which Hatch dies. Eighty minutes later, however, he is revived by Jonas Nyebern, a specialist in resuscitation. Grateful for Hatch's second chance, the Harrisons work out their grief over their dead son and adopt a disabled teenager named Regina.

The Harrisons happy home life is interrupted, however, when Hatch begins to have troubling and violent dreams—dreams that revolve around an evil character named Vassago, who claims to have visited hell and returned. Vassago, on the other hand, has visions of Hatch's life, and has marked

Lindsey and Regina as murder candidates. Struggling desperately to save his loved ones, Hatch learns from Nyebern that only one other patient survived the resuscitation procedure: Vassago. The two, it seems, developed a mysterious psychic bond and their visions of each other draw them together for a final confrontation between good and evil. Critics again praised Koontz's ability to produce a gripping narrative with both a frightening plot and positive conclusion.

With a growing core of loyal readers who propel his works to the best-seller lists, Koontz continues to produce his unique brand of suspense novels. Although he focuses on frightening events, the author remains firm in his belief that life—like his books—will have a positive outcome. "I think we live in a time of marvels, not a time of disaster, and I believe we can solve every problem that confronts us if we keep our perspective and our freedom," Koontz explained. "For all its faults, I find the human species—and Western culture—to be primarily noble, honorable, and admirable. In an age when doomsayers are to be heard in every corner of the land, I find great hope in our species and in the future we will surely make for ourselves."

Sources

Adelson, Suzanne, and Andrea Chambers, article on Dean R. Koontz, *People,* April 13, 1987, p. 58.

Campbell, Don G., "Storyteller: New in February," *Los Angeles Times Book Review,* January 21, 1990, p. 12.

Donovan, Mark, review of *Midnight, People,* April 24, 1989, pp. 35–36.

Klett, Rex. E., review of *Whispers, Library Journal,* May 15, 1980, p. 1187.

Lochte, Dick, "The Perils of Little Laura," *Los Angeles Times Book Review,* January 31, 1988, p. 8.

Mitchell, Sean, "America's Least-Known Best-Selling Author," *Los Angeles Times Magazine,* January 7, 1990, pp. 17–19, 38.

Pitts, Denis, review of *Whispers, Punch,* July 15, 1981, p. 109.

Review of *Hideaway, Publishers Weekly,* November 22, 1991, p. 37.

Review of *The Mask, Publishers Weekly,* September 25, 1981, p. 86.

See, Lisa, interview with Dean R. Koontz, *Publishers Weekly,* December 18, 1987, pp. 44–45.

Slung, Michele, review of *Lightning, New York Times Book Review,* April 3, 1988, p. 14.

Wiater, Stanley, interview with Dean R. Koontz, *Writer's Digest,* November, 1989, pp. 34–38.

William Kotzwinkle

Born: November 22, 1938, Scranton, Pennsylvania

William Kotzwinkle is a versatile writer whose works include straightforward stories for children, wildly fantastic science fiction novels for adults, and novelizations of popular movies such as *E.T.: The Extra-Terrestrial* and *Superman*. His works for adults—such as the cult classic *The Fan Man* and *Fata Morgana*—are characterized by intricate plots and a startling mixture of reality and playful fantasy. But his simpler books for children enter freely into the imaginative states of younger readers. The reclusive author, who lives with his novelist wife in remote coastal Maine, does not consider himself a children's writer, but told *Publishers Weekly* interviewer Walter Gelles, "I always think I'll never do another [children's book], but something in me keeps bubbling up, the inner child who wants us to reexperience the world in a spontaneous way."

The author of the novelization of E.T.: The Extra-Terrestrial *writes books for readers of all ages that give voice to the child within.*

Peter Pan and the Gifted Bard

Born in 1938, Kotzwinkle is an only child. He told Gelles that being an only child developed his introspective outlook, and admits that he "was deeply in love with Wendy of *Peter Pan*. She was one of my early muses." Although he majored in literature at Penn State University, he spent most of his time in the theater. In fact, he attributes his discovery of an authentic writing voice to an improvisational theater class, admitting that until then he had imitated Jack Kerouac, a noted free-spirit author of the time. Inspired by Kerouac's *On the Road*—and kicked out

Best Bets

1982 ***E. T.: The Extra-Terrestrial***
An adaptation of the screenplay about a cute creature from outer space.

1983 ***Superman III***
A computer genius devises a scheme to create a computer that will control every computer in the world, and only Superman can stop him.

1985 ***E. T.: The Book of the Green Planet***
Back on his home planet, E.T. longs to return to earth to help his friend Elliott survive the trials of teenhood.

1986 ***Hearts of Wood and Other Timeless Tales***
A collection of fairy tale-like stories, including "The Fairy King," in which a logger descends into the core of a tree, lives as the king of the fairies, and then wonders if it was all a dream.

1994 ***The Game of Thirty***
An antiques dealer is murdered while playing "The Game of Thirty," a game once enjoyed by the pharaohs.

of Penn State—Kotzwinkle hitchhiked to New York City in 1957. While there he worked odd jobs, involved himself in the active Greenwich Village art scene, and wrote. One of his better known books for adults, *The Fan Man,* is rooted in these experiences.

Kotzwinkle has a rare ability to stir up strong emotions—both positive and negative—among those who comment on his works. His tendency to scramble reality and devote himself wholeheartedly to an idea (such as vegetarianism in *Doctor Rat*) either pleases or perturbs his reviewers. Thomas Lask, reviewing the short story collection *Elephant Bangs Train* in the *New York Times,* praised Kotzwinkle as "the fabulist, the gifted bard, the natural storyteller," and a *New York Times Book Review* critic said that he is "a writer with an original bent for wildly funny imagery." Others, however, have been less than amused by Kotzwinkle's work. Richard P. Brickner, writing in the *New York Times Book Review,* called *Doctor Rat* "recklessly sentimental in its argument" and "disturbingly frivolous," while Anne Larsen, in her review of the same book for *Village Voice,* claimed that "it's simply a bad book, a puffed-up book."

Kotzwinkle has had his moment in movie writing, too. Kotzwinkle's pen brought back the indomitable Freddy Krueger in *Nightmare on Elm Street Four: The Dream Master,* and in 1991, the 1950s slice-of-life *Book of Love* hit the theaters, with a script adapted by the author from his novel *Jack in the Box.*

Phoning Home

Writing the novel version of the movie *E.T.,* Kotzwinkle abandoned his idiosyncratic style, producing a book that has been well received and has sold over three million copies. Reviewing *E.T.: The Extra-Terrestrial: A Novel* for *Village Voice,* Ariel Dorfman remarked that Kotzwinkle's adaptation of Melissa Mathison's screenplay has "removed the pulsing, dancing core of the movie," giving the reader a "blueprint with which to interpret the original. By reading this book, we can come to terms with the real reasons for that film's phenomenal success." The book version of *E.T.* allows Kotzwinkle to explore the character of the cute creature from outer space—to show how he feels about the strange world and the strange people around him. The author also explores the motivations of the adults in the story, something that the movie failed to do. Kotzwinkle insisted to Gelles that the book communicates—to adults as well as to children—"a powerful archetype that is dawning for humanity, the little helper from the stars. UFO visitations represent the alien within us. The alien is a missing link for us, a missing piece of our awareness."

Kotzwinkle has already written a second book on the subject, *E.T.: The Book of the Green Planet,* based on a story by filmmaker Steven Spielberg. This book finds E.T. back on his home planet, but longing to return to earth to help his friend Elliott survive the trials of adolescence. According to Jill Grossman, who reviewed the book in the *New York Times Book Review,* the author's "strong suit here is his imagination and playfulness with language."

Cover of the *Great World Circus,* a mythical tale of adventure and romance by William Kotzwinkle.

Dry Humor and Insulated Wet Suits

Kotzwinkle has a low opinion of much of children's literature, as he explained to Gelles: "So much of this writing is condescending, permeated with an austere sense of looking down at the child, or of deliberately writing *for* the child." In such books as *Trouble in Bugland: A Collection of Inspector*

Reel Life

Usually a book precedes a movie—and leads to all sorts of interesting problems and possibilities in rendering the written word on the big screen. With *E. T.* and *Superman*, however, the book *followed* the movie—leading to a whole new set of problems and intriguing possibilities. Writing the novelization of *E. T.*, Kotzwinkle was able to probe into the endearing alien's character more than was possible on the silver screen.

Mantis Mysteries, Kotzwinkle challenges readers with Sherlock Holmes-style mysteries—mysteries set in a world inhabited solely by bugs. According to Ann Cameron, who reviewed the book in the *New York Times Book Review,* even readers who are not familiar with the famed sleuth will "appreciate the book's sly mock seriousness and flights of rhetoric and imagination."

Kotzwinkle's regimen of work and play may strike some readers as a bit eccentric. He wakes every morning at sunrise, writes until 2:00 or 3:00 P.M., swims in the Atlantic Ocean every day—even during the winter (but then he dons an insulated wetsuit). Though uncertain of what books lie ahead, Kotzwinkle told *People* magazine's Brenda Eady, "I know I'll end up a little old guy telling stories on a mountain somewhere."

Sources

Brickner, Richard P., review of *Doctor Rat, New York Times Book Review,* May 30, 1976, p. 8.

Cameron, Ann, review of *Trouble in Bugland, New York Times Book Review,* January 1, 1984, p. 23.

Dorfman, Ariel, "Norteamericanos, Call Home," *Village Voice,* August 24, 1982, pp. 39–40.

Eady, Brenda, "From Any Angle, E.T.'s Biographer William Kotzwinkle Is Not an Alien to Success," *People,* May 27, 1985.

Easterman, Daniel, review of *The Game of Thirty, New York Times Book Review,* June 19, 1994, p. 18.

Gelles, Walter, interview with Kotzwinkle, *Publishers Weekly,* November 10, 1989, pp. 46–47.

Grossman, Jill, review of *E.T.: The Book of the Green Planet, New York Times Book Review,* May 5, 1985, p. 24.

Larsen, Anne, "Did Doctor Rat Sell Out?," *Village Voice,* June 28, 1976, p. 45.

Lask, Thomas, "Of Elephants and Air Strikes," *New York Times,* April 9, 1971, p. 29.

Manuel, Diane, review of *The Hot Jazz Trio, New York Times Book Review,* February 25, 1990, p. 13.

Schumacher, Michael, "The Inner Worlds of William Kotzwinkle" (interview), *Writer's Digest,* July 1992.

Ursula K. Le Guin

Born: October 21, 1929, Berkeley, California

Critics have often found it difficult to classify Ursula Le Guin: While some consider her writing to be science fiction, the author—who has also written several volumes of poetry and essays—avoids narrow categorization. "Some of my fiction is 'science fiction,'" she has conceded, " some of it is 'fantasy,' some of it is 'realist,' [and] some of it is 'magical realism.'" Although Le Guin is best known for her fantasy fiction—particularly the acclaimed "Earthsea" books—her science fiction novels have also won her a wide following.

Tales, Myths, and a Non-religious Upbringing

Le Guin was born to Theodora, a writer, and Alfred Kroeber, a professor of anthropology at the University of California. She once remarked that their summer house was "an old, tumble-down ranch in the Napa Valley ... [and] a gathering place for scientists, writers, students, and California Indians. Even though I didn't pay much attention, I heard a lot of interesting, grown-up conversation." She grew up hearing a variety of Native American tales from her father, and she loved to read mythology; she particularly liked Norse myths.

Le Guin—who has three older brothers—feels her upbringing was totally nonsexist: Her parents expected the same level of achievement from her and her brothers. Her home was also non-religious. "There was no religious

The National Book Award-winning author of the Earthsea series writes everything from science fiction and fantasy to realistic fiction.

Best Bets

practice of any kind," she once related, "There was also no feeling that any religion was better than another or worse; they just weren't part of our life. They were something other people did." Eventually, Le Guin arrived at a strong respect for Taoism, an Eastern religion of simplicity and acceptance; a Taoist text, the *I Ching,* has influenced many of her books.

Romance Languages and a Romantic Encounter

Le Guin made her first short-story submission at the age of 12 to *Amazing Stories*—a magazine that she and one of her brothers enjoyed—but the story was rejected. "It was all right with me," she later said of her first rejection. "It was junk. At least I had a real rejection slip to show for it."

Although Le Guin always thought of herself as a writer, she decided, after earning her bachelor's degree from Radcliffe, to follow her father's advice and find a marketable career. Planning to teach, she studied Romance languages, eventually earning a master's degree from Columbia University. While pursuing a doctorate in French and Italian Renaissance literature on a Fulbright fellowship, she met Charles Le Guin; both were traveling to France on the *Queen Mary.* "We had a shipboard romance and, as the French have developed bureaucracy into a way of life, spent our first six months trying to marry," Le Guin recalled. After returning to the States, the couple moved to Atlanta, Georgia, where Le Guin wrote and worked as a secretary, while her husband taught at Emory University. She spent the next several years balancing part-time work, writing, and her family, which came to include three children: Elisabeth, Caroline, and Theodore.

Fairy Tales in Space Suits

During the 1950s, Le Guin wrote five novels—four of which were set in the imaginary country of Orsinia—but she was unable to find a publisher willing to take a risk on her unusual style. Having turned to the science fiction/fantasy genre in order to get published, Le Guin made her first sale—a time-travel fantasy—to *Fantastic Stories and Imagination* magazine. Developing a science fiction style took time, and Le Guin calls her first published novels "fairy tales in space suits." These early works, part of the Hainish cycle, branch off from a central idea: that humanity came from the planet Hain, which colonized several other planets and whose colonies were separated by a galactic war. The cycle includes *Rocannon's World, Planet of Exile, City of Illusions, The Left Hand of Darkness, The Dispossessed, The Word for World Is Forest,* and some short stories.

Le Guin's fiction is extraordinarily risky: it is full of hypotheses about morality, love, society, and ways of enriching life expressed in the symbolic language found in myth, dream, or poetry. However, the greater the risk, the greater the reward, and for the reader ... the reward is a glimpse of something glowing, something very much like truth."

—Brian Attebery, Dictionary of Literary Biography

In the late 1960s Herman Schein, the editor of Parnassus Press, asked Le Guin to write a novel for 11- to 17-year-olds. Le Guin answered Schein's request with *A Wizard of Earthsea,* a fantasy that deals with the adventures of the apprentice sorcerer Ged. Critics praised the novel both for the story and the complexity of Le Guin's created world, which consists of a chain of islands; in fact, many compared *Earthsea* to J. R. R. Tolkien's *Middle-earth* and C. S. Lewis's *Narnia.* Fellow author Eleanor Cameron wrote "To me, it is as if Ursula Le Guin herself has lived on the Archipelago, minutely observing and noting down the habits and idiosyncrasies of the culture from island to island.... Nothing has escaped the notice of her imagination's seeking eye."

Plastic Suburbs and Twilight Lands

Le Guin followed up *A Wizard of Earthsea* with *The Tombs of Atuan,* a darker novel. Tenar, Le Guin's first female character, is a young priestess who discovers Ged wandering through sacred places forbidden to anyone but the priestesses and their eunuchs. Tenar's life changes through this meeting,

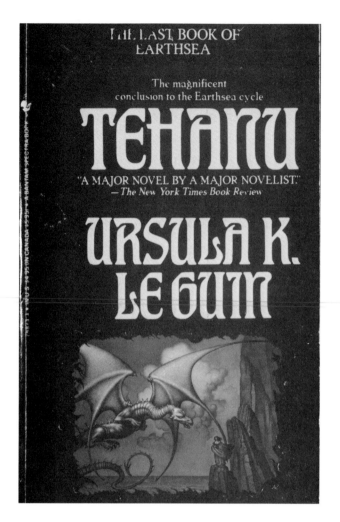

THE LAST BOOK OF EARTHSEA

The magnificent conclusion to the Earthsea cycle

TEHANU

"A MAJOR NOVEL BY A MAJOR NOVELIST."
— *The New York Times Book Review*

URSULA K. LE GUIN

Cover to *Tehanu: The Last Book of the Earthsea,* by Ursula K. Le Guin.

prompting Le Guin to call the story "a feminine coming of age." *The Farthest Shore,* for many years the last book of the series, "is about the thing you do not live through and survive," Le Guin continues. The plot concerns Ged, now a mature wizard, and his journey with a young prince to the westernmost end of the world to discover why Earthsea is losing its magic. Praised as "a novel of epic scope," *The Farthest Shore* won the National Book Award for Children's Literature.

Very Far Away from Anywhere Else, a realistic young adult novel, describes the deepening relationship between two extremely talented but lonely teenagers. Some critics, however, consider *The Beginning Place,* written a few years later, to be a more successful novel. The story of two young adults who, at different times, discover a strange world on the borders of their dull suburb, *The Beginning Place* mixes fantasy and reality. Critic Andrew Gordon believes "the achievement of the novel is its vivid, detailed realism, which brings alive both the plastic suburb and the haunting twilight land, and makes us believe in the possibility of crossing the threshold between the two."

In 1990 Le Guin published the sequel to *The Farthest Shore* as *Tehanu: The Last Book of Earthsea,* a story concerned less with the magic of wizards than with the importance of everyday life. In *Tehanu,* Tenar, now a farmer's widow, finds a little girl who has been raped by her gypsy father and his friends and left to die. Adopting the child, Tenar is eventually joined by Ged, who arrives drained of power and strength; the three form an unlikely family to battle an unexpected threat to Tenar's island home.

Adored by Critics

Critics have praised Le Guin's books for young readers—as well as her books for adults—for their variety, force, and depth. "Can one find a common denominator in the work and thought of Ursula K. Le Guin?" asks author Theodore Sturgeon in a *Los Angeles Times* article. "Probably not; but there are some notes in her orchestrations that come out repeatedly and with power. A cautionary fear of the development of democracy into dictatorship. Celebrations of courage, endurance, risk. Language, not only loved and shaped, but investigated in all its aspects; call that, perhaps, communication. But above all, in almost unearthly terms Ursula Le Guin examines, attacks, unbuttons, takes down and exposes our notions of reality."

Sources

Allen, Frank, review of *Going Out with the Peacocks and Other Poems, Library Journal,* June 1, 1994, p. 110.

Attebery, Brian, "Ursula K. Le Guin," *Dictionary of Literary Biography,* Volume 8: *Twentieth-Century American Science Fiction Writers, Part 1,* Gale, 1981, pp. 263-280.

Cameron, Eleanor, "High Fantasy: *A Wizard of Earthsea,*" *Horn Book,* April 1971, pp. 129-138.

Engel, Monroe, review of *Searoad: Chronicles of Klatsand, New York Times Book Review,* January 12, 1992, p. 10.

Kessel, John, review of *The Norton Book of Science Fiction, The Magazine of Fantasy and Science Fiction,* April 1994, p. 18.

Le Guin, Ursula K., "Recreating Reality: Making It Happen for Your Reader," *The Writer,* October 1991, p. 11.

Le Guin, Ursula K., "Talking about Writing," *The Writer,* December 1992, p. 9.

Olander, Joseph D., and Martin Harry Greenberg, *Ursula K. Le Guin,* Taplinger, 1979.

Slusser, George Edgar, *The Farthest Shores of Ursula Le Guin,* Borgo, 1976.

Madeleine L'Engle

Born: November 29, 1918, New York, New York

The Newbery Medal-winning author pits good against evil in the Time Fantasy series.

Madeleine L'Engle is a writer who resists easy classification. She has successfully published plays, poems, essays, autobiographies, and novels for both young people and adults. Best known for her Time Fantasy series—*A Wrinkle in Time, A Wind in the Door, A Swiftly Tilting Planet,* and *Many Waters*— L'Engle combines elements of science fiction and fantasy with themes of family love and moral responsibility.

An Only Child with an Active Imagination

As the daughter of a respected journalist and a gifted pianist, L'Engle was surrounded by creative people from birth. An only child, she wrote her first stories at the age of five. About her childhood, L'Engle explains in *The Summer of the Great-Grandmother*, "My mother was almost 40 when I was born.... Once she and Father had their long-awaited baby, I became a bone of contention between them. They disagreed completely on how I ought to be brought up. Father wanted a strict English childhood for me, and this is more or less what I got—nanny, governesses, supper on a tray in the nursery, dancing lessons, music lessons, skating lessons, art lessons." The product of a strict upbringing, L'Engle later wrote in her autobiographies about her fondness of solitude and of the rich fantasy life she created for herself.

When her father's failing health sent her parents to Switzerland, young Madeleine attended a series of boarding schools, where she found herself very unpopular because of her shy, introspective ways. "I learned," L'Engle recounts in *The Summer of the Great-Grandmother,* "to put on protective coloring in order to survive in an atmosphere which was alien; and I learned to concentrate. Because I was never alone ... I learned to shut out the sound of the school and listen to the story or poem I was writing when I should have been doing schoolwork. The result of this early lesson in concentration is that I can write anywhere."

L'Engle transformed these unpleasant boarding school memories into her first published novel, written shortly after she graduated from Smith College. The novel, entitled *The Small Rain,* features Katherine Forrester, a boarding-school student who, comforted by her music, becomes increasingly dedicated to her art. *The Small Rain* thus featured "one of L'Engle's predominant themes: that an artist must constantly discipline herself; otherwise her talent will become dissipated and she will never achieve her greatest potential," commented Marygail G. Parker in the *Dictionary of Literary Biography.*

*M*adeleine L'Engle is a curiously-gifted, curiously-learned, curiously-imperfect writer.... And yet I find her an extraordinarily interesting writer. She aims high, and will risk a few misses for the sake of the hits."

—John Rowe Townsend in A Sense of Story: Essays on Contemporary Writers for Children

Best Bets

1962 ***A Wrinkle in Time***
A girl travels in time to rescue her father, a scientist, from the evil forces that hold him prisoner on another planet. The first book of the Time Fantasy series; followed by *A Wind in the Door, A Swiftly Tilting Planet,* and *Many Waters.*

1989 ***An Acceptable Time***
Two students and a retired bishop travel through time to the land of druids and warriors.

Art Irritates Life

After publishing several books in the late 1940s, L'Engle postponed her career as a writer in favor of raising a family. During the 1950s, while running a general store in rural Connecticut with her husband, L'Engle continued to write stories in her spare time. Much to her disappointment, however, magazine editors were not interested in publishing her stories. She recounts in *A Circle of Quiet,* "During the long drag of years before our youngest child went to school, my love for my family and my need to write were in acute conflict. The problem was really that I put two things first. My husband and children came first. So did my writing."

Einstein, Quantum Theory, and *A Wrinkle in Time*

Shortly after her 40th birthday, L'Engle's luck shifted, and her writing began to sell again. Getting a publisher to purchase *A Wrinkle in Time,* however, proved difficult. In two years, 26 publishers rejected the novel, citing various reasons. Neither science fiction nor fantasy, the book was impossible to pigeonhole. "Most objections," L'Engle recalled in an interview with *Children's Literature in Education,* "were that it would not be able to find an audience, that it was too difficult" for young readers.

Finally, an editor at Farrar, Strauss accepted L'Engle's oft-rejected tale. "He had read my first book, *The Small Rain,* liked it, and asked if I had any other manuscripts," L'Engle recalled for *More Books by More People.* "I gave him *Wrinkle* and told him, 'Here's a book nobody likes.' He read it and two weeks later I signed the contract. The editors told me not to be disappointed if it doesn't do well and that they were publishing it because they loved it." The editors weren't alone: The public loved *A Wrinkle in Time,* which won the Newbery Medal in 1963, the Lewis Carroll Shelf Award in 1965, and was a runner-up for the Hans Christian Andersen Award in 1964.

Time Travel, ESP, and an Author Possessed

In *A Wrinkle in Time,* Meg Murry—a girl with the gift of extrasensory perception (ESP)—travels in time to rescue her father, a gifted scientist, from the evil forces that hold him prisoner on another planet. To release him, Meg must learn the power of love. Writing in *A Critical History of Children's Literature,* Ruth Hill Viguers called *A Wrinkle in Time* a "book that combines devices of fairy tales, overtones of fantasy, the philosophy of great lives, the visions of science, and the warmth of a good family story.... It is an exuberant book, original, vital, exciting. Funny ideas, fearful images, amazing characters, and beautiful concepts sweep through it. And it is full of truth." Arriving at this truth, however, involved a mysterious process: Explaining how *A Wrinkle in Time* "possessed" her, L'Engle said, "I can't possibly tell you how

I came to write it. It was simply a book I had to write. I had no choice. And it was only *after* it was written that I realized what some of it meant."

L'Engle went on to write three more books featuring the characters introduced in *A Wrinkle in Time*. In each of the books in the Time Fantasy series, she further develops the theme of love as a weapon against darkness. Although some critics claim that the series is too complicated for young readers, many have praised the series for its willingness to take risks. Writing about *A Wind in the Door, School Library Journal* contributor Margaret A. Dorsey asserted, "Complex and rich in mystical religious insights, this is breathtaking entertainment."

Cover from Madeleine L'Engle's *A Wrinkle in Time.*

Sources

Hopkins, Lee Bennett, *More Books by More People,* Citation, 1974.

Horowotz, Shel, "The Story of Truth and Fact: Madeleine L'Engle," *Writer's Digest,* April 1992, p. 6.

L'Engle, Madeleine, *A Circle of Quiet,* Farrar, Straus, 1972.

L'Engle, Madeleine, *The Summer of the Great-Grandmother,* Farrar, Straus, 1974.

Parker, Marygail G., "Madeleine L'Engle," *Dictionary of Literary Biography,* Volume 52: *American Writers for Children since 1960: Fiction,* Gale, 1986.

Rausen, Ruth, "An Interview with Madeleine L'Engle," *Children's Literature in Education,* Number 19, winter 1975.

Townsend, John Rowe, "Madeleine L'Engle," *A Sense of Story: Essays on Contemporary Writers for Children,* Lippincott, 1971, pp. 120-129.

Viguers, Ruth Hill, "Golden Years and Time of Tumult, 1920-1967: Worlds without Boundaries and Experiences to Share," *A Critical History of Children's Literature,* revised edition, edited by Cornelia Meigs, Macmillan, 1969, p. 481.

C. S. Lewis

Born: November 29, 1898, Belfast, Ireland
Died: November 22, 1963, Oxford, England

A Christian convert Lewis discovered his "imaginative self" in The Chronicles of Narnia.

As a sworn bachelor and respected lecturer in medieval and Renaissance studies at England's Oxford University, C. S. Lewis was an unlikely candidate to author one of the most popular series of books for a young audience written in the twentieth century. But as the author of The Chronicles of Narnia, Lewis became so well known as a writer for children that, in some circles, his accomplishments as literary critic, religious apologist (someone who writes in defense of a faith), poet, and science fiction novelist were nearly forgotten.

Security Lost and Paradise in a Toy Garden

Born to a solicitor (a British lawyer who prepares cases for barristers to try in court) and a clergyman's daughter, Lewis and his older brother, Warren, came from a well-educated and prosperous family. Although their mother's serene temperament balanced their father's moody disposition, the family's happiness was relatively short-lived: Lewis's mother contracted cancer when he was nine years old and slowly died at home. In *Surprised by Joy: The Shape of My Early Life,* Lewis wrote, "With my mother's death all settled happiness, all that was tranquil and reliable, disappeared from my life. There was to be much fun, many pleasures, many stabs of Joy; but no more of the old security."

Lewis believed that what he called "Joy" played an important role in the development of his imagination. In later life, the author recalled that a toy garden his brother had built on the top of a biscuit tin prompted his first experience of "joy." "It made me aware of nature," he wrote in *Surprised by Joy*, "not, indeed, as a storehouse of forms and colors but as something cool, dewy, fresh, exuberant.... As long as I live my imagination of Paradise will retain something of my brother's toy garden." When Lewis was six, his father moved his family to the "new house," a larger home in the country. It was here that Lewis first remembered the toy garden.

Best Bets

1950 ***The Lion, the Witch, and the Wardrobe***
The noble lion Aslan fights the forces of evil to save the people of Narnia. The first book of The Chronicles of Narnia; followed by *Prince Caspian: The Return to Narnia*, *The Voyage of the "Dawn Treader," The Silver Chair, The Horse and His Boy, The Magician's Nephew*, and *The Last Battle*.

Boarding School

After his mother's death, Lewis and Warren drifted from their father, who had become emotionally distant. Sent to boarding school—as was common among middle- and upper-class children of the early twentieth century— Lewis suffered through unpleasant times, so much so, in fact, that he abandoned his childhood belief in God. After his first teacher (who regularly beat his students) lost his school due to his cruelty and poor financial practices, Lewis was moved to another school. Lewis disliked this school as well, and his father hired a former school headmaster, W. T. Kirkpatrick, to prepare the boy for college. With Kirkpatrick—whom Lewis called "Kirk"—he lived a "perfect" life, focusing on studying and writing, interrupted only by meals and daily walks.

He aroused warm affection, loyalty, and devotion in his friends, and feelings of almost equal strength among innumerable persons who knew him only through his books. But he also aroused strong antipathy, disapproval, and distaste among some of his colleagues and pupils, and among some readers. It was impossible to be indifferent to him."

—*Helen Gardner, quoted by Eugene McGovern in* Dictionary of Literary Biography

Lewis first saw Oxford University in 1916, when he arrived as a scholarship candidate; he was delighted with the place. Writing to his father, as

Cover of *Prince Caspian,* Book 2 in The Chronicles of Narnia series by C. S. Lewis.

recorded in *Letters of C. S. Lewis,* he beamed, "This place has surpassed my wildest dreams; I never saw anything so beautiful, especially on these frosty nights." World War I, however, interrupted Lewis's studies. After having been stationed in France, he was wounded and returned to England to recuperate. There Lewis resumed his studies, convinced that teaching was the only profession that suited him. In 1925, elected to a five-year teaching fellowship at Oxford's Magdalen College, Lewis was asked to teach philosophy as well as English. A letter he wrote at the time—also collected in *Letters of C. S. Lewis*—expresses his eagerness: "I need hardly say," he tells his father, "that I would have coached a troupe of performing bagbirds in the quadrangle."

A Cure for Spiritual Illness

Although he had previously published books of poetry, Lewis's first truly successful work was a study on medieval love poems. Begun in 1928, *The Allegory of Love* was finally published in 1936, to much critical and scholarly acclaim. Also during these years, Lewis began to form relationships that would affect the rest of his life. One of the most puzzling of these was his tie to Mrs. Moore, the mother of a companion who had died during World War I. Although the two seemed incompatible, Lewis lived as a kind of son to Mrs. Moore until her death in 1951, often shouldering many of the household chores despite his many other responsibilities.

Nineteen thirty-one brought an important milestone in Lewis's life: The author—who had lost his religion as a child—converted to Christianity. In the preface to *Letters of C. S. Lewis,* his brother, Warren, wrote that "this seemed to me no sudden plunge into a new life, but rather a slow steady convalescence from a deep-seated spiritual illness of long standing—an illness that had its origins in our childhood, in the dry husks of religion offered by the semi-political church-going of Ulster, in the similar dull emptiness of compulsory church during our schooldays."

Friends, Inklings, and Spiritual Leanings

Reel Life

The Chronicles of Narnia, 1989.

BBC production about four brave young souls who battle evil in a mythical land where the animals talk and strange creatures roam the countryside. In three volumes: *The Lion, the Witch, and the Wardrobe, Prince Caspian and the Voyage of the "Dawn Treader,"* and *The Silver Chair.* Aired on PBS as part of the Wonderworks family movie series.

Lewis forged many strong friendships in the 1930s and 1940s with other Christians; among his circle of friends were J. R. R. Tolkien, metaphysical writer Charles Williams, and others who formed a group called the Inklings. In the group, members and visitors read from their writings—which were then vigorously praised or criticized. Among the works read at these meetings was Tolkien's *The Lord of the Rings*. Lewis described the Inklings in a letter collected in *Letters of C. S. Lewis*: "We meet on Friday evenings in my rooms, theoretically to talk about literature, but in fact nearly always to talk about something better. What I owe to them all is incalculable. Dyson and Tolkien were the immediate human causes of my conversion."

In 1939 England entered World War II. During the war—while Lewis and his brother took in some London children to shelter them from the bombings—the author composed *The Screwtape Letters,* a series of notes from a senior devil to a junior tempter. A popular hit, the book was Lewis's first "Christian" success. Also during that time, Lewis became known for his radio broadcasts aimed at explaining theology to laymen.

The Imaginative Self and a Significant Other

During the 1950s, Lewis embarked on The Chronicles of Narnia, stories of a fairy-tale land and the eight children who visit it. The author believed that his "imaginative self" inspired the series, which represented his personality more than did his work in either apologetics or criticism. In 1953 Lewis met Joy Davidman—a woman with whom he had corresponded—who had become a

Christian through his influence. The pair became good friends and fell in love, but in 1956 Joy discovered she had cancer. Although doctors gave her only a few weeks to live, the two married. As it turned out, Joy lived for four years, during which time the couple enjoyed a happy union. Lewis did not live long after her death, dying one week before his 64th birthday—the same day that Aldous Huxley and John F. Kennedy died.

Sources

Dictionary of Literary Biography, Gale, Volume 15: *British Novelists, 1930-1959,* 1983, Volume 100: *Modern British Essayists, Second Series,* 1990.

Lewis, C. S., *Surprised by Joy: The Shape of My Early Life,* Bles, 1955, pp. 3-21.

Lewis, W. H., editor, *Letters of C. S. Lewis,* Harcourt 1966, pp. 1-26, 32-33, 101-102, 196-198.

Wilson, A. N., *C. S. Lewis: A Biography,* Norton, 1990.

H. P. Lovecraft

Born: August 20, 1890, Providence, Rhode Island
Died: March 15, 1937, Providence, Rhode Island

H. P. Lovecraft is widely considered the twentieth century's most important writer of supernatural horror fiction. Forging a unique niche within the horror genre, he created what have become known as "weird tales," stories containing a distinctive blend of dreamlike imagery, Gothic terror, and elaborate mythology. During his lifetime Lovecraft's work appeared almost exclusively in pulp magazines; only since his death in 1937 has it received a wide readership and critical analysis. While many criticize his writings for being wordy and melodramatic, others praise his precise narrative skills and unique ability to unsettle his readers.

A Victorian Childhood and Gothic Fiction

Born in 1890 in Providence, Rhode Island, Lovecraft grew up in the affluent and intellectual surroundings of his grandfather's Victorian mansion. Sickly as a child and only able to attend school sporadically, he became an avid reader of

The so-called "Master of the Macabre" is sometimes compared to Edgar Allan Poe.

eighteenth-century history and Gothic horror stories. Fascinated by science, he began to write about it at an early age. After his grandfather died in 1904, Lovecraft moved with his mother from the family mansion to a nearby duplex—his father, a virtual stranger to the boy, had died some years earlier after spending the last years of his life in a sanatorium. Lovecraft later related that, having been raised by a sensitive and overprotective mother, he grew up in relative isolation, believing that he was unlike other people. Chronic ill-

Best Bets

ness as a teenager prevented Lovecraft from finishing high school or attending college. He continued to educate himself, however, and supported himself by working as a ghostwriter and revisionist—work that he disliked, but depended on throughout his life. An admirer of Edgar Allan Poe, Lovecraft began to write horror tales; he didn't consider these stories to be important, however, so he devoted himself to amateur journalism and contributed nonfiction and poetry to magazines.

In 1914 Lovecraft joined the United Amateur Press Association, a group of nonprofessional writers who produced a variety of publications and exchanged letters, and one year later he began publishing his own magazine, *The Conservative*. The numerous letters and essays he wrote during this time focus on his deep respect for scientific truth, his love of the past, and his disdain for the present-day world. Lovecraft, Darrell Schweitzer wrote in *The Dream Quest of H. P. Lovecraft,* developed the belief that "only by clinging to tradition could we make life worth living amidst the chaos of modern civilization."

Weird Tales and Spooky Stories

Lovecraft resumed writing fiction in 1917 and, encouraged by friends, began submitting stories to *Weird Tales*—a pulp magazine that would print the majority of Lovecraft's writings published during the author's lifetime. Such stories as "Dagon," "The White Ship," "The Silver Key," "The Doom That Came to Sarnath," and "The Cats of Ulthar" stem from fairy-tale tradition, exhibiting rich dreamlike descriptions and imaginary settings. Lovecraft's early cycle culminated in a short novel called *The Dream Quest of Unknown Kadath*. The story of protagonist Randolph Carter's search for a magnificent city he once envisioned, *The Dream Quest of Unknown Kadath* depicts Carter's voyage into the world of his dreams, where incredible landscapes and fantastic creatures exist. "Few more magical novels of dream-fantasy exist than this phantasmagoric adventure," Lin Carter declared in his introduction to Ballantine's edition of the work.

Contrasting with Lovecraft's stories of fantasy are his tales of horror, remarkable for their bizarre supernatural conceptions rooted in the realism of a New England setting. Lovecraft was captivated by what he considered the ideal beauty of the area's unspoiled landscape and traditional colonial architecture; he was also intrigued by what he considered to be New England's darker dimension. "The Unnameable" and "The Picture in the House," for example, depict corruption and superstition that persist in secluded New England areas; "The Festival" portrays unearthly rituals that are practiced in the picturesque town of Kingsport—a village Lovecraft modeled after Marblehead, Massachusetts; and "Pickman's Model" focuses on a group of ghouls inhabiting the Boston that Lovecraft knew. Similar to these stories is the novel *The Case of Charles Dexter Ward,* in which the title character uses magic to bring back to life a seventeenth-century ancestor named Curwen. Once a practitioner of the black arts in Salem, the resurrected Curwen is determined to inflict evil on modern Massachusetts; he consequently takes over the identity of Ward, who is later saved by the family doctor.

Lovecraft's admirers point to several elements in his writing that distinguish him as a master of supernatural horror. Foremost is his ability to arouse terror by creating an unseen and unearthly presence. In fact, the author once explained in his lengthy essay *Supernatural Horror in Literature* that in order for fiction to instill fear "a certain atmosphere of breathless and unexpected dread of outer, unknown forces must be present."

Black Magic and "Cosmic Indifferentism"

Lovecraft's best-known stories came later, and centered on the Cthulhu Mythos—a term critics use to describe the distinctive universe of landscape, legends, and mythology that the author invented. Like his earlier tales, the Cthulhu Mythos works are inspired by New England locales. But their settings are reworked to form Arkham, Innsmouth, and Dunwich, fictional worlds overseen by gods like Cthulhu and Yog-Sothoth. These stories, August Derleth quoted Lovecraft as saying, "are based on the fundamental lore or legend that

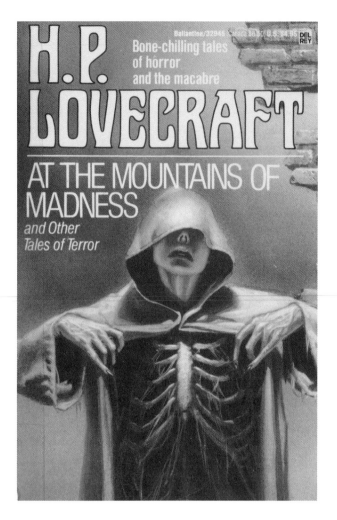

Cover of H. P. Lovecraft's *At the Mountains of Madness and Other Tales of Terror.*

this world was inhabited at one time by another race who, in practicing black magic, lost their foothold and were expelled, yet live on outside, ever ready to take possession of this earth again." Tales governed by this principle include "The Nameless City," "The Call of the Cthulhu," "The Whisperer in the Darkness," and "At the Mountains of Madness."

In addition to writing weird tales, Lovecraft wrote many letters and continued to generate a number of essays. Through these nonfiction outlets, he expounded on the aesthetics of supernatural horror fiction and on such philosophies as "mechanistic materialism" and "cosmic indifferentism"—the idea that the universe is a purposeless mechanism in which humankind is largely insignificant. Lovecraft also produced a relatively large body of poetry, mostly imitating eighteenth-century masters. Though he wrote prolifically, only one book, *The Shadow over Innsmouth,* was published during his lifetime. When Lovecraft died of intestinal cancer at the age of 46, the bulk of his writings remained either scattered in magazines or unpublished.

A Painter of Moods and Mind-Pictures

Later, Lovecraft's friends—and fellow writers August Derleth and Donald Wandrei—brought his writings to a wider readership. Establishing the publishing house of Arkham expressly to bring Lovecraft's work into book form, Derleth and Wandrei edited such early collections as *The Outsiders and Others* in 1939 and *Beyond the Wall of Sleep* in 1943; in later decades, Arkham and other publishers produced numerous volumes of the horror writer's work.

Critics, however, have not all been kind to the dean of cosmic indifferentism. While Dirk Mosig wrote in *Whispers* that "the Lovecraft oeuvre [body of work] can be regarded as a significant contribution to world literature," author Larry McMurtry commented in the *Washington Post* that Lovecraft is "a totally untalented and unreadable writer." Even more scornful was science fiction writer Ursula Le Guin, who announced in the *Times Literary Supplement* that "Lovecraft was an exceptionally, almost impeccably, bad writer.... Derivative, inept, and callow, his tales can satisfy only those who believe that a capital letter, some words, and a full stop make a sentence."

Lovecraft did not pretend to possess great writing talent. "No one is more acutely conscious than I of the inadequacy of my work.... I am a self-confessed amateur and bungler, and have not much hope of improvement," the author confessed in "The Defense Reopens!," an article later collected in S. T. Joshi's *In Defense of Dagon*. He did, however, consider himself a serious artist, practitioner, and theorist. Lovecraft "demanded that the fantastic tale be treated as art, not just a frivolous parlor game or an easy way to make a buck," wrote Schweitzer. "The imaginative writer," Lovecraft explained in "The Defense Reopens!, "devotes himself to art in its most essential sense.... He is the painter of moods and mind-pictures—a capturer and amplifier of elusive dreams and fancies—a voyager into those unheard-of lands which are glimpsed through the veil of actuality but rarely, and only by the most sensitive.... Most persons do not understand what he says, and most of those who do understand object because his statements and pictures are not always pleasant and sometimes quite impossible. But he exists not for praise, nor thinks of his readers. His only [goal is] to paint the scenes that pass before his eyes."

Sources

Burleson, Donald, *H. P. Lovecraft: A Critical Study,* Greenwood Press, 1983.

Carter, Lin, *Lovecraft: A Look Behind the "Cthulhu Mythos,"* Ballantine, 1972.

Caywood, Carolyn, "The Book Whose Reputation Preceded It," *School Library Journal,* November 1993, p. 48.

Derleth, August, *H. P. L.: A Memoir,* Ben Abramson, 1945.

Joshi, S. T., editor, *In Defense of Dagon,* Necronomicon, 1985.

Lovecraft Studies, spring 1986.

Schweitzer, Darrell, editor, *Discovering H. P. Lovecraft,* Starmont House, 1987.

Steinberg, Sybil, review of *Tales of the Cthulhu Mythos, Publishers Weekly,* January 5, 1990, p. 66.

Times Literary Supplement, March 26, 1976.

Washington Post, February 17, 1975; October 25, 1985.

Whispers, December 1976.

George MacDonald

Born: December 10, 1824, Huntly, Aberdeenshire, Scotland
Died: September 18, 1905, Ashstead, Surrey, England

A pastor-writer whose fairy tales speak to the child within.

George MacDonald was one of the founding fathers of modern fantasy. Although he wrote many different kinds of books—including realistic novels, poetry, sermons, and literary criticism—his imaginative fairy tales of growth and redemption were his most influential. Critics believe that MacDonald's works, which successfully mingled the real and the fantastic, inspired prominent literary figures such as T. S. Eliot, C. S. Lewis, and J. R. R. Tolkien.

A Preacher Without a Pulpit

Born in northern Scotland, MacDonald drew on his own background in his writings. Having grown up in a rural, hilly area near a ruined castle and a large manor house, he filled his fairy tales with castles and landscapes. After losing his mother when he was a child, young MacDonald was influenced by his loving grandmother, who later became the model for wise women who inhabited the author's stories. MacDonald's reading also inspired his writings. Reviewers have noted that he was profoundly influenced by the German and English romantic writers whose works he read during his college years. MacDonald's Christian faith also played a major role in his writings. As a Congregational pastor during the early 1850s, he gave sermons "bereft of doctrine and promising salvation to heathens and even animals"; this, Marjory Lang explained in the *Dictionary of Literary Biography,* alarmed his conser-vative parishioners. A self-described independent, MacDonald lost his position because of his unconventional views. Losing his official pulpit, however, did not prevent

MacDonald from preaching. Lecturing to whomever would listen, he also incorporated his spiritual messages into his various writings. As author and illustrator Maurice Sendak observed in the *Washington Post Book Week,* MacDonald was "a novelist, poet, mythmaker, allegorist, critic, essayist, and, in everything, a preacher."

The Peaks of Spirituality and the Depths of Fantasy

MacDonald's best-known writings mingle fairy-tale worlds with imagination and spirituality. According to Lang, his first fantasy novel, *Phantastes: A Faerie Romance for Men and Women*—an episodic tale of a young man's wanderings and spiritual rebirth in a magical land—"firmly established his literary reputation." With its union of poetic symbolism, fairy-tale characters, and spiritual sensibility, the critically praised *Phantastes* marked the beginning of MacDonald's experimentation with the literary parable.

"The Light Princess" may be the best known and most representative of MacDonald's shorter works aimed at a younger audience. First published in the 1867 collection *Dealings with the Fairies,* it relates the story of a child who is cursed as an infant with the loss of her gravity—that is, she has lost both her weight and her seriousness. Not until much later, when she risks her life to save her beloved, does she reclaim what she's been missing since childhood.

Critics have found several ways to interpret this story. In the opinion of Richard H. Reis, writing in his book *George MacDonald,* it is "a parable of puberty ... designed to convince children that sooner or later childhood's frivolity must be abandoned for the sake of mature seriousness, which has its own rewards." Glenn Edward Sadler, on the other hand, suggested in *Writers for Children* that the princess's self-sacrifice represents her spiritual rebirth, while her gradual spiritual growth is reflected in her learning to walk.

MacDonald's other well-known fantasies touch upon spiritual struggles as well. Virtuous young people triumph over evil goblins and corrupt adults in *The Princess and the Goblin* and *The Princess and Curdie.* The novel

Best Bets

1867 ***Dealings with the Fairies***
A collection of stories including "The Light Princess," in which a child is cursed by the loss of her gravity.

1871 ***At the Back of the North Wind***
A young boy meets the fairylike Mistress North Wind as he progresses from illness to death.

1872 ***The Princess and the Goblin***
Virtuous young people triumph over evil goblins and corrupt adults.

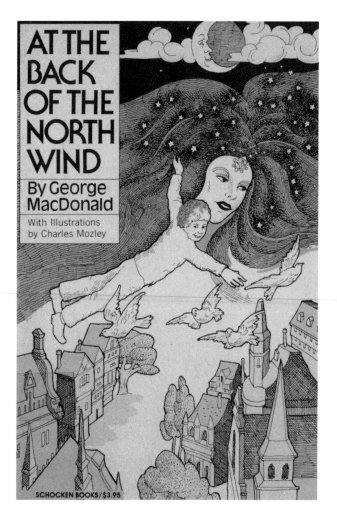

AT THE BACK OF THE NORTH WIND

By George MacDonald

With Illustrations by Charles Mozley

SCHOCKEN BOOKS/$3.95

Cover of *At the Back of the North Wind* by George MacDonald.

Lilith deals with spiritual redemption and resurrection and *At the Back of the North Wind* uncovers divine goodness where others might see only tragedy.

North Wind, the story of a young London boy's progression from illness to death, describes the boy's introduction to the fairylike Mistress North Wind, their airborne journeys together, and his final trip to "the back of the North Wind." Considered to be the only tale in which MacDonald fully mingles the real with the fantastic, it is also regarded as one of the author's most impressive works for young people. Eric S. Rabkin asserts that *At the Back of the North Wind* defends God's goodness and omnipotence in the presence of evil. In his essay "The Fantastic and Perspective," Rabkin wrote, "the North Wind (whose other name is never mentioned but we know it is Death) is revealed as a perfect servant of some higher good (again unnamed, again we know: God)." What's more, the critic argues, MacDonald "takes the bold step of calling death the best thing in the world." A devout and mystical Christian, MacDonald presented death not as the end of life but as the gateway to greater life.

Fairy Tales and the Child Within

Sometimes criticized for lacking literary polish, MacDonald was less interested in technique than in evoking an emotional or spiritual response from his readers. As he commented in his essay "The Fantastic Imagination," published in *A Dish of Orts: Chiefly Papers on the Imagination and on Shakespeare,* "The best thing you can do for your fellow, next to rousing his conscience, is ... to wake things up that are in him."

Of all MacDonald's dozens of books, critics view his fantasies as his greatest contribution to literature. Rich in symbolism and moral and spiritual conviction, they gave "a new dimension to the world of faerie, one that his imitators would find it difficult to equal," Sadler declared in *Writers for Children*. Author C. S. Lewis agreed, writing, "What [MacDonald] does best is fantasy ... and this ... he does better than any man."

Sources

Lang, Marjory, "George MacDonald," *Dictionary of Literary Biography,* Volume 18: *Victorian Novelists,* Gale, 1983, pp. 158-163.

Lewis, C. S., preface to *George MacDonald: An Anthology,* Bles, 1946, pp. xxx-xxxiv.

Phelan, Carolyn, review of *The Lost Princess: A Double Story, Booklist,* January 15, 1993, p. 908.

Rabkin, Eric S., "The Fantastic and Perspective," *The Fantastic in Literature,* Princeton University Press, 1976, pp. 74-116.

Reis, Richard H., *George MacDonald,* Twayne, 1972.

Sadler, Glenn Edward, "George MacDonald," *Twentieth-Century Children's Writers,* 3rd edition, St. James Press, 1989, pp. 1105-1106.

Sadler, Glenn Edward, "George MacDonald," *Writers for Children,* edited by Jane M. Bingham, Scribner, 1988, pp. 373-380.

Sendak, Maurice, "The Depths of Fantasy," *Washington Post Book Week,* July 24, 1966, pp. 14-15.

Margaret Mahy

Born: March 21, 1936, Whakatane, New Zealand

The author of The Haunting *writes of family relationships, faith, fact, and fiction.*

F antastical adventures that tell about how people get along with their families have made New Zealand author Margaret Mahy well known around the world. In more than 50 titles since her first book, *A Lion in the Meadow*, Mahy has written about a world full of surprising possibilities and of friendship tested by adventure. Wounded by childhood experiences, her young characters find healing that helps them to continue their journeys into adulthood. Critics place Mahy's work, which appeals to readers of all ages, with the best works of young people's literature. Whether writing about aliens with unusual powers, intelligent adolescents, or New Zealand, "she writes with all the force and precision and richness of a poet," Elizabeth Ward observed in the *Washington Post Book World*.

Family Ties

Employing a variety of storytelling methods, Mahy describes the problems that plague teens everywhere. In her first book, *A Lion in the Meadow*, she features a mother whose trouble stems from neglecting to take her son seriously. In *The Haunting*, a young man named Barney Palmer finds out he is in line to inherit psychic powers that he feels are a curse more than a blessing. Critics praise Mahy's ability to develop likeable characters and ambitious themes. Sarah Hayes observed in the *Times Literary Supplement* that "*The Haunting* manages to combine a realistic approach to family life—in which how you feel about your parents and yourself is actually important—with a strong and terrifying line in fantasy." Mahy combines these themes again in *Dangerous Spaces*, about one young woman's struggle to control her habit of trying to avoid life's difficulties by escaping to a private world inhabited by her great-uncle's ghost. Anthea's own parents have died suddenly and she lives with relatives whose complicated and noisy lives are no comfort to her. When she retreats to the spacious dream-world Viridian, her nightly trips soon become so dangerous they threaten her life. Flora, Anthea's down-to-earth cousin, charges in to Viridian to rescue Anthea and put an end to the haunting that has plagued the family for generations. As is typical of Mahy's tales, the story skillfully weaves adventure with insights into family relationships.

More of Life's Lessons

The importance of family relationships to young adults is just one of the major themes that pervade Mahy's work. She also finds intriguing "the double aspect of things—man and beast, [good] and evil, young and old," Hayes observed in the *Times Literary Supplement*. The author explores this "double aspect of things" in *The Catalogue of the Universe,* in which the main characters are high school seniors who are working out the problems of identity. Angela has lived without a father for many years, and feels that the blessings of beauty, a loving mother, and intelligence do not compensate for his absence. Tycho—her friend since early childhood, who looks to science and astronomy to provide a rational basis for his life—helps Angela in her search for her missing father. When they finally encounter Angela's lost father, however, the young woman is disappointed and realizes that she must find out who she is apart from family ties.

The truest thing in science is wonder just as it is in story. And I never forget that story is as important to human beings as science."

—Margaret Mahy

Best Bets

1982 ***The Haunting***
Barney Palmer finds out that he is in line to inherit psychic powers he considers to be more of a curse than a blessing.

1984 ***The Changeover***
After an antique shop owner assumes control of Jacko's life, Laura seeks the help of a white witch to save her friend.

1987 ***Memory***
Jonny, a troubled teenager, comes to terms with his life after meeting an old woman suffering from Alzheimer's disease.

1989 ***The Blood-and-Thunder Adventure on Hurricane Peak***
A romance between a school principal and scientist Belladonna Doppler dramatizes the rivalry between magic and science.

1991 ***Dangerous Spaces***
"Dangerous spaces" in Flora's haunted house draw her and her cousin Anthea into the dream-world Viridian.

Cover of *Memory,* by Margaret Mahy.

The young adults in Mahy's story discover that it takes both faith and facts to survive their experiences and to achieve their goals. What's more, although forgiveness can help relationships to survive, it doesn't change the faults of others; in short, it's difficult to forgive. Mahy's characters accept these lessons without feeling sorry for themselves and without giving up on life.

Mahy compares the powers and the limitations of both magic and science in the well-received junior novel *The Blood-and-Thunder Adventure on Hurricane Peak. Times Literary Supplement* reviewer John Mole observed that in the romance between a school principal and the scientist Belladonna Doppler, "the rival claims of magic and science argue their way towards a happy marriage"; as the scientist realizes near the end of the book, although sorcery brought them into the forest, it took science to get them out.

Truth and Fiction

Combining fantasy with themes that are relevant to young adults, Mahy consistently takes a nonsexist view of roles and relationships. Jan Dalley, writing in the *Times Literary Supplement,* pointed out that Mahy "continually pushes at the boundaries of [fairy-tale] conventions," and dispels the sexism that used to be common in fiction for young readers. For example, although male characters have traditionally been cast in the roles of rescuers, leaders, and problem solvers, Mahy assigns these roles as often to female characters; what's more, her female leaders are both young and old, and have different levels of social status. And Mahy assigns the roles of home economist and nurturer—traditionally assigned to women—to men as well. The experience of sexual awakening is as exciting and frightening for her female teens as it is for her male adolescents, too. Men and women in Mahy's stories are equally prone to weakness, and both fail to discern the needs of their children. All of Mahy's characters face the same challenges to strike a balance between freedom and commitment, reason and emotion; and they all benefit from recognizing the power of the imagination—which they learn to celebrate as well as to contain.

In addition to being valued for their themes, Mahy's books for young readers are popular—and highly regarded—because of her skills as a poet. The rhythmic verses in *17 Kings and 42 Elephants*—which describe a parade of kings, elephants, tigers, and other jungle animals—are as memorable as "The Congo" and other masterpieces by American poet Vachel Lindsay. As Arthur Yorinks commented in the *New York Times Book Review,* the language of *17 Kings and 42 Elephants* is both precise and creative, entertaining and thought-provoking, silly and serious. Patricia MacCarthy's brightly colored batik illustrations make the second edition particularly pleasing to the eye: so much so that, in 1987, the *New York Times Book Review* named it one of the year's ten best illustrated books.

Sources

Cart, Michael, review of *The Haunting, School Library Journal,* August 1982, p. 119.

Dalley, Jan, "Fantastical Flights," *Times Literary Supplement,* November 25, 1988, p. 1323.

Fargnoli, Harriett, review of *Tick Tock Tales: Twelve Stories to Read Around the Clock, School Library Journal,* April 1994, p. 110.

Hayes, Sarah, "Adding Another Dimension," *Times Literary Supplement,* July 13, 1984, p. 794.

Hayes, Sarah, "Unearthing the Family Ghosts," *Times Literary Supplement,* September 17, 1982, p. 1001.

Hower, Edward, reviews of *Dangerous Spaces* and *The Door in the Air and Other Stories, New York Times Book Review,* June 23, 1991, p. 23.

Jones, Malcolm, Jr., review of *The Seven Chinese Brothers, Newsweek,* December 3, 1990, p. 65.

Mahy, Margaret, "May Hill Arbuthnot Lecture, A Dissolving Ghost: Possible Operations of Truth in Children's Books and the Lives of Children," *Journal of Youth Services in Libraries,* summer 1989, pp. 313–329.

Mole, John, "Abandoning Reality," *Times Literary Supplement,* April 7, 1989, p. 378.

Ward, Elizabeth, "Space to Dream," *Washington Post Book World,* October 12, 1986, p. 11.

Watson, Elizabeth S., "*The Pirates' Mixed-up Voyage:* Dark Doings in the Thousand Islands," *Horn Book,* May-June, 1993, p. 334.

Yorinks, Arthur, "Lots of Pachyderms," *New York Times Book Review,* November 8, 1987, p. 40.

Anne McCaffrey

Born: April 1, 1926, Cambridge, Massachusetts

The award-winning author of the Dragonrider series features strong women and girls in unusual tales of science fantasy.

Anne McCaffrey's emphasis on the conflicts between individuals, the fight against Thread (deadly spores on the Pern—a former colony of Earth), and the unique telepathic relationship between dragon and rider makes her popular with readers of all ages. Her books have made frequent appearances on the best-seller charts, and she has earned a number of prestigious awards, including a 1968 Hugo Award for best novella (for *Weyr Search*) from the World Science Fiction Society; a 1969 Nebula Award for best novella (for *Dragonrider*) from Science Fiction Writers of America; and a 1979 Gandalf Award for *The White Dragon*. As the first woman to win Hugo and Nebula awards, McCaffrey is often credited with bringing more women writers into the field.

Self-Fulfillment and a Horse of One's Own

After earning a B.A. from Radcliffe College in 1947, McCaffrey worked as a copywriter, studied theater and voice, and directed operas and operettas. Married to H. Wright Johnson from 1950 to 1970, she had three children—two boys and a girl. Although her first story was published in 1953, she prefers to acknowledge her 1959 novella *The Lady in the Tower* (published in the *Magazine of Fantasy and Science Fiction*) as her first. Now living in Ireland, she says that she imagines interesting people or concepts to write about and then finds conflicts for them.

McCaffrey's characters are often women or children who are looking for their niche in society and frequently must struggle against convention and adversity to succeed. These struggles reflect the author's own childhood determination to make something of herself, as she once commented: "When I was a very young girl, I promised myself fervently (usually after I'd lost another battle with one of my brothers) that I would become a famous author and I'd own my own horse." McCaffrey credits her parents for raising her to believe she could do anything.

Dragons and Fire Lizards

McCaffrey's Harper Hall series, a popular Pern trilogy for younger readers, follows a teenage girl who comes from a very different situation. In *Dragonsong,* the first book, Menolly has been forbidden to play or sing her music solely because she is a girl and "girls aren't harpers." After her hand is accidentally injured—and deliberately mistreated to prevent proper healing that would allow her to play again—Menolly runs away. Outside the Hold, she faces the dangers of the Thread and the challenges of survival by herself. But when she discovers she isn't alone, she befriends and cares for a set of young fire lizards, small cousins to Pern's mighty dragons. By the end of the story, Menolly is rescued from Threadfall and the Harper Guild discovers her talent.

Menolly encounters a new set of problems in *Dragonsinger,* the second book in the series. Although she has arrived at the Harper Hall and has started training to be a harper, she still must face the prejudice of some teachers and the resentment of students who are jealous of her talent and her fire lizards. With her usual determination—not to mention the help of some new friends, such as the apprentice Piemur—Menolly conquers her troubles and ultimately finds happiness. Piemur takes center stage in the third Harper Hall book, *Dragondrums,* and together the first three contain "strong characters" as well as "a nice balance between problems that are present in any civilized

Best Bets

1976 ***Dragonsong***
Flying, fire-breathing, genetically engineered dragons and their human partners protect Pern—a former colony of Earth—from deadly spores called Thread. The first book of the Dragonriders of Pern series, followed by *Dragonsinger, Dragondrums, Dragonsdawn,* and *All the Weyrs of Pern.*

1994 ***Lyon's Pride***
The fourth book in the Damia series (preceded by *The Rowan, Damia,* and *Damia's Children*) continues to spin far-future galactic empire yarns about the descendants of The Rowan, who are blessed with telepathic and teleportational abilities.

1994 ***Power Lines***
The sentient planet Petaybee and its inhabitants join in a battle to prevent a powerful company from razing the country in search of valuable minerals. A sequel to *The Powers That Be.*

society and a sense of humor," Zena Sutherland wrote in the *Bulletin of the Center for Children's Books.*

A Recipe for Science Fantasy

Although Pern is inhabited by flying dragons and dominated by a near-feudal society—elements typical of fantasy worlds—McCaffrey's creation is based on solid scientific principles. The author frequently consults with scientific experts in order to make her ideas realistic and believable; 1988's *Dragonsdawn,* for instance, reveals the story of how the original colonists of Pern used genetic manipulation to develop the colony's dragons. The book features two of Pern's first dragonriders, young lovers Sean and Sorka, as they participate in the daring experiment and take up the battle against Threadfall.

All the Weyrs of Pern, published in 1991, brings the human settlers full swing: As the past and future meet, the knowledge of the first settlers becomes a part of the wisdom of the descendants. Lord Jaxom of Ruatha and his white dragon, Ruth, lead the rediscovery of the Landing and the revitalization of Avivas—an Artificial Intelligence Voice-Address System that has survived on minimum power for more than 5,000 years. Avivas then attempts to reeducate Pern's inhabitants in the lost sciences in order to end the threat of the Thread forever.

I am a storyteller of science fiction and wish that label attached to my work in that field. I make this point as I am often classified, erroneously, as a fantasy writer."

—Anne McCaffrey

But the emotional focus of the Dragonrider series—and other McCaffrey works such as *Crystal Singer* and the Raven Women novels—forces technology into the background. This emphasis on people and feelings—which is unusual among science fiction novels—has led some critics to christen the Pern books "science fantasy." McCaffrey, however, believes the use of emotion is appropriate to science fiction. In fact, one of her first (and most popular) stories, "The Ship Who Sang," was born of her grief over her father's death: "'Ship' taught me to use emotion as a writing tool," she later wrote. "And I do, with neither apology nor shame, even though I am writing science fiction, a genre not often noted, in those days, for any emotions, only intellectual exercise and scientific curiosities."

Genre-bending Tales of Heroic Girls and Women

McCaffrey's approach also allows her to weave serious social commentary into her work, according to Edra C. Bogle in the *Dictionary of Literary Biography.* "Most of McCaffrey's protagonists are women or children, whom she treats with understanding and sympathy," Bogle said. "The injustices imposed on these women and children by powerful men," she continued, "aided by the social system, are at the heart of most of McCaffrey's books." In fact, the majority of McCaffrey's novels feature strong heroines: the ruling Weyrwomen of the Dragonrider books; the determined young musician of *Crystal Singer* and *Killashandra;* the talented psychics of *To Ride Pegasus* and the Raven Women series; and Helva, the independent starship "brain" of *The Ship Who Sang* all demonstrate McCaffrey's interest in forceful and self-possessed female characters.

Cover of the 1976 multi-award-winning novel *Dragonsong* by Anne McCaffrey.

"Anne McCaffrey succeeds so well because she presents a colorful, ideally traditional culture in which each person has his or her place, with corresponding duties and privileges; in which the moral choices are clear; and in which, 'if you try hard enough, and work long enough, you can achieve anything you desire,'" Gary K. Reynolds asserted in the *Science Fiction and Fantasy Book Review.* Apparently, McCaffrey's optimism appeals to the public. With each new volume hitting the best-seller lists, the Dragonriders series has proved so popular that James and Eugene Sloan conclude in the *Chicago*

Tribune Book World that it "must now rank as the most enduring serial in the history of science fantasy."

Sources

Bogle, Edra C., "Anne McCaffrey," *Dictionary of Literary Biography,* Volume 8: *Twentieth-Century American Science Fiction Writers,* Gale, 1981.

Klein, Jay Kay, column on Anne McCaffrey, *Analog,* August 1991, p. 77.

McCaffrey, Anne, entry in *Something about the Author Autobiographical Series,* Volume 11, Gale, 1991, pp. 241-257.

Reynolds, Gary K., article in *Science Fiction and Fantasy Book Review,* July 1979.

Sloan, James, amd Eugene Sloan, article in *Chicago Tribune Book World,* July 13, 1986.

Sutherland, Zena, review of *Dragondrums, Bulletin of the Center for Children's Books,* July-August, 1979, p. 195.

Patricia A. McKillip

Born: February 29, 1948, Salem, Oregon

Patricia A. McKillip is a critically acclaimed author of works in three literary genres: fantasy, science fiction, and the young adult novel. With the publication of her ambitious Riddle of Stars, a fantasy adventure in three parts, McKillip was recognized as one of the leading writers of fantasy literature. Roger C. Schlobin wrote in *Science Fiction and Fantasy Book Review* that "McKillip's series delves deeply into the rich earth of full human characterization and creates a world elaborate in both magic and mythology."

From Baby-sitting to Storytelling

In her youth McKillip became an expert storyteller; she was the second of six children and always entertained her siblings with tall tales of adventure as she baby-sat them. She began working on her first novel, *The House on Parchment Street,* as a teenager. "I was living in England at the time (my father was stationed at a local air base) in a big old house facing a grave-

The World Fantasy Award-winning author of the Riddle of the Stars trilogy shifts easily between science fiction and fantasy.

yard: the 'house on Parchment Street,'" she recalled. She had hopes of becoming a musician, but soon realized that her real talent was for writing. "Since I didn't think I was capable of holding down a full-time job," she later said in an interview, "I thought I'd better get published before I left college, so I could support myself. I have been writing full-time since then."

Best Bets

Choosing Between the Lesser of Two Ills

Many reviewers of McKillip's work have noted her ability, regardless of the genre in which she is writing, to touch on basic human traits and themes. *The Forgotten Beasts of Eld,* published in 1974, has all the trappings of the fantasy adventure novel: dragons, talking animals, doorless towers, and glass mountains. "*The Forgotten Beasts of Eld* works on a strictly human level," wrote *New York Times Book Review* contributor Georgess McHargue. "Trust, loneliness, love's responsibilities and the toxicity of fate are the themes that underlie the fantasy love story." Riddle of Stars, McKillip's famous fantasy trilogy, garnered similar praise. The plot follows the fortunes of Morgan from his beginnings as ruler of Hed, a peaceful, sleepy kingdom, to his ultimate destiny as a trained "riddle-master." Referring to the first volume of the three, Glenn Shea stated in the *New York Times Book Review* that McKillip "understands that we spend much of our time choosing, not between good and evil, but the lesser of two ills."

*F*or my own purposes, I try to keep [fantasy and science fiction] separate. If I'm writing fantasy I use elements of epic, fantasy, myth, legend; and if I put magic in it, it's magic out of the imagination and out of the heart."

—Patricia McKillip

Switch-hitting: Science Fiction and Fantasy

In 1982 McKillip published the young adult novel *Stepping from the Shadows* in what—on the surface at least—seemed like a movement away from the fantasy adventure format. In fact, *Stepping from the Shadows,* in terms of its concentration on universal human themes, develops very naturally from McKillip's earlier work. The book revolves around the very private torments of Frances, a young girl who shares, through conversation and writing, her rich fantasy life with an imaginary sister.

With the publication of *Moon-Flash* in 1984, *The Moon and the Face* in 1985, and *Fool's Run* in 1987, McKillip achieved distinction in yet another literary genre: science fiction. "When I write science fiction ... I try to turn my back on traditional fantasy elements and extrapolate a plot from history, or daily life, or whatever science happens to stick in my head," McKillip explained. "The heritage, the roots and background of science fiction are very different from those of fantasy. The language is different; the images I find in my mind when I contemplate a science fiction plot are different. The stars in *Riddle-Master* are a symbol. The stars in science fiction are real." In 1991 McKillip returned to fantasy with the debut volume of another series, *The Sorceress and the Cygnet.*

Cover of *Heir of Sea and Fire,* the second book from the Riddle of the Stars trilogy by Patricia McKillip.

The story of Corleu, a young man who is different in appearance and interests from his Wayfolk kin, is "a richly imagined tale of enchantment, intrigue, and romance," according to *Voice of Youth Advocates* contributor Carolyn Shute. Corleu's story continues in the 1993 novel *The Cygnet and the Firebird.* "I'd like to do more of everything," McKillip observed. "There are so many backgrounds and people I'd like to write about—not in any personal way, but just people I know who suggest stories that might be nice to write."

Sources

Baun, Grace, review of *The Sorceress and the Cygnet, School Library Journal,* October 1991, p. 160.

McHargue, Georgess, review of *The Forgotten Beasts of Eld, New York Times Book Review,* October 13, 1974, p. 8.

McKillip, Patricia A., interview in *Contemporary Authors New Revision Series,* Volume 18, Gale, 1986, pp. 316–320.

Schobel, Richard, review of the Riddle of the Stars trilogy, *Science Fiction and Fantasy Book Review,* May 1979, pp. 37–38.

Shea, Glenn, review of *The Riddle-Master of Hed, New York Times Book Review,* March 6, 1977, p. 29.

Shute, Carolyn, review of *The Sorceress and the Cygnet, Voice of Youth Advocates,* June 1991, p. 112.

Robin McKinley

Born: November 16, 1952, Warren, Ohio

Retelling familiar fairy tales and legends, Robin McKinley interprets the original stories for contemporary young readers. Having adapted such classics as Rudyard Kipling's *The Jungle Book,* Anna Sewell's *Black Beauty,* and Hans Christian Andersen's *The Little Mermaid,* she has also created her own fantasy world—Damar—where *The Blue Sword, The Hero and the Crown,* and *Kirith* take place.

A Young Girl Who Never Stayed Put

With her father dedicated to his navy career, McKinley grew up all over the world. By the third grade, she was already a well-traveled girl: Born in Warren, Ohio, she spent her earliest childhood in Arlington, Virginia, attended kindergarten in Long Beach, California, and, during her first three grades, lived in upstate New York. Reflecting on her childhood, McKinley concludes that because she moved too often to make lasting friendships, her best friends were always

A Newbery Medal-winning author says she writes about "girls who do things."

books, which always accompanied her to her new home. "My mother ... would read to me before I was old enough to sit up by myself," she remembers, while her father brought home "suitcases of books and rolls of film" from his navy assignments.

At the age of ten, while living in Japan—where her family stayed for four years—McKinley took her first horseback-riding lessons. After her family returned to the United States, she worked in a stable every day after her eighth-grade classes. While she was still in her teens, her father retired from the navy

Best Bets

1978 ***Beauty: A Retelling of the Story of Beauty and the Beast***
A new version of an old story featuring a heroine named Honour.

1982 ***The Blue Sword***
The medieval atmosphere of the mythical world of Damar is the backdrop for magic and mysterious events. Followed by a Newbery award-winning sequel, *The Hero and the Crown.*

1988 ***The Outlaws of Sherwood***
A retelling of the legend of Robin Hood in which Maid Marian plays a prominent role.

1994 ***A Knot in the Grain***
A collection of stories including four Damarian tales about adventurous heroines.

and the family moved to Vinalhaven, an island off the coast of Maine. She spent her last high school years at Gould Academy in western Maine, later taking a job in Washington, D.C. Back in Maine, she enrolled in Bowdoin College, and, after graduating, worked as a dorm counselor at a prep school in Massachusetts and then as a reader for the children's department of Little, Brown Publishers.

Twice-Told Tales and Writing by Ear

Watching a television presentation of the fairy tale *Beauty and the Beast,* McKinley concluded that "they did everything wrong." "I sat down at my desk that same night," she relates, "to write what I intended to be a short story, my version of my favorite fairy tale." In the fall of 1978, the novel *Beauty: A Retelling of the Story of Beauty and the Beast*—with a heroine named Honour—was published. The book attracted much attention, and McKinley went on to retell other fairy tales, which were printed as *The Door in the Hedge.*

McKinley envisioned the stories that would become her Damar series early in her writing career. She writes, "I had plots and characters multiplying like mice and running in all directions." Moving to New York City, she shared half of a large rented house on Staten Island with some friends and began writing in earnest. She claims that she always writes the first draft in longhand, "turning what I see and hear into a story"; she also says that she "writes by ear," and tries to get her story right the first time. Since the stories "tell themselves" to McKinley, she is often as surprised as her readers by plot twists and other revelations.

A Girl Who Does Things

In 1983 *The Blue Sword,* McKinley's first book about the fantasy world of Damar, was runner-up for the coveted Newbery Medal. Her next book, *The Hero and the Crown,* which tells of the events that happen before those described in *The Blue Sword,* won the Newbery Medal in 1985. In spite of her mounting success as a writer, McKinley says that her Newbery Medal acceptance speech was the hardest thing she had ever had to write. In her speech, published in *Horn Book,* McKinley states, "You see, it's finally occurred to me that I'm myself a girl who does things."

Fond of traveling, McKinley has had many opportunities to do so. In addition to having lived as a child in Japan and in various parts of the United States, she has had speaking engagements all across the United States—including Alaska—and has traveled around the world. Particularly fond of England, she retells the legend of Robin Hood in *The Outlaws of Sherwood;* breathing new life into the old stories, she concludes *Sherwood* with a surprise ending: Maid Marian becomes one of McKinley's "girls who do things."

In 1992 McKinley married Peter Dickinson, a noted English mystery author who also writes stories for young readers. Although McKinley maintains her home in Maine, the couple live in southern England with three whippets and their books.

Cover of *Beauty: A Retelling of the Story of Beauty and the Beast* by Robin McKinley.

Sources

Cassada, Jackie, review of *Deerskin, Library Journal,* April 15, 1993, p. 130.

Dictionary of Literary Biography, Volume 52: *American Writers for Children since 1960: Fiction,* Gale, 1986, pp. 262-266.

McKinley, Robin, "Newbery Medal Acceptance," *Horn Book,* July/August 1985.

Review of *A Knot in the Grain and Other Stories, New York Times Book Review,* June 5, 1994, p. 30.

Review of *Rowan, Publishers Weekly,* August 31, 1992, p. 78.

Windling, Terri, and Mark Alan Arnold, "Robin McKinley," *Horn Book,* July/August 1985, pp. 406-409.

Michael Moorcock

Born: December 18, 1939, Mitcham, Surrey, England

The Guardian *Literary Prize-winning author of the Jerry Cornelius tetralogy writes science fiction that traverses space and time—and even personality.*

Michael Moorcock was associated with the New Wave, an avant-garde science fiction of the 1960s that introduced a wider range of subject matter and style to the science fiction field. As editor of *New Worlds,* the most prominent of the New Wave publications, Moorcock promoted the movement and provided a showcase for its writing.

A Man of Many Genres

Moorcock's own writing covers a wide range of science fiction and fantasy genres. He has written science fiction adventures in the style of Edgar Rice Burroughs's Mars novels, sword and sorcery novels, comic and satirical science fiction, and time-travel science fiction. Moorcock's fantasy novels have earned him major genre awards and popularity among literary critics: Tom Hutchinson of the *London Times,* for example, called Moorcock's sword and sorcery novel *The Chronicles of Castle Brass* "a masterpiece of modern high fantasy."

I have read about half his prodigious output ... and on the strength of that sample Moorcock strikes me as the most prolific, probably the most inventive and without doubt the most egalitarian writer practicing today."

—Philip Oakes writing in the London Times Magazine

The genre books that brought Moorcock to critical attention—and those he considers to be his most important—combine standard science fiction trappings with experimental narrative structures. His *Breakfast in the Ruins: A Novel of Inhumanity,* for instance, contains a number of historical vignettes featuring the protagonist Karl Glogauer. In each of these, Karl is a different person in a different time, participating in such examples of political violence as the French Revolution, the Paris Commune, a Nazi concentration camp, and a My Lai-style massacre. Interwoven with these vignettes is a homosexual love scene, involving Karl and a black Nigerian, which takes on a mystical connotation as the two lovers seem to merge into each other's identities. Helen Rogan of *Time* described the book as "by turns puzzling, funny, and shocking," calling Moorcock "both bizarrely inventive and highly disciplined."

Space, Time, and Apocalyptic Disaster

Best Bets

1972 ***Breakfast in the Ruins***
Karl Glogauer travels through time, participating in episodes ranging from the French Revolution to a Nazi concentration camp.

1977 ***The Condition of Muzak***
Jerry Cornelius—a man with no consistent character or appearance—travels through time in a world brimming with alternative histories. The final book of the Jerry Cornelius series.

1981 ***The Nomad of Time***
A collection of three short stories—"The Warlord of the Air," "The Land Leviathan," and "The Steel Tsar"—that describe the bizarre experiences of Oswald Bastable (fomerly a captain in the Royal Lancers) as told by Moorcock's grandfather.

1986 ***The Brothel in Rosenstrasse***
An aging hedonist tells the story of his fruitless life in the doomed and decadent city of Mirenburg.

In books and stories featuring Jerry Cornelius, Moorcock experiments with character as well as with narrative structure. Cornelius has no consistent character or appearance; he is, as Nick Totton wrote in *Spectator,* "a nomad of the territories of personality; even his skin color and gender are as labile [open to change] as his accomplishments." Cornelius's world is just as flexible, containing a multitude of alternative histories, all contradictory, and peopled with characters who die and are resurrected as a matter of course. Within this mutable landscape, Cornelius travels from one inconclusive adventure to another, trapped in an endless existence.

The Condition of Muzak, completing the initial Jerry Cornelius tetralogy, won the *Guardian* Literary Prize in 1977, bringing Moorcock acceptance in a wider literary world. "Moorcock," Angus Wilson wrote in the *Washington Post Book World,* "is emerging as one of the most serious literary lights of

Cover of *The Nomad of Time* by Michael Moorcock.

our time.... For me his Jerry Cornelius quartet [of novels] assured the durability of his reputation."

The Twentieth Century through the Eyes of an Egomaniac

The publication of *Byzantium Endures* and *The Laughter of Carthage* substantially enhanced Moorcock's literary standing. The "autobiography" of the fictitious Russian émigré Colonel Pyat, these two novels are the closest Moorcock has come to conventional literary fiction. Born on January 1, 1900, the colonel relates a life story that is essentially a history of the twentieth century. Pyat—who survived the Russian Revolution, traveled throughout Europe and America, and participated in a number of important historical events—is a megalomaniac who imagines himself to be a great inventor—the equal of Thomas Edison—and a major figure on the stage of world history. He is also an anti-Semite [hostile toward Jews as a religious or racial group] who believes that true Christianity—as embodied in the Russian Orthodox Church—is engaged in a battle against the Jews, Asians, Bolsheviks, and other destroyers of order. Needless to say, Pyat's account of his life is riddled with factual errors and distorted by his sense of self-importance.

Pyat's narration, because it is colored by his eccentric, offensive views and a distorted sense of his place in things that take place around him, gives a fantastic sheen to the familiar historical events he relates. "This is Moorcock's achievement: he has rewritten modern history by seeing it in the distorting mirror of one man's perceptions so that the novel has the imaginative grasp of fantasy while remaining solidly based upon recognizable facts," Peter Ackroyd wrote in the *London Times*. Although some critics, like Richard Eder of the *Los Angeles Times,* found Pyat's narrative an "extremely long-winded unpleasantness" because of his political views, others, like the *New York Times Book Review*'s Thaddeus Rutkowski, forgave the "sometimes tedious" nature of Pyat's narration. "Most often," Rutkowski found, "Pyat's tirades are beguiling. They are the pronouncements of a singularly innocent intelligence gone awry."

Moorcock Moves to Mainstream

Moorcock combined mainstream fiction with a bit of fantasy in *The Brothel in Rosenstrasse,* a novel set in the imaginary city of Mirenburg. The city's brothel is the center of social life, as well as a "microcosm of *fin de siècle* [end-of-the-century] Central Europe; hedonistic [pleasure-seeking], decadent, deluded and heedless of an inevitable future," Elaine Kendall wrote in the *Los Angeles Times*. Narrated by an aging hedonist who relates the story of his long and dissipated life, the novel follows a handful of decadent characters to their eventual destruction during the bombardment of Mirenburg. Suffering makes the characters finally come alive in a way they have never been before. "They begin to engage our full attention," Kendall concluded, "and earn not only our sympathy but in some cases, our respect. By then it's too late; Mirenburg and all the good and evil it represented has vanished forever. If there's no parable here, surely there's a moral."

In *Mother London,* Moorcock presents a "complex, layered history of London since the war, seen through the stories of a group of psychiatric patients," Brian Appleyard explained in the *London Times*. The novel earned high praise from several critics. Nigel Andrew of the *Listener* called the book "a prodigious work of imaginative archaeology.... [Moorcock] displays the generosity of spirit, the sweep and sheer gusto of Dickens." Similarly, writing in the *Washington Post Book World,* Gregory Feeley states that *Mother London* "often indulges its author's crotchets and biases, [but] it also proves warm and humane, often surprisingly funny, and moving in a way Moorcock has never before succeeded in being." "If," wrote Andrew, "this wonderful book does not finally convince the world that [Moorcock] is in fact one of our very best novelists and a national treasure, then there is no justice."

Moorcock has his own thoughts about his life as a writer. "The job of a novelist," he explained, "has its own momentum, its own demands, its own horrible power over the practitioner. When I look back I wonder what I got myself into all those years ago when I realized I had a facility to put words down on paper and have people give me money in return. For ages the whole business seemed ludicrous. I couldn't believe my luck. Frequently, I still can't but it seems an unnatural way of earning a living. Of course, it's no longer easy. It's often a struggle. It spoils my health.... I suppose it must be an addiction. I'm pretty sure, though I deny it heartily, that I could now no longer give it up. I'm as possessed as any fool I used to mock."

Sources

Callow, A. J., compiler, *The Chronicles of Moorcock,* A. J. Callow, 1978.

Cassada, Jackie, review of *The Revenge of the Rose, Library Journal,* November 15, 1991, p. 111.

Clute, John, review of *Jerusalem Commands, New Statesman,* July 24, 1992, p. 38.

Dictionary of Literary Biography, Volume 14: *British Novelists Since 1960,* Gale, 1983.

Easton, Tom, reviews of *The City in the Autumn Stars* and *The Fortress of the Pearl, Analog,* March 1990, pp. 179-180.

Greenland, Colin, *The Entropy Exhibition: Michael Moorcock and the British "New Wave" in Science Fiction,* Routledge & Kegan Paul, 1983.

Listener, June 23, 1988; January 18, 1990.

Los Angeles Times, January 9, 1985; November 10, 1987.

New York Times Book Review, April 5, 1970; May 19, 1974; April 25, 1976; February 21, 1982; February 10, 1985; November 23, 1986.

Spectator, April 1, 1969; August 10, 1974; November 20, 1976; April 9, 1977; December 24, 1977; June 27, 1981; February 9, 1985.

Time, August 5, 1974; January 28, 1985.

Washington Post Book World, March 21, 1982; December 23, 1984; September 28, 1986; May 14, 1989.

Wollheim, Donald A., *The Universe Makers,* Harper, 1971.

Joan Lowery Nixon

Born: February 3, 1927, Los Angeles, California

J oan Lowery Nixon has won the Mystery Writers of America's coveted Edgar Allan Poe Award for best juvenile mystery three times—the only writer to do so—and three of her other works have been nominated for that honor, including her 1992 novel *The Weekend Was Murder.* "In the field of young adult mystery writers, a field crowded with authors," stated Melissa Fletcher Stoeltje in the *Houston Chronicle,* Nixon "is by all accounts the grande dame."

A Youthful Poet and Playwright

As a child, Nixon lived with her parents, grandparents, and two younger sisters in a large double house. She wanted to be a writer even at a very young age, and began teaching herself how to read by memorizing the words of her favorite books. She also began composing poetry, asking her mother to write down the verses she thought up. Her first published work, a poem, appeared in *Children's Playmate* magazine when she was ten

The author of The Mystery of Hurricane Castle *pens Westerns and historical novels, too.*

years old. The young writer was also enamored of mysteries; "from the time I discovered mysteries," she would later recall, "I was in love with them."

Famous Neighbors and School Newspapers

When Nixon was 12, her grandfather died and the family moved to a large house in East Hollywood, where they had some famous neighbors, including

Best Bets

1964 ***The Mystery of Hurricane Castle***
Left behind during a hurricane evacuation, two girls and their younger brother seek shelter in a house that's said to be haunted.

1980 ***The Seance***
A game soon becomes terrifying after one girl disappears and another dies.

1989 ***Whispers from the Dead***
When Sarah moves with her family to Houston, the ghost of a murdered Spanish girl attempts to communicate with her.

1992 ***The Weekend Was Murder***
During a murder mystery enactment weekend at the Ridley Hotel, hotel worker Liz is supposed to "discover" a body in room 1927, a room inhabited by a ghost. When she finds a real corpse, she, her boyfriend, and a detective friend team up to solve the mystery.

filmmaker Cecil B. DeMille, the comedian W. C. Fields, and the champion boxer Jack Dempsey. After entering ninth grade at Le Conte Junior High in Hollywood—in 1941, the year of the attack on Pearl Harbor—Nixon became interested in journalism, editing the school newspaper. At the age of 17, Nixon wrote her first article for a magazine, selling it to *Ford Times*.

The Road to *Hurricane Castle*

One week after her high school graduation, Nixon entered the University of Southern California (USC) as a journalism student. "My training in journalism taught me discipline," she recalled in an interview. "I had to sit down and *write,* whether I felt like it or not—no waiting for inspiration. I learned the skill of finding the important facts in a story, and how to isolate them from all of the unnecessary details."

Nixon's degree in journalism did not lead to a job in that field, partly because of competition from returning war correspondents. Eventually landing an assignment to teach kindergarten in Ramona Elementary School, Nixon took education courses in night school at the nearby Los Angeles City College campus. While at USC, Nixon had also met her future husband, Hershell "Nick" Nixon, who was a student majoring in naval science. During the three years Nixon taught at Ramona, their first daughter, Kathleen Mary, was born. After Nick graduated from USC in 1952, the family moved several times, and by the time they settled in Corpus Christi, Texas, Kathy had been joined by Maureen, Joe, and the youngest, Eileen.

The move to Texas marked an important event in Nixon's life. When she read an announcement of the upcoming Southwest Writers Conference shortly after her arrival, she became enthusiastic about writing for children. "I had children, I had taught children, and I have the vivid kind of memory which enables me to remember all the details I saw and the emotions I felt when I was a child," she recalled. "I made a mental note to myself. Maybe I'd try writing something for children."

Kathy and Maureen discussed this development and announced to their mother, "We've decided. If you're going to write for children, you have to write a book, and it has to be a mystery, and you have to put us in it." Each day after school, Nixon read the material she had completed that day to her children, and she joined the Byliners, a local group of writers who read and criticized each other's manuscripts. In spite of all this input, *The Mystery of Hurricane Castle* was rejected 12 times by different publishers before Criterion finally accepted it.

All in the Family

The Mystery of Hurricane Castle tells the story of two girls—the Nickson sisters, Kathy and Maureen—and their younger brother, Danny, who are left behind during an evacuation just before a hurricane. The book follows them as they seek shelter in a house that, according to local legend, is haunted. Nixon declares in *The Writer* that the plot of the book came from a family experience: "When we moved to Corpus Christi, Texas, we found ourselves in the middle of a hurricane. The area had been evacuated," Nixon continues, "but I wondered what someone would have done who couldn't leave—who, for some reason, had been left behind in the confusion. The beach houses could not withstand the force of the storm, or stay intact, but what if high on the hill there stood a stone 'castle,' strong enough to survive the storm and to shelter its occupants? And what if this castle were known to have as its only occupant a ghost?"

That first book convinced Nixon to continue writing. After *Hurricane Castle,* she wrote *The Mystery of the Grinning Idol,* a story about smuggling Mexican artifacts (which starred her youngest child, Eileen), and *The Mystery of the Hidden Cockatoo,* about a jewelled pin lost in a house in the French Quarter of New Orleans. The Nicksons returned in *The Mystery of the Haunted Woods,* and son Joe finally got a starring role in *The Mystery of the Secret Stowaway.*

Nixon soon found herself busy writing children's books, teaching creative classes at local children's schools, libraries, and colleges, and writing a humor column for the *Houston Post.* Deciding to give up teaching, Nixon was able to concentrate on storytelling; admitting that writing is difficult, Nixon explained that "it's such a fulfilling, enjoyable occupation that it's worth all the effort."

Writing for a New Audience

Nixon did not begin writing for young adults until later in her career: In 1975, attending the first International Crime Writers Congress in London, England, the author decided to try writing a mystery for young adults. *The Kidnapping of Christina Lattimore* received the Edgar Award for best juvenile mystery by the Mystery Writers of America in 1980. Told in the title character's own words, *The Kidnapping of Christina Lattimore* describes a young girl's ordeal as she is kidnapped, held for ransom, and then suspected of having engineered the whole project to get money from her grandmother for a school trip. When she is rescued, she dedicates herself to bringing the criminals to justice to prove that she did not try to defraud her grandmother. *New York Times Book Review* contributor Paxton Davis found this part of the novel particularly intriguing, writing that "Christina's inability to persuade the authorities or her family that she was not an accomplice in the crime makes for good narrative."

One year after *The Kidnapping of Christina Lattimore* won the Edgar Award for best juvenile novel, Nixon repeated the accomplishment with *The Seance,* and in 1987 *The Other Side of Dark* made her a three-time recipient of the prize. The latter book presents quite a different type of problem to the reader; in it, 17-year-old Stacy wakes up to find that she has lost four years of her life in a coma after an intruder shot her and killed her mother. Faced with the challenge of adapting to a new lifestyle and catching up on the missing years, Stacy must also identify the killer before she becomes his next victim. "Stacy is a vivid character," David Gale wrote in *School Library Journal,* "whose need to be brought up to date provides some comic moments." Also praising the story, *Voice of Youth Advocates* reviewer Mary L. Adams found "believable characters, suspense, mystery, a little romance" in the book, which she was convinced would "make its readers want to read Nixon's other books."

A Western State of Mind

Nixon has also won awards for her historical fiction. Two volumes of her Orphan Train quartet, *A Family Apart* and *In the Face of Danger,* won the Golden Spur Award—the Western Writers of America's equivalent of the Edgar. The idea, she noted in an interview, came from a publisher who asked

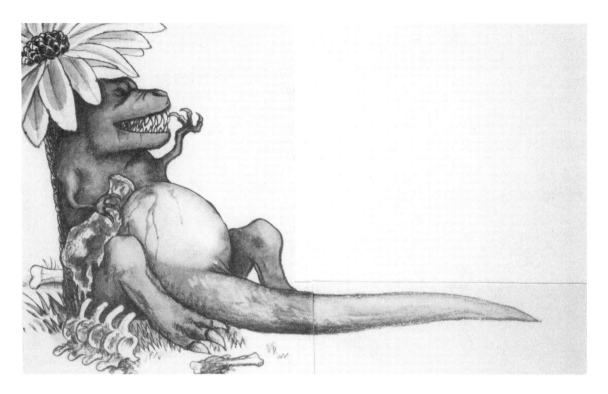

An illustration from the 1978 book *Danger in Dinosaur Valley* by Joan Lowery Nixon. Illustrated by Marc Simont.

her if she had ever heard of the "Orphan Train children." The historical Children's Aid Society, an organization of social activists, operated between 1854 and 1929 to place more than 100,000 children with foster families in the West. The children—not necessarily orphans—were usually from immigrant families living in slums in New York City.

Nixon's popular Claude and Shirley series for younger readers is also set in the West. Betsy Hearne, writing in the *Bulletin of the Center for Children's Books,* noted that the series contains "endearing characters, adroit writing, and an action-packed feminist pioneer."

"The West to me is a state of mind," Nixon declared in *The Writer.* "Writing western historical novels for young adults is immensely satisfying. It gives me the opportunity to show that history isn't simply a collection of dates and wars and kings and presidents, but that *children* have always helped make history, that *children* are not only important to the past but are helping to shape history being made today."

Hollywood High and More About Maggie

Nixon also draws on her own past for inspiration. Her Hollywood Daughters series, she related in an interview, is based on "some of the kids I knew at Hollywood High during the 1940s—kids who had been stars as children but who were 'has-beens' by the time they were teenagers."

Nixon's Maggie stories deal with the problems of growing up in an unstable environment, too. Young Maggie lost her mother in an accident several years before the opening chapters of *Maggie, Too,* and she has little contact with her filmmaker father. Over the course of the book and its two sequels, *And Maggie Makes Three* and *Maggie Forevermore,* Maggie learns to love her grandmother, to lose her resentment toward her father and his new wife, and to appreciate her own life. "Generation to generation, emotions don't change," Nixon stated in *The Writer.* "Loneliness, fear, joy, sorrow, embarrassment.... External situations may differ greatly, but the emotions they cause are always the same. Our basic needs—such as the need to be loved, to be comforted, and to be secure—remain constant."

Hope and Hot-air Balloons

In *The Writer* Nixon discussed writing mysteries for young adults. "Appreciating them, really liking them ... I think, is an essential part of the answer." Nixon explained that she always has two levels in her books: "a problem to solve, and a mystery to solve." "Later," she added, "the characters can weave them together." And Nixon has a few words for aspiring writers: "For those of you who have hopes of becoming writers, it's important to know that you'll need that determination and persistence and the courage to continue, no matter what might happen.... If you want to be successful, published writers, you'll have to be able to take editorial direction."

After more than three decades and 90 books, Nixon's popularity shows no signs of flagging. Why is her work so popular with young people? "It's because her writing gives them a feeling of hope," the author's son, Nick Nixon, told Stoeltje in the *Houston Chronicle.* "Through her heroines, she tells children that anything is possible for them. 'Be strong, be confident. You can do things.'" Clearly, Nixon's imagination never idles. Describing a hot-air balloon trip she took with her son, she said, "I glanced down and a man just happened to be in his driveway, putting something in the trunk of his car. I said to Nick, 'Suppose he had just committed a crime and was stuffing the body bags in the trunk?' And Nick sort of gave this exasperated sigh and said, 'Can't you just enjoy this lovely scenery and forget about mysteries for a while?'"

Sources

Davis, Paxton, review of *The Kidnapping of Christina Lattimore, New York Times Book Review,* May 13, 1979, p. 27.

Gale, David, review of *The Other Side of Dark, School Library Journal,* September 1986, pp. 145–146.

Hearne, Betsy, review of *Fat Chance, Claude, Bulletin of the Center for Children's Books,* September 1987, p. 15.

Nixon, Joan Lowery, "Clues to the Juvenile Mystery," *The Writer,* February 1977, pp. 23–26.

Nixon, Joan Lowery, autobiographical sketch in *Something about the Author Autobiography Series,* Volume 9, Gale, 1990, pp. 267–284.

Nixon, Joan Lowery, "Writing Mysteries Young Adults Want to Read," *The Writer,* July 1991, pp. 18–20.

Nixon, Joan Lowery, "Writing the Western Novel for Young Adults," *The Writer,* June 1992, pp. 21–23.

Review of *Fat Chance, Claude, Publishers Weekly,* September 25, 1987, p. 107.

Review of *The Name of the Game Was Murder, Publishers Weekly,* May 24, 1993, p. 89.

Review of *Shadowmaker, Publishers Weekly,* April 11, 1994, p. 66.

Something about the Author, Volume 8, Gale, 1976, pp. 143–144; Volume 44, Gale, 1986, pp. 131–139.

Stoeltje, Melissa Fletcher, "Murder for Gentle Readers," *Houston Chronicle Magazine,* June 20, 1993, pp. 8–11.

André Norton

Born: February 17, 1912, Cleveland, Ohio

The author of Star Hunter *penned the first science fiction tale to feature a female heroine.*

Although Alice Mary Norton writes books primarily for young readers, adults enjoy her many novels as well. In 1934 she legally changed her name to André Norton, believing that a masculine-sounding name would make her books more acceptable to publishers and male readers. She has written over one hundred books (many of them best-sellers), including historical romances, adventure stories, and science fiction and fantasy tales about worlds of the future and outer space. Her awards are numerous, and in some cases, she was the first woman to be so honored. Her novels include a number of firsts: *Ordeal in Otherwhere* is the first science fiction story to feature a female heroine, while the first African American science fiction hero appears in *Storm over Warlock.*

The Children's Hour and the Road to André

With pioneer settlers and a Wyandot Indian as ancestors, Norton has had a lifelong interest in American history. Both parents were avid readers and read to their daughter daily; young Norton's favorites included the Uncle Wiggley and Oz books. Fond of toy animals and animal stories, Norton began writing tales of her own at the age of eight.

In school at Collinwood High in Cleveland, Norton had an inspiring teacher who started her on a literary career. Editor of the school newspaper and annual, the budding author wrote short adventure stories for the literary magazine and was elected president of the honor society for girls; Norton became a member of Quill and Scroll, an honorary society of high school journalists, and won the English trophy, all while aspiring to a career as a history teacher. She also wrote her first novel while in high school. Later, in 1938, she rewrote it and published it under the title of *Ralestone Luck,* having been encouraged by the success of her first published book, *The Prince Commands,* in 1934.

Norton attended Western Reserve University, but financial problems during the Great Depression caused her to accept a position at the Cleveland Public Library. Continuing her college courses at night, Norton took—as she told *Luna Monthly* interviewer Paul Walker—"every writing course they offered." Her job in the children's section of the library included hosting a "Children's Hour," for which she had to find suitable material; often, she wrote her own stories to read at the story hour. While employed at the library, Norton produced nine novels and two short stories. As she became more interested in writing science fiction, however, she felt that her woman's name hindered her ability to find publishers, so she legally changed her given name to André. Eventually, due to her deteriorating health, Norton turned to freelance writing.

Espionage, Adventure, and Gender Bending

During World War II, Norton met members of the *Cleveland Press*'s World Friends Club, who gave her access to some exciting letters from the Netherlands. These letters inspired her novels of espionage. Norton also loved legends, translating and adapting two cycles of tales (which she had used for story hours at the library) into *Rogue Reynard* and *Huon of the Horn.* She

Best Bets

1963 ***Witch World***
Simon Tregarth stumbles upon an entranceway to alternate dimensions and arrives in Witch World, where witches, known as Estcarpians, use magic to battle their enemies.

1992 ***The Mark of the Cat***
Ignored, bullied, and disliked, Hynkkel goes on a coming-of-age solo where he blood-bonds with Murri, a fearsome sandcat, in an event foretold by the bards.

1992 ***Songsmith***
Eydryth the Songsmith looks for her missing mother and for a cure for her father, who lost his mind attempting to use magic to find his wife. A Witch World novel.

1993 ***Brother to Shadows***
On the planet Asborgan, offworld-born Jofre battles a jealous Shagga priest and his allies who wish to prevent an off-worlder from acquiring the powers of Lair Master.

1994 ***The Hands of Lyr***
The tale about a priestess and a young warrior who set out to restore their dying planet by finding the magical hands of Lyr.

1994 ***Firehand***
Erstwhile criminal Ross Murdock—now a reluctant hero—teaches guerilla warfare to a not-quite-human nonterrestrial group, so as to ready them for a future plagued by vicious aliens. Part of the Time Traders series, coauthored by P. M. Griffin, who also collaborated on several Witch World books.

Cover of *The Wraiths of Time* by André Norton.

wrote four historical novels for young people: novels about the settlement of Maryland, pirates in the West Indies, and adventures during the Revolutionary and the Apache wars. In 1941 Norton moved to Mt. Ranier, Maryland, where she opened a bookshop and lending library; later, she worked as a librarian for a government agency, rewrote material in basic English for immigrants, and also worked at the Library of Congress.

I'm drawn to the science-fiction genre because it imposes no limits on my imagination."

—André Norton

In 1952 Norton's first science fiction novel, *Star Man's Son,* enjoyed such a positive reception that she wrote many more such adventures. The author confided to a *Starlog* interviewer that she likes to write sequels—because it allows her to "revisit" characters she has written about previously. She has also invited other authors to contribute "Witch World" stories to her anthologies; this, she says, is "pooling strengths and ideas." Commenting on the content of her books over the years, Norton once explained, "My themes haven't really changed over the years. I've always written stories about the loner, the person who doesn't give up. I use female protagonists because it makes for a better story. When I started writing, you couldn't put a female character in an adventure story, it was taboo. The first story I wrote had a female protagonist, and nobody would publish it at first because editors believed that girls didn't read science fiction, and boys wouldn't read about girls. Now more than half of the readers of science fiction are women, and the writers of fantasy ... are most all women."

When her health began to fail, Norton decided to try to make a living solely by writing. Although the first years were slow (she admitted in *Starlog* that one year her total income from writing was 37 cents), she became a very popular author of adventure and historical novels. Since 1968 Norton has lived in Florida in a home called Avalon with her cats, a large library, windows that resemble the eyes of a cat, and a replica of King Arthur's sword, Excalibur, hanging over the mantel. And, to the pleasure of her many fans, the so-called Sorceress of the Witch World continues to pen her unique brand of stories.

Reel Life

Beastmaster, 1982.

Beastmaster battles overwhelming forces of evil, thereby irritating critics and author Norton. "It had nothing to do with my book," lamented the disgruntled author in a *Starlog* interview. But did she *like* it? In a word, no: Norton calls the film version of her 1959 tale "dreadful."

Sources

Cassada, Jackie, "*The Elvenbane:* Epic High Fantasy of the Halfblood Chronicles," *Library Journal,* October 15, 1991, p. 127.

Cassada, Jackie, review of *Golden Trillium, Library Journal,* June 15, 1993, p. 104.

Crispin, A. C., "André Norton: Sorceress of the Witch World," *Starlog,* September 1989, pp. 33–36, 52.

Crispin, A. C., "André Norton: Notes from the Witch World," *Starlog,* October 1989, pp. 54–57, 96.

Easton, Tom, review of *Brother to Shadows, Analog,* May 1994, p. 163.

Review of *The Hands of Lyr, Publishers Weekly,* May 23, 1994, p. 82.

Schlobin, Roger C., *André Norton,* Gregg, 1979.

Staicar, Tom, editor, *The Feminine Eye: Science Fiction and the Women Who Write It,* Ungar, 1982.

Steinberg, Sybil, review of *Four From the Witch World, Publishers Weekly,* January 27, 1989, p. 456.

Walker, Paul, "An Interview with André Norton," *Luna Monthly,* September 1972.

George Orwell

Born: June 25, 1903, Motihari, Bengal (now Bihar)
Died: January 21, 1950, London, England

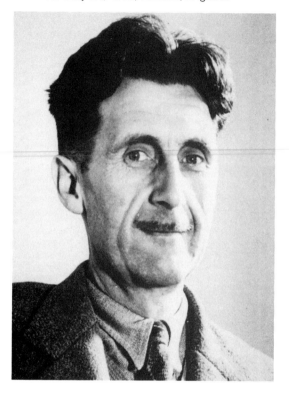

The author of Animal Farm *wrote cautionary tales whose morals have not diminished over time.*

George Orwell is best remembered for his unwavering commitment—both as an individual and as an artist—to personal freedom and social justice. Of his many works, the novels *Animal Farm* and *Nineteen Eighty-Four* are best known and most widely read. Orwell's ability to grasp the social effects of political theories—from communism to fascism to capitalism—inspired *Harper's* contributor Irving Howe to call him "the greatest moral force in English letters" of the first part of the twentieth century.

A Literary Conscience

Eric Arthur Blair—best known today under the pen name George Orwell—was born into a lower-middle-class family that struggled to provide him with an education. His mother managed to find him a place—at reduced rates—in a preparatory school. Despite his academic accomplishments, however, young Orwell was keenly aware of his low social standing. In his essay "Such, Such Were the Joys" Orwell explained the guilt and shame he felt throughout his school years and how those experiences fostered his keen sensitivity to social victimization. After attending Eton College on scholarship, Orwell left England by enlisting in the Indian Imperial Police. Stationed in Burma, he encountered the harsh realities of colonial rule: He vividly depicts his reactions in the essays "Shooting an Elephant" and "A Hanging," and in the 1934 novel *Burmese Days*. Although critics faulted *Burmese Days* for its awkward attempts at descriptive writing, it is nonetheless an excellent study of the guilt, hypocrisy, and loneliness that infects the rulers of a subject population.

Disgusted with colonial life, Orwell left the police after five years, determined to become a writer. His first novel, 1933's *Down and Out in Paris and London*—which was based on a year he spent in self-imposed poverty—sympathetically examines the life of the poor. The author concluded that the lower classes of society are exploited much as colonial subjects are, and his later works would also reflect his indignation at this exploitation. Other novels Orwell wrote during the thirties deal with victimization as well: His protagonists—confused individuals who are preyed upon by society and their own weaknesses—attempt to rebel against their lot but ultimately fail.

Liberty is telling people what they do not want to hear."

—*George Orwell*

In December 1936 Orwell traveled to Barcelona, Spain, to write about the causes and progress of the Spanish Civil War. Joining a militia unit, he fought with the Republicans. After being wounded, he returned to England and wrote *Homage to Catalonia,* a 1938 account that depicts the absurdities of warfare, the duplicity of every political ideology, and the essential decency of ordinary people caught up in events beyond their control.

Political Purpose and Artistic Purpose

Orwell's first major critical and popular success as an author came with the publication of *Animal Farm* in 1945. A deceptively simple animal fable about a barnyard revolt, *Animal Farm* satirizes the consequences of the Russian Revolution while suggesting why most revolutionary ideals fail. Critics applauded Orwell's ability to create a narrative that functions on several levels, and the novel is generally regarded as a masterpiece of English prose. "*Animal Farm* was the first book in which I tried, with full consciousness of what I was doing, to fuse political purpose and artistic purpose into one whole." His

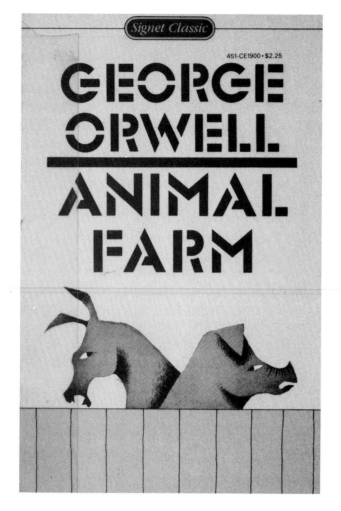

Signet Classic

451-CE1900 • $2.25

GEORGE
ORWELL
ANIMAL
FARM

Cover of *Animal Farm*, by George Orwell

income from the book's sales, though not great, enabled him to rent a house on the Scottish island of Jura in the spring of 1947, and there begin work on a new novel.

By December 1947 Orwell was hospitalized for treatment of tuberculosis, from which he had suffered since his mid-30s. He spent the first half of 1948 in Hairmyres Hospital in Glasgow, and on his release returned to Jura to complete the novel, tentatively titled *The Last Man in Europe;* it would eventually be published as *Nineteen Eighty-Four.*

Nineteen Eighty-Four attacks totalitarianism, warning that absolute power in the hands of any government can deprive a people of all basic freedoms. Although Orwell based the novel in part on the Soviet example, he set the story in England to underscore his conviction that unchecked power—even in the hands of a Western democracy—can result in a repressive regime.

Although very ill and under a doctor's orders to work no more than an hour each day, Orwell was unable to find a typist willing to come to the isolated island, so he prepared the final manuscript of *Nineteen Eighty-Four* himself. Collapsing almost immediately after he completed the task, he was bedridden for the remaining two years of his life. Many critics contended that the overwhelming pessimism of *Nineteen Eighty-Four* was directly related to the author's fatal illness—a position that is supported by Orwell's remark that the novel "wouldn't have been so gloomy if I hadn't been so ill."

Friends and acquaintances of Orwell, however, have emphatically maintained that *Nineteen Eighty-Four* was not meant to be Orwell's last book; nor was it meant to be his last word on the future. Orwell was a prolific writer who had lived by his pen for years, and often spoke of plans for essays and for another novel he hoped to write upon his recovery. He also remarried just three months before his death, telling his friend T. R. Fyvel that the marriage would give him another reason to live.

Animal Stories

Nothing in Orwell's career indicated that his desire to write politically committed literature that was "also an aesthetic experience" would find expression in a skillfully executed animal fable. J. R. Hammond described *Animal Farm* as "totally different in style and conception from anything Orwell had previously written"; similarly, Laurence Brander said the book was "a sport, out of [Orwell's] usual way; and yet more effective in the crusade to which he was dedicated than anything else he wrote."

Animal Farm represents a radical departure from the documentaries, essays, and novels that Orwell wrote in the 1930s; the author, however, was undoubtedly aware that the beast fable was uniquely suited to his own purposes of social and political satire. In such fables, each animal traditionally represents not only itself but an individual aspect of human nature as well; by drawing such simple characters, the author may thus avoid the psychological complications that go along with fully developed human characters. The conventions of the animal fable enabled Orwell to examine simply and directly the many levels of moral decisions made within a political system.

"In *Animal Farm*," Rama Rani Lall noted, "the animals are consistently animals and Orwell keeps the reader conscious simultaneously of the human traits satirized and of the animals as animals. He has successfully played upon the two levels of perception, making us feel that his animals are really animals and are yet as human as ourselves. Though he has couched his criticism in the simplest of terms, it is convincing because of the realistic pictures of animal life."

Reel Life

Animal Farm, 1955.

A barnyard full of animals start to fall into totalitarian habits in this animated version of Orwell's classic political satire.

1984, 1984.

Orwell's vision of the future (now past) comes to the big screen for the second time in this British version starring John Hurt and Richard Burton. Edmond O'Brien, Michael Redgrave, and Donald Pleasance appeared in a 1955 version of Orwell's tale—when 1984 was still the future.

Big Brother Is Watching

Nineteen Eighty-Four vividly portrays life in Oceania, a totalitarian state controlled by a mysterious Inner Party that exacts blind devotion to the Party and to its leader, Big Brother; this it accomplishes by constantly rewriting history (editing events to make the Party appear infallible) and by installing two-way telescreens monitored by Thought Police. The world is divided into three superstates—Oceania, Eastasia, and Eurasia—that are constantly realigning and continually at war. The constant warfare cripples the productive capabilities of each superpower so that the population of each exists in poverty and ignorance; meanwhile, reports of glorious victories on the battlefields, parades of captured enemy soldiers, and frequent public executions of spies and traitors to the State work the people into a patriotic frenzy. The novel recounts the brief revolt of one man, Winston Smith, against the control of the Party, and his eventual, inevitable defeat.

Beginning with the earliest reviews of *Nineteen Eighty-Four,* critics have tended to interpret the novel in one of three ways: as a satire of the contemporary social and political scene; as an attack on a specific political party or system (most often thought to be Stalinist communism); or as a general warning about the dangers of totalitarianism, which could result if any government were to assume absolute power. After noting that many early reviews of the book—particularly in the United States—assumed that the novel was meant as a pointed attack on a particular government, Orwell issued a statement to clarify his intentions in writing the book: The novel, he declared, was set in Britain "in order to emphasize ... that totalitarianism, if not fought against, could triumph anywhere."

The Wintry Conscience of a Generation

Orwell's fiction has left its mark on the modern imagination. The seventh commandment of Animalism in *Animal Farm*—that "all animals are equal, but some animals are more equal than others"—is widely known (and paraphrased). Various terms Orwell employed in *Nineteen Eighty-Four*—such as "Newspeak" and "double-think"—are part of our contemporary vocabulary; and "Big Brother"—perhaps the work's most famous coinage—has become synonymous with oppressive government.

Orwell's long struggle for success, his willingness to brave controversy, and his untimely death helped make him a figure of legend. In a famous obituary for *New Statesman,* V. S. Pritchett called Orwell "the wintry conscience of a generation" and "a kind of saint." Orwell's strengths were difficult to summarize. He may have done the best job himself when he described Charles Dickens, an author whose social concern and faith in human decency he greatly admired. The virtues Orwell saw in Dickens were perhaps those he valued in himself. "I see ... a man who is always fighting against something," Orwell wrote, "but who fights in the open and is not frightened ... a man who is generously angry—in other words ... a nineteenth-century liberal, a free intelligence, a type hated with equal hatred by all the smelly little orthodoxies which are now contending for our souls."

Sources

Aldritt, Keith, *The Making of George Orwell,* St. Martin's, 1961.

Bloom, Harold, *Modern Critical Views: George Orwell,* Chelsea House, 1987.

Gardner, Averil, *George Orwell,* Twayne, 1987.

Harper's, January 1969; January 1983.

Rodden, John, *The Politics of Literary Reputation: The Making and Claiming of "St. George" Orwell,* Oxford University Press, 1989.

Shelden, Michael, *Orwell: The Authorized Biography,* HarperCollins Publishers, 1991.

Woodcock, George, *The Crystal Spirit: A Study of George Orwell,* new edition, Schocken, 1984.

Meredith Ann Pierce

Born: July 5, 1958, Seattle, Washington

The author of the Darkangel trilogy creates a world where Alice in Wonderland meets Prince Valiant.

Meredith Ann Pierce's novels are full of imaginative plots and settings, poetic language, and determined, independent characters. Her most noted work, the Darkangel fantasy series, relates a young girl's struggle to free herself, her friends, and her world from an evil witch's power. Pierce's work "combines a mythic inventiveness with such elemental themes as love, conflict and quest," Joan Nist observed in the *ALAN Review;* she added that Pierce "is one of the foremost young authors of fantasy today." As a *Publishers Weekly* reviewer wrote, "The author's imagination seems boundless and she writes with such assurance that readers believe in every magic being and occurrence."

An Appetite for Information

"I was a great collector of stuffed animals and had several entire imaginary lives," Pierce once recalled of her childhood. As a little girl with an active imagination, she would spend hours talking and playing with her unseen companions. She also entertained herself with books, making trips to the library with her parents, who frequently read aloud to her. With their encouragement, she began to read by herself when she was about three years old. "I was extremely self-contained," she remembered. "Since I could read real young, I could get my hands on all this information—a book."

Wonderland and Writing for Profit

Pierce has fond memories of Lewis Carroll's classic *Alice's Adventures in Wonderland,* having read it over and over as a child. "*Alice in Wonderland* is like my religion," she says. "It was introduced into my system before my immune system was complete, so it's wired into my psyche. I can't distinguish between my own mythology and early influences like *Alice in Wonderland* or the movie *The Wizard of Oz.* Some of the stuff that I saw really impressed me when I was very little and just went straight into my neurons—it's inseparable from my way of thinking."

Although she constantly wrote down ideas and stories when she was a student, Pierce didn't realize that people could actually make a living writing novels. "My parents always treated my writing as another one of those obsessive little hobbies," she recalled, "Since they were the authority figure I had to pretend that this wasn't the most important thing in my life and find some other career." But at the University of Florida Pierce met professor and children's writer Joy Anderson, who showed her that writing could turn into a successful career. "Through her I got a much better idea of what writing is all about. She taught not just the craft of writing, but also the marketing aspect."

Anderson helped develop Pierce's talent. As part of her class assignments, she asked students to prepare a manuscript to be submitted to a publisher. "Joy was very good about shoring up my confidence and giving me real specific criticism," Pierce recalled. "If someone says 'Oh that's good, oh what a good writer you are, oh that's nice,' that's emotional stroking and I just hate that.... Joy would give me very precise suggestions and comments that would leave the solution up to me."

Best Bets

1982 ***The Darkangel***
A young girl struggles to free her world from an evil witch's power. First book in the Darkangel series, followed by *A Gathering of Gargoyles* and *The Pearl of the Soul of the World.*

1985 ***Birth of the Firebringer***
The story of Jan, the prince of the unicorns. Followed by a sequel, *Dark Moon,* in which Jan's father goes mad and brings the tribe to the brink of disaster.

1985 ***The Woman Who Loved Reindeer***
Mythical tale about a young woman who searches for the love she lost for the answer to problems that plague her homeland.

1992 ***Wild Magic***
Orphaned Daine—whose only family is the Long Lake wolf pack—is able to mind-speak with animals. The sequel, *Wolf-Speaker,* picks up with Daine and her friends opposing the "two-leggers" who are ruining the pack's home.

Cover of *The Woman Who Loved Reindeer* by Meredith Ann Pierce.

Vampires, Gargoyles, and Human Relationships

Pierce developed her first novel, *The Darkangel,* in this fashion. The story—set on the moon—follows the journey of Aeriel, a servant girl who sets out to rescue her mistress from a vampire who is evil but strangely attractive. Because of her experience in college, Pierce was not intimidated by having to find a publisher for the novel. Pierce's intuition proved right: *The Darkangel* was soon accepted by Little, Brown, and, published in 1982, it garnered much critical praise.

One outstanding feature of *The Darkangel* is Aeriel's determination to stand her ground in the face of danger. Although she is threatened by the vampire Irrylath, she frees his gargoyles and returns to his castle to confront him. According to Pierce, Aeriel's courage and persistence grew out of one of her own childhood experiences—when she was forced, as a young girl, to deal with an alcoholic and abusive relative who was much older and stronger than she. "One day I found myself in the absurd position of facing someone twice my size who, for no cause, had made up his mind to do me violence," Pierce related in a *Horn Book* article. "I found myself being filled by the most supernal fury. How dare this person believe I was just going to stand there and take this?" At that point Pierce determined not to give in, whatever the consequences, and the relative left her alone.

This showdown was "a little bit of a revelation," Pierce confided in an interview, "that a lot of human relationships are bluff, and that's an important thing to know." She continued, "Just because somebody tells you, 'This is the situation and I have great power over you,' doesn't mean it's true."

*P*ierce is intensely visual, even poetic, in her descriptions and
imaginative in her surprising plot turns."

—*Eleanor Cameron in the* New York Times Book Review

A Medieval Sensibility

In the second volume of the trilogy, *A Gathering of Gargoyles,* Aeriel discovers that Irrylath is still bound to the evil White Witch and cannot love another. To release him, Aeriel searches the moon to find their world's lost lons, ancient animal guardians who will help lead the battle against the Witch's forces. In the last novel of the series, *The Pearl of the Soul of the World,* Aeriel must bring the White Witch a gift and persuade her to renounce evil. This results in a showdown between good and evil, something that has fascinated Pierce for many years—ever since she discovered the comic strip "Prince Valiant."

Pierce would like to serve as an example for aspiring writers. "Anybody who's out there who's interested in writing I hope they'll read my stuff and say 'Gee, I'd like to write books like that,'" she said. "That is what I used to do when I would read one of my favorite authors when I was little." Pierce is also able to help aspiring young writers through her work as a librarian. "I see myself in them; I see them as not having the information that they need to decide whether or not they want to be a writer. So I try to supply [them] with as much information as they ask for on publishing."

Sources

Cameron, Eleanor, review of *A Gathering of Gargoyles, New York Times Book Review*, December 30, 1984, p. 19.

Nist, Joan, review of *The Woman Who Loved Reindeer, ALAN Review,* winter 1985, p. 31.

Pierce, Meredith Ann, "A Lion in the Room," *Horn Book,* January-February, 1988, pp. 35-41.

Rees, JoAnn, review of *Dark Moon, School Library Journal,* June 1992, p. 139.

Review of *A Gathering of Gargoyles, Publishers Weekly,* November 30, 1984, p. 92.

Roback, Diane, review of *The Pearl of the Soul of the World, Publishers Weekly,* February 9, 1990, p. 63.

Christopher Pike

The author of Slumber Party *writes mystery and suspense tales that seem to have "a hotline to the teenage psyche."*

"I'm often called the young Stephen King," said Christopher Pike (a pseudonym taken from a character on an early episode of *Star Trek*). "But I prefer to call King the old Christopher Pike." Pike is kidding, of course, but critics do often compare his books to King's, and the comparison is apt. Both authors write well-crafted, taut suspense novels that fans (and even critics) find nearly impossible to put down; both writers also regularly make the best-seller lists. But, while King writes for and about adults, Pike's characters and his audience are mainly comprised of teenagers.

Smells Like Teen Angst

Pike originally had his sights set on a career writing science fiction, which he had loved as a child growing up in southern California. A college dropout, Pike was unable to get his adult novels published; when his agent suggested he take a stab at writing for teens, Pike figured he had nothing to lose. The result was *Slumber Party,* which did very well for a "first" novel.

Pike commented that "I did sort of fall into writing for teens, but I think I've stayed with it, not just because of the money, but because I have a very romantic idea of high school. I guess I'm very nostalgic." While nostalgia may draw Pike to his teenage characters, he doesn't present a rosy, romantic view of the teen years; the characters in his books have serious problems. Dusty Shame (*The Wicked Heart*) lives with his mother, who has been ravaged by Alzheimer's, a disease that has destroyed her mind. Marvin Summer

(*Master of Murder*) supports his alcoholic mother and his little sister, sometimes having to defend them against his abusive father. Shari Cooper (*Remember Me*), looking on from beyond the grave, knows she was murdered even though her death is treated as a suicide. Still other Pike characters have more commonplace problems—like a jealous boyfriend or an unrequited love—which they take very much to heart.

Adolescent and Alone

When it comes to the problems that Pike's characters face, the adults in their lives aren't much help. If parents—or other "responsible" adults—aren't actually the cause of the kids' problems, they offer very little in the way of support or aid. Most of Pike's characters come from single-parent families, and that one parent is often somehow incapacitated. On the other hand, when Pike's characters have parents who truly serve as authority figures, they manage to be out of touch at climactic moments.

Left to their own devices and buffeted by the intense emotions of adolescence, Pike's characters frequently resort to extreme actions in an attempt to solve a problem, or at least to find some kind of escape. Herb Trasker (*Die Softly*), tired of lusting after girls who won't give him a second look, sets up a hidden camera in the girls' locker room to take pictures of the cheerleaders as they shower. Jane Retton (*Gimme a Kiss*) wants revenge too: Publicly humiliated when a page of her diary is circulated around school, she fakes her own death so that it appears her tormentors have killed her. Not surprisingly, Pike's teens tend to land in deep trouble.

A Hot Line to the Teenage Psyche

Critics have repeatedly praised Pike's ability to create believable and interesting characters; he has what Amy Gammerman of the *Wall Street Journal* described as an "apparent hot-line to the teenage psyche." Carefully examining his characters' motivations, he leads his readers to believe they really know the kids who

Best Bets

1989 ***Remember Me***
In a tale from beyond the grave, Shari Cooper knows she was murdered even though her death is treated as a suicide.

1991 ***Bury Me Deep***
On vacation in Hawaii, Jean Fiskal finds that her scuba instructors once gave lessons to the young man who died a gruesome death in the plane seat next to her.

1992 ***Monster***
Angela starts to understand why her friend Mary killed two people at a party because "they were no longer human."

1994 ***The Midnight Club***
Terminally ill teens spin tales in their posh private hospice.

A teenage ghost comes back to solve her own murder in Christopher Pike's *Remember Me*. Cover illustrated by Brian Kotzky.

inhabit his books. As Sue Tait and Christy Tyson stated in a review of *Last Act* in *Emergency Librarian*, "It is the relationship between the characters that makes (the book) work.... These are people who are really involved with each other, and when they are in danger the reader can't help but feel it too. Again, Pike's clear portraits provide the hook that is missing in many mysteries written for young adults."

Pike earns raves for his skill at creating suspense as well. In a review of *Scavenger Hunt,* Joyce Hamilton of *Voice of Youth Advocates* (*VOYA*) commented that "readers looking for a horror book will love it.... [*Scavenger Hunt*] will be impossible to put down." JoEllen Broome, in a review of *Spellbound* in *VOYA,* wrote that "This well-told tale of horror sparkles ... with high adventure, daring and romance.... A fun, frightening frolic indeed." And in a review of *Gimme A Kiss,* a *Booklist* critic claimed that "Pike pulls out all the stops," calling the story a "fast, suspenseful tale."

Violence, Villains, Heroes, and Morality

While critics often applaud Pike's characters and the pace of his novels, they are sometimes less than thrilled with his willingness to use graphic violence. In *Harper's,* Tom Engelhardt called Pike's books "novelizations of horror films that haven't yet been made," and claimed that in them, "junior psychos reign supreme," and "no mutilation is too terrible for the human face." But Pike believes that the criticism of the violence in his books is unjustified: "I feel that in order to have a great hero," he has said, "you have to have a great villain. Much of the classic literature that has been written is very violent. Look at *The Lord of The Rings,* which may be the classic work of our time—

it's a very violent book. Yet the heroes in that book are very noble, and it's only because the villains are so atrocious that the heroes can be so great. I feel that the moral center of my books is very good. The 'point of view' character usually is a good person, someone who is trying to do what is right.... I don't feel like I ever glorify violence."

A Dark Story for Dark Nights

Pike doesn't often base a character's feelings or experiences on his own. Again, *The Wicked Heart* was an exception to that rule. The physical pain Dusty feels and the emotional pain Sheila feels both grew out of real-life ordeals for Pike. "My girlfriend had just left me, and I'd had an injury to my side which ran into complications with my liver, so I was in tremendous pain. I remember writing that book in incredible pain, sometimes just sweating to death. It was a very hard book to write. I wrote it mainly at night, because I couldn't sleep at all. And when Sheila is pining away for her boyfriend—I just took that out of my own life," Pike said. The circumstances under which the book was written explain the unusual dedication in the book, which reads, "For myself. This dark story for those dark nights."

Sources

Broome, JoEllen, review of *Spellbound, Voice of Youth Advocates,* August 1988, p. 135.

Engelhardt, Tom, "Reading May Be Harmful To Your Kids," *Harper's,* June 1991, pp. 55–62.

Gamerman, Amy, "Gnarlatious Novels: Lurid Thrillers for the Teen Set," *Wall Street Journal,* May 28, 1991, p. A20.

Hamilton, Joyce, review of *Scavenger Hunt, Voice of Youth Advocates,* February 1990, p. 346.

Moy, Suelain, "To Shock Is the System," *Entertainment Weekly,* January 31, 1992, p. 68.

Pike, Christopher, interview with Sarah Verney for *Authors and Artists for Young Adults,* Gale, November 1993.

Review of *Gimme a Kiss, Booklist,* October 15, 1988, p. 400.

Review of *The Immortal, Publishers Weekly,* June 14, 1993, p. 72.

Review of *The Midnight Club, Publishers Weekly,* January 24, 1994, p. 57.

Tait, Sue, and Christy Tyson, "Paperbacks for Young Adults," *Emergency Librarian,* January–February 1989, pp. 53–54.

Wagner-Mees, Drue, review of *Gimme A Kiss, Voice of Youth Advocates,* April 1989, p. 31.

Daniel Manus Pinkwater

Born: November 15, 1941, Memphis, Tennessee

An accomplished illustrator, the author of Borgel *encourages readers to use their imaginations in everyday life.*

Were a blue moose to come striding into Daniel Manus Pinkwater's living room one day and ask for a cup of coffee, Pinkwater wouldn't be at all surprised: That's exactly the kind of situation he has been describing for years in his books for young readers. From his home in upstate New York, Pinkwater writes and illustrates books about the lives of such characters as Aunt Lulu, the Muffin Fiend, and the Frankenbagel Monster. Though Pinkwater's characters are absurd, his intent in writing is not; "I want my readers to feel encouraged and snarky, because basically they are kids taking on a hostile and/or indifferent world," the author confided in an interview. "My books are about finding favoring signs in the world, about discovering riches—things which are not dead. My stories are about people prevailing."

A Well-Sculpted Story

Born in Memphis, Tennessee, Pinkwater grew up in Chicago. He remembers the kids in his neighborhood acting out the stories that they had read in adventure books like Jules Verne's *20,000 Leagues under the Sea* and the *Three Musketeers* by Alexandre Dumas. "We heard about books by word of mouth—the kid next door had an older brother who told me about the *Three Musketeers*," the author recalled. "I got to read good books, although mainly adventure stories." Much like the characters in his stories, Pinkwater considered himself an oddball as a child; he was lucky enough, however, to find a group of boys who shared his interests, which kept him from feeling alienated.

During his time at Bard College in Annandale-on-Hudson, New York, Pinkwater decided to become a sculptor in order to become a good writer. By the time he finished college and a three-year apprenticeship with a sculptor, however, he had changed his mind. When he returned to writing four years later, he realized that he *was* a better writer thanks to his sculpting experience. Hence the author's advice to aspiring authors: Learn to do something other than writing.

Sweaty, Spotty, Stinky Kids

Pinkwater once noted that he didn't "decide" to write books for young readers; he "floated into it." Having produced a set of illustrations for the book that was to become *The Terrible Roar,* he didn't want to deal with someone else writing the text for the book. So he wrote it himself. Though his first few books were "just a giggle" for him, he found them more and more interesting and soon committed himself to writing full-time. "I thought after two or three books I would have saturated my audience, whom I imagined as fat, bespectacled, intellectual boys," he commented. "I often receive photographs from my readers, including good-looking ... kids, who are captains of their soccer teams. It's not just the sweaty, spotty, stinky, pimply kids who do college physics in middle school who read my work, although, of course those are my favorites."

Art and Everyday Reality

Although Pinkwater's books have been classified as fantasy and science fiction, Janice Alberghene argued in *Twentieth-Century Children's Writers* that the author "is less interested in the creation of a separate secondary world or alternate universe ... than he is in the eruption of the fantastic into everyday

Best Bets

1975 ***Blue Moose***
A blue moose walks into a restaurant and is hired as a waiter.

1979 ***Yorborgle: Mystery Monster of Lake Ontario***
Eugene Winkelman accompanies his Uncle Mel—a fast food fanatic—on a dull business trip that perks up after Eugene meets a number of interesting characters after viewing a movie about monster Yorborgle.

1982 ***The Snarkout Boys and the Avocado of Death***
Walter, Winston, and Rat must find Rat's uncle and save the world from space-realtors.

1986 ***Moosepire***
A railroad boxcar operates as a time machine.

1990 ***Borgel***
Borgel invites Melvin and Fafner on a magical ride in an old 1937 sedan through "Space, Time and the Other"; they meet strange characters, search for the "Great Popsicle," and, eventually running out of steam, head home to watch television.

Cover of *The Snarkout Boys & The Baconburg Horror*, from The Snarkout Boys series, by Daniel Pinkwater. Illustrated by the author.

reality." Introducing extraordinary events into rather ordinary situations, Pinkwater has a knack for making commonplace situations stand out. In *Blue Moose,* for example, the title character walks into a restaurant and is hired as a waiter, and in *The Moosepire,* a railroad boxcar operates as a time machine. By putting a new twist on everyday occurrences, both books show how imagination can animate even the most mundane situation.

Some critics, however, think that Pinkwater overindulges in absurdity. Reviewing *Yobgorgle: Mystery Monster of Lake Ontario* for *Children's Book Review Service,* John Cech found that the continual "weirdness" of Pinkwater's story drains the reader's patience. Further, he suggested that the story is "without substance." On the other hand, many reviewers find that Pinkwater's books—as a *Publishers Weekly* critic commented—"have all been notably imaginative and appealing." Michele Landsberg wrote in the Toronto *Globe & Mail* that "my entire family, in fact, relishes Pinkwater's benign surrealism, his deadpan post-[Monty] Python humor and rich allusiveness, and his hidden but unmistakable tenderness for underdogs and oddballs."

Though Pinkwater's stories are not serious, he is very serious about his work. "I think ... books [for young readers] are the most important thing you can do," Pinkwater told Joann Davis in *Publishers Weekly,* "because these are people who are learning about reading." He says that one of his goals as a writer is to celebrate dying cultural treasures such as beer gardens, used bookstores, old railroad cars, and other aspects of urban life. Pinkwater doesn't hesitate to mention the names of authors and artists in his works, hoping to encourage young readers to learn more about those people.

It is par for the course to find James Dean, The Sorrows of Young Werewolf, and a giant avocado capable of being modified into a thought-wave producing 'Alligatron' all within the covers of the same [Pinkwater] book."

—Janice M. Alberghene writing in Twentieth-Century Children's Writers

Even though Pinkwater's books don't focus on teaching, the author admitted that "it is an intention of my books to present the sheer pleasure of the phenomena of civilized life." What's more, Pinkwater has firm convictions about the role of art in life: "I also believe it is impossible to make sense of life in this world except through art.... The only way we can deal with the proliferation of ideas ... is to make a story or a picture out of it. At present, there are things happening that I like, as well as things I don't like; by participating I'm able to put some weight on the side of the things I like."

Sources

Alberghene, Janice M., essay in *Twentieth-Century Children's Writers,* 3rd edition, St. James Press, 1989, pp. 781–782.

Cech, John, review of *Yobgorgle: Mystery Monster of Lake Ontario, Children's Book Review Service,* winter 1980, pp. 68–69.

Davis, Joann, "Spring Is a Season of Plenty for Children's Author Daniel Pinkwater," *Publishers Weekly,* May 7, 1982, pp. 53–54.

Engelfried, Steven, review of *The Phantom of the Lunch Wagon, School Library Journal,* December 1992, p. 88.

Janick, Lori A., review of *Author's Day, School Library Journal,* July 1993, p. 68.

Landsberg, Michele, "A Loopily Sane Social Satirist," *Globe & Mail* (Toronto), April 18, 1987.

Peters, John, review of *Guys From Space, School Library Journal,* June 1989, p. 91.

Pinkwater, Daniel M., interview in *Something about the Author,* Volume 46, Gale, 1987, pp. 178–191.

Review of *Lizard Music, Publishers Weekly,* October 18, 1976, p. 64.

Scanlon, Donna L., review of *Spaceburger: A Kevin Spoon and Mason Mintz Story, School Library Journal,* February 1994, p. 90.

Edgar Allan Poe

Born: January 19, 1809, Boston, Massachusetts
Died: October 7, 1849, Baltimore, Maryland

The author of such horror classics as The Murders in the Rue Morgue *is also considered to be the Great-Grandfather of Science Fiction and Detective Fiction.*

Edgar Allan Poe stands as a major figure in world literature. In his ingenious and profound short stories, his many poems, and his critical theories, he demonstrated a brilliant command of language and technique as well as an inspired and original imagination. Regarded as the architect of the modern short story, Poe was also the principal forerunner of the "art for art's sake" movement in nineteenth-century European literature. Stories like "The Fall of the House of Usher" and "The Masque of the Red Death" are classics of macabre literature and have made a lasting mark on the collective imagination of generations of readers.

A Poet in the Military

Poe's parents were professional actors who, at the time of his birth, belonged to a repertory company in Boston, Massachusetts. Before Poe was three years old both his father and mother had died; he was raised by John Allan, a prosperous exporter living in Richmond, Virginia, who never legally adopted his foster son. As a boy, Poe attended the best schools available, and was admitted to the University of Virginia at Charlottesville in 1825. While there he distinguished himself academically but was forced to leave after less than a year because of bad debts and inadequate financial support from Allan.

Poe's relationship with his foster father fell apart when he returned home to Richmond in 1827; soon thereafter he left for Boston, where he enlisted in the army and published his first poetry collection—*Tamerlane, and Other*

Poems. The volume went unnoticed by readers and reviewers, and a second collection—*Al Aaraaf, Tamerlane, and Minor Poems*—received only slightly more attention when it appeared in 1829.

That same year Poe was honorably discharged from the army, having attained the rank of regimental sergeant major. He then gained admission to the U.S. Military Academy at West Point. However, because Allan would neither provide his foster son with sufficient funds to maintain himself as a cadet nor give the parental consent necessary to allow Poe to resign from the academy, Poe managed to get himself dismissed by ignoring his duties and violating regulations. He later moved to New York City, where *Poems,* his third collection of verse, was published in 1831, and then to Baltimore, where Poe lived at the home of his aunt, Mrs. Maria Clemm.

Best Bets

1840 ***Tales of the Grotesque and Arabesque***
A collection of offbeat stories from the master of the macabre.

1845 ***Prose Romances: The Murders in the Rue Morgue and The Man That Was Used Up***
More macabre musings about gruesome deaths and mutilated corpses.

1976 ***The Science Fiction of Edgar Allan Poe***
Speculative and fantastic narratives that anticipate a genre that didn't come into its own until nearly a century after Poe's stories were first published.

A Short Life Filled with Short Stories

Over the next few years Poe's first short stories appeared in the *Philadelphia Saturday Courier* and his "MS. [manuscript] Found in a Bottle" won a cash prize for best story in the *Baltimore Saturday Visitor.* Still, Poe was not earning enough to live independently, nor did Allan's death in 1834 provide him with a legacy. The following year, however, the writer's financial problems were temporarily eased when he accepted an editorship at *The Southern Literary Messenger* in Richmond, bringing with him his Aunt Clemm and his 12-year-old cousin Virginia, whom he married in 1836. *The Southern Literary Messenger* was the first of several journals Poe would direct over the next ten years, and he soon became a leading man of letters in America.

Known not only as a talented author of poetry and fiction, Poe established himself as a literary critic whose imagination and insight distinguished him from his predecessors. While his writings garnered attention in the late 1830s and early 1840s, the profits from his work remained meager; Poe supported himself by editing *Burton's Gentleman's Magazine* and *Graham's Magazine* in Philadelphia and New York City's *Broadway Journal.* After his young wife died from tuberculosis in 1847, Poe became involved in a number

Reel Life

Masque of the Red Death, 1965.

As the deadly plague rages outside his castle, an evil prince (Vincent Price) practices black magic and tempts a village lass to join him.

Murders in the Rue Morgue, 1986.

In 19th-century Paris, the actors in a mystery play find their roles are coming to life before their very eyes. George C. Scott, Rebecca DeMornay, and Val Kilmer star in this made-for-television version of the Poe story—its fifth screen incarnation.

The Raven, 1963.

Rival sorcerers battle amongst themselves in this tongue-in-cheek rendering of the classic Poe poem. Vincent Price and Boris Karloff play rival sorcerers while Peter Lorre, as their unfortunate associate, is turned into the title character.

of romantic affairs and eventually became engaged. As he prepared for his second marriage in late September of 1849, Poe inexplicably made his way to Baltimore. On October 3, he was discovered there in a state of semiconsciousness; he died four days later without ever having been able to explain what had happened during the last days of his life.

The Father of Many Genres

A certain psychological intensity is characteristic of Poe's writings, especially the tales of horror that comprise his best and best-known works. Poe often recounts these stories—which include "The Black Cat," "The Cask of Amontillado," and "The Tell-Tale Heart"—through a first-person narrator; in this way Poe probes the workings of his character's psyche. In his Gothic tales, Poe also employed an essentially symbolic, almost allegorical [having a hidden spiritual meaning] method which gives such works as "The Fall of the House of Usher," "The Masque of the Red Death," and "Ligeia" a mysterious quality that accounts for their enduring popularity.

In addition to his achievement as creator of the modern horror tale, Poe is also credited with inspiring two other popular genres: science fiction and the detective story. In such works as "The Unparalleled Adventure of Hans Pfaall" and "Von Kempelen and His Discovery," Poe took advantage of the nineteenth century's fascination for science and technology to produce narratives—filled with fantasy and speculation about the future—that look toward a type of literature that did not become widely practiced until after 1900. Similarly, critics recognize Poe's three tales of ratiocination [the process of reasoned thinking]—"The Murders in the Rue Morgue," "The Purloined Letter," and "The Mystery of Marie Roget"—as the models that established the major character types and literary conventions of detective fiction. The amateur sleuth who solves a crime that has confounded the authorities and whose feats of deductive reasoning are documented by an admiring associate was a creation, first, of Poe.

Poetic Journeys into the Imagination

While Poe is most often remembered for his short fiction, his first love as a writer was poetry, which he began writing during his adolescence. His early verse reflects influences of such nineteenth-century English romantic poets as Lord Byron, John Keats, and Percy Bysshe Shelley, while foreshadowing the subjective outlook and surreal, mystic vision of his later poetry. "Tamerlane" and "Al Aaraaf" exemplify Poe's evolution from portraying heroes inspired by Byron to the depiction of journeys within his own imagination and subconscious.

In "The Raven," Poe investigates the loss of ideal beauty and the difficulty in regaining it. In this psychological piece, a young scholar is emotionally tormented by a raven's ominous repetition of "Nevermore" in answer to his question about the probability of an afterlife with his deceased lover. Charles Baudelaire noted in his introduction to the French edition of "The Raven," "It is indeed the poem of the sleeplessness of despair; it lacks nothing: neither the fever of ideas, nor the violence of colors, nor sickly reasoning, nor drivelling terror, nor even the bizarre gaiety of suffering which makes it more terrible."

Wood engraving by Fritz Eichenberg, from "The Fall of the House of Usher." (From *Tales of Edgar Allan Poe,* 1944.)

Ludwig's Legacy

While his works weren't fully appreciated during his lifetime, Poe was respected as a gifted fiction writer, poet, and man of letters—and he occasionally achieved a measure of popular success, especially following the appearance of "The Raven." After his death, however, the author suffered from gross misinterpretation—a trend initiated by Poe's one-time friend R. W. Griswold. In a libelous obituary notice in the *New York Tribune* bearing the byline "Ludwig," Griswold attributed the depravity and psychological aberrations [abnormalities] of many of the characters in Poe's fiction to the author himself. But Griswold's claims seem to have aroused as much sympathy as censure with respect to Poe and his work, leading later biographers to defend—sometimes too devotedly—Poe's name.

It was not until 1941 that A. H. Quinn, in a biography of Poe, offered a balanced view of the relationship between the author's life and his imagination. Nevertheless, twentieth-century readers continued to identify Poe with the murderers and madmen of his works. Adding to the controversy over Poe's sanity, critics questioned the value of his works as serious literature. At the forefront of Poe's detractors were such eminent figures as novelists Henry James and Aldous Huxley, and poet T. S. Eliot, who dismissed Poe's works as juvenile, vulgar, and artistically debased; in contrast, writers such as Bernard Shaw and William Carlos Williams have judged these same works to be literary masterpieces.

Sources

Bloom, Harold, editor, *Edgar Allan Poe,* Chelsea House, 1985.

Campbell, Killis, *The Mind of Poe and Other Studies,* Harvard University Press, 1933.

Gould, Stephen Jay, "Poe's Greatest Hit," *Natural History,* July 1993, p. 10.

Harrison, J.A. *The Life of Edgar Allan Poe,* Crowell, 1902.

Smith, Gary, "Once Upon a Midnight Dreary: Cognac, Roses and Edgar Allan Poe: A Graveyard Mystery," *Life,* July 1990, p. 48.

Wagenknecht, Edward, *Edgar Allan Poe: The Man Behind the Legend,* Oxford University Press, 1963.

Woodbury, George Edward, *The Life of Edgar Allan Poe, Personal and Literary,* Chelsea House, 1980.

Terry Pratchett

Born: 1948, Buckinghamshire, England

First a journalist and then a press officer for the Central Electricity Board in Britain, Terry Pratchett eventually turned his talents to writing science fiction. Winner of the 1990 British Science Fiction Award, he combines clever storylines, exotic settings, and humor to create some of the most promising works of science fiction and fantasy being written today.

Romps with Dragons

In *Strata,* Pratchett's protagonist is a woman whose job is to oversee the construction of planets. But her job, it seems, is not entirely straightforward: She must take great pains to ensure that her subordinates do not plant anachronistic items [items that are out of their chronological context] in the strata of these worlds. When a mysterious visitor informs her of the existence of a flat world—which is lost in space and is inhabited by people who appear to be human—she sets off with a number of companions—some human, some not—to find the flat planet. Unfortunately,

The author of the Discworld series writes tales of witches, wizards, and sons of Satan—all with a sly sense of humor.

a series of mishaps results in the loss of their guide and the eventual incapacitation of their spacecraft. They do manage, however, to land at their destinations, and what ensues is a hilarious romp among dragons, robots, aliens, and other creatures.

The Dark Side of the Sun is a slightly more serious work. The protagonist—a rich heir to a powerful title—sets off on a quest to find the Jokers' World, home of a legendary space-alien species. In *The Dark Side of the Sun,*

Cover of *The Wyrd Sisters* by Terry Pratchett.

the laws of chance can be manipulated, and coincidence can save lives. Again, Pratchett's novel takes place in a richly creative world rife with aliens, religious and philosophical speculations, and exotic settings. What's more, the author's light-hearted approach turns what would otherwise be a standard adventure story into a witty exercise of the imagination.

A Giant Tortoise Swimming in Space

It was with *The Colour of Magic,* however, that Pratchett hit his stride. This first volume of the ongoing Discworld series consists of four interrelated adventures. A flat planet, Discworld is not set in a rational universe: The planet is supported on the backs of four gigantic elephants astride the shell of an immense tortoise swimming in space. A wild worldview, perhaps; but the inhabitants know that their view of the universe is correct because they have lowered observers over the edge to see for themselves.

Rincewind—one of the least likely magicians ever to grace the pages of fiction—appears ian *The Colour of Magic* as well as later chronicles of Discworld. In this instance, he agrees to provide his services as a guide to a visitor from another planet interested in exploration. Their travels result in encounters with malevolent animals, wizards, monsters, and other villains in what is essentially a satire on the fantasy genre itself.

Misdirected Magic

Pratchett has since produced fairly regular chronicles of Discworld. Magical madness continues as Rincewind combats the appearance of a strange new star in *The Light Fantastic*. Granny Weatherwax, a canny old witch, takes center stage in *Equal Rites*, trying to straighten out the problems that ensue when the eighth son of an eighth son is ... a daughter. More misdirected magic dominates the scene in *Sourcery* and in *Wyrd Sisters*, a retelling of the traditional story of the prince regaining his throne. To Pratchett nothing is sacred; ancient Egypt gets raked over the coals in *Pyramids*. Possibly the funniest of this hilarious series is *Mort*, in which Death goes on a holiday after taking on an inept apprentice who is just too kindhearted to harvest all the souls who are scheduled to pass on. Considering the number of volumes in this series, readers might expect Pratchett to begin repeating himself; each book, however, is as fresh, inventive, and hilarious as its predecessors.

Pratchett's recent novel *Good Omens: The Nice and Accurate Predictions of Agnes Nutter, Witch* (written in collaboration with comic-book writer Neil Gaiman), is a send-up of modern horror themes, particularly the Omen series of films and its imitators. When the son of Satan is misplaced and raised as a nice child, the schedule of Armageddon is thrown awry, and the powers of Heaven and Hell must pitch together to work things out. A rare novel, *Good Omens* proves that humor can be more than just great entertainment.

Best Bets

1991 *Reaper Man*
When Death is relieved of his duties, nothing on Discworld dies and zombies become a serious problem in the city of Ankh-Morpork. The 10th book of the Discworld series.

Sources

Chang, Margaret A., review of *Wings, School Library Journal,* September 1991, p. 258.

Easton, Tom, review of *Good Omens: The Nice and Accurate Prophecies of Agnes Nutter, Witch, Analog,* February 1991, p. 180.

Flowers, Anne A., review of *Diggers, Horn Book,* May-June 1991, p. 332.

Kaganoff, Penny, review of *Mort, Publishers Weekly,* February 24, 1989, p. 226.

Kaganoff, Penny, review of *Sourcery, Publishers Weekly,* November 10, 1989, p. 57.

Roback, Diane, review of *Truckers, Publishers Weekly,* February 9, 1990, p. 63.

Anne Rice

Born: October 4, 1941, New Orleans, Louisiana

The author of the Vampire Chronicles breathes new life into well-worn coffins and terrifying tombs.

A nne Rice will live on through the ages of literature.... To read her ... is to become light-headed as if our blood is slowly being drained away," exclaimed the *San Francisco Chronicle*. Crafting novels about the bizarre and the supernatural, Rice—who is probably best known for her Vampire Chronicles—has won both critical acclaim and a readership of cult proportions.

Light Years from the Garden

Rice grew up with three sisters in an area of New Orleans called the Irish Channel. Her father worked for the post office and wrote unpublished fiction, while her mother, Katherine, was an alcoholic who combined southern-belle enchantment with strict Catholicism. Rice enjoyed a close relationship with her mother, who, despite her strictness, was also a magnificent storyteller and an advocate of freedom of expression and originality. At the age of 14, however, Rice lost her mother to alcoholism.

Throughout her childhood Rice constantly imagined what life would be like in the majestic homes of New Orleans's Garden District. The marked differences between her own life in the Irish Channel and the lives of those inside these grand houses of the Garden District often made her feel like an outsider, a feeling shared by many of the characters she creates. Daydreams filled Rice's early years, and she developed a vivid imagination. In a *Rolling Stone* article, Gerri Hirshey pointed out that Rice "was a fifth grader at the Holy Name of Jesus School when she filled a notebook with her first novel about two kids from Mars who commit suicide."

Grief, an Insatiable Thirst, and Eternal Life

Rice married her high school sweetheart, poet Stan Rice, at the age of 20. The following year they had a daughter, Michele; then Rice had a prophetic dream. "I dreamed my daughter, Michele, was dying—that there was something wrong with her blood," she recalled in a *People* interview. Several months later, Michele was diagnosed with a rare form of leukemia and died shortly before her sixth birthday. "Two years later," Hirshey observed, "her image was reincarnated as the child vampire Claudia in *Interview* [*with the Vampire*], Anne's first published work." Claudia, like Michele, is beautiful and blond; unlike Michele, however, she is granted eternal life at the age of six. "It was written out of grief, the author says, in five weeks of 'white-hot, access-the-subconscious' sessions between 10:00 P.M. and dawn," added Hirshey.

Vampire as Metaphor

As its title describes, *Interview with the Vampire,* the first book of the Vampire Chronicles, is the result of an evening in which Louis—who wrestles with morality as a vampire—tells his story to a fascinated young mortal. Poignantly, he speaks of Lestat, his creator, Claudia, his creation, and his former life as an eighteenth-century mortal.

The novel, which actually began in the late 1960s as a short story, developed into something much larger following Michele's death. "Suddenly, in the guise of Louis, a fantasy figure, I was able to touch the reality that was mine," explained Rice in a *Publishers Weekly* interview.

Best Bets

1976 ***Interview with the Vampire***
Vampire Louis recounts the story of his creation and his former life as a mortal. The first book of the Vampire Chronicles, followed by *The Vampire Lestat* and *The Queen of the Damned.*

1989 ***The Mummy: Or Ramses the Damned***
When an Egyptologist finds his tomb, Egyptian ruler Ramses wakes from a very long sleep.

1990 ***The Witching Hour***
Generations of witches inhabit a New Orleans mansion while an evil spirit waits his turn to become flesh. The first book of a trilogy; followed by *Lasher* and *Taltos: Lives of the Mayfair Witches.*

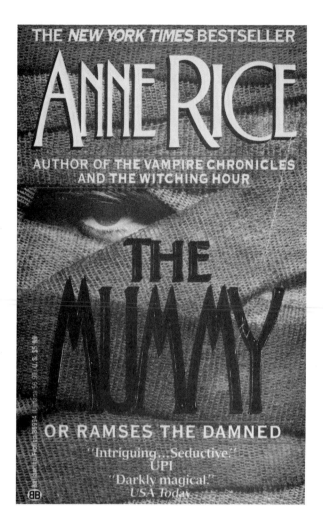

THE *NEW YORK TIMES* BESTSELLER

ANNE RICE

AUTHOR OF THE VAMPIRE CHRONICLES
AND THE WITCHING HOUR

THE MUMMY

OR RAMSES THE DAMNED

"Intriguing...Seductive."
UPI
"Darkly magical."
USA Today

Cover from the best-seller *The Mummy* by Anne Rice.

Undead Again

The Vampire Lestat appeared in 1985. In this second novel of the Vampire Chronicles, Lestat, who has returned to America and buried himself, awakens from his sleep of many years to find himself in the 1980s. The novel, in the form of an autobiography, is part of a marketing campaign to launch Lestat's new rock and roll career. Nina Auerbach found the novel "ornate and pungently witty in the classic tradition of gothic fiction, it teases and tantalizes us into accepting its kaleidoscopic world. Even when they annoy us or tell us more than we want to know, its undead characters are utterly alive."

The Queen of the Damned, the third book in the Vampire Chronicles, opens before Lestat's concert, following the wrathful vampires in the crowd as they plot his destruction. He has some supporters, though, among them Akasha, the mother of all vampires and queen of the damned, who has been awakened by Lestat from her several-centuries-long sleep. Far from a nurturing character, however, Akasha wants to bring peace to the world by killing 90 percent of all males and creating a kingdom ruled by women.

Mummy Dearest

In 1988, after several years of writing romance and historical novels under pseudonyms, Rice returned to both New Orleans and to writing about the supernatural world under her own name. In 1989 she released *The Mummy: Or Ramses the Damned,* and *The Witching Hour* followed in 1990. *The Mummy* tells the story of Ramses the Great, who ruled Egypt 3,000 years ago; having taken an elixir that gives him eternal life, Ramses is awakened from his sleep by a British Egyptologist who finds his tomb.

Rice brings a fresh and powerful imagination to the staples of vampire lore; she makes well-worn coffins and crucifixes tell new tales that compose a chillingly original myth."

—Nina Auerbach, New York Times Book Review

Rice's large, antebellum mansion in New Orleans becomes the setting for *The Witching Hour*. Inhabiting the old mansion is the Mayfair family, whose generations of witches have had to contend with Lasher, a spirit who patiently awaits his opportunity to become flesh. While some reviewers agreed with Patrick McGrath's assessment in the *New York Times Book Review* that "the book is bloated, grown to elephantine proportions," others praised the story's believability. Susan Isaacs, in her *Washington Post Book World* review, asserted that "halfway through the novel, even the most skeptical reader has no trouble believing in the existence of witches and—yes—in The Man, Lasher, the devil incarnate."

Spending most of her time with her husband and son, Christopher, and the rest writing, Rice seeks immortality through her books. "I want my books to live, to be read after I'm dead," the author confided in her *Lear's* interview. "That will be justification enough for all the pain and work and struggling and doubt."

Sources

Auerbach, Nina, "No. 2 with a Silver Bullet," *New York Times Book Review,* October 27, 1985, p. 15.

Current Biography, H. W. Wilson, July 1991, p. 54.

Ferraro, Susan, "Novels You Can Sink Your Teeth Into," *New York Times Magazine,* October 14, 1990, p. 26.

Hirshey, Gerri, "Flesh for Fantasy," *Rolling Stone,* November 20, 1986, pp. 91-94, 155.

Holditch, W. Kenneth, "Interview With Anne Rice," *Lear's,* October 1989, pp. 87-89, 155.

Isaacs, Susan, "Bewitched and Bewildered," *Washington Post Book World,* October 28, 1990, pp. 1-2.

Kirchhoff, H. J., "Adventure, Romance and a Modern Vampire," *Globe & Mail* (Toronto), March 15, 1986.

Lovell, James Blair, "The Call of the Wild," *Washington Post Book World,* June 18, 1989, p. 4.

McGrath, Patrick, "Ghastly and Unnatural Ambitions," *New York Times Book Review,* November 4, 1990, p. 11.

Preston, John, and Silvia Taccani, interview with Anne Rice, *Interview,* December 1990, p. 126.

Prial, Frank J., "Undead and Unstoppable," *New York Times Book Review,* June 11, 1989, p. 8.

Review of *The Queen of the Damned, Publishers Weekly,* August 12, 1988, p. 40.

Wadler, Joyce, and Johnny Greene, "Anne Rice's Imagination May Roam Among Vampires and Erotica, but Her Heart Is Right at Home," *People,* December 5, 1988, pp. 131-134.

Mary Wollstonecraft Shelley

Born: August 30, 1797, London, England
Died: February 1, 1851, Bournemouth, England

Mary Wollstonecraft Shelley is best known for *Frankenstein; or, The Modern Prometheus*—a novel that has transcended the gothic and horror genres to gain recognition as a work of philosophical and psychological depth. Critics agree Shelley's depiction of a seemingly godless universe where science and technology have gone awry was a powerful metaphor for the modern age. Indeed, the Frankenstein myth—which has been adapted to stage, film, and television—has become part of modern culture. Shelley's achievement is considered remarkable, moreover, because she completed the book before her twentieth birthday. She also wrote several novels that, while mildly successful in their time, are little known today, and issued an edition of poetry by her husband—the Romantic poet Percy Bysshe Shelley—with notes that are now regarded as indispensable. Shelley's reputation continues to rest, however, on what she once called her "hideous progeny," *Frankenstein*.

This accomplished writer, poet, and critic is best remembered as the author of Frankenstein.

Feminists and Freethinkers

Shelley's personal life has sometimes overshadowed her literary work. She was the daughter of Mary Wollstonecraft, an early feminist who authored *A Vindication of the Rights of Woman,* and William Godwin, a political philosopher and novelist. Her parents' wedding, which occurred when Wollstonecraft was five months pregnant with Mary, was the marriage of two of the era's most noted freethinkers; while both parents objected to the

Best Bets

institution of matrimony, they agreed to marry to ensure their child's legitimacy. Ten days after Mary's birth, Wollstonecraft died from complications, leaving Godwin, an undemonstrative and self-absorbed intellectual, to care for both Mary and Fanny Imlay, Wollstonecraft's daughter from an earlier relationship.

Mary's home life improved little with the arrival four years later of a stepmother and her two children. The new Mrs. Godwin, who contemporaries described as petty and disagreeable, favored her own offspring over the daughters of the celebrated Wollstonecraft, and Mary often found herself alone and unhappy. Although not formally educated, she absorbed the intellectual atmosphere created by her father and such visitors as poet Samuel Taylor Coleridge. She read a wide variety of books, notably those of her mother, whom she idolized. Young Mary's favorite retreat was Wollstonecraft's grave in the St. Pancras churchyard, where she went to read and write and eventually to meet her lover, Percy Shelley.

Trying Times

An admirer of Godwin, Percy Shelley visited the author's home and briefly met Mary when she was 14, but their attraction did not take hold until they met again two years later. At 22, Percy Shelley was married and his wife was expecting their second child. He and Mary, however—like Godwin and Wollstonecraft—believed that ties of the heart were more important than legal ties. In July 1814, one month before her 17th birthday, Mary eloped with Percy, and they spent the next few years traveling in Switzerland, Germany, and Italy. These years were characterized by financial difficulty and personal tragedy. Percy's father, Sir Timothy Shelley, a wealthy baronet, cut off his son's substantial allowance after he deserted his family; in 1816 Mary's half-sister Fanny committed suicide; and weeks later, Percy's wife, Harriet, drowned herself.

Mary and Percy were married in London, in part because they hoped to gain custody of his two children by his first wife—but custody was denied. Three of the couple's own children died in infancy, and Mary fell into a deep depression that didn't lift until after Percy Florence—her only surviving

From the movie *Bride of Frankenstein* (1935), starring Elsa Lanchester and Boris Karloff.

child—was born in 1819. The Shelleys' marriage suffered, too, in the wake of their children's deaths, and Percy became involved with other women. Despite these trying circumstances, both Mary and Percy continued to study rigorously—applying themselves to European literature and Greek, Latin, and Italian language, art, and music. They also wrote ambitiously: During this period Mary completed *Frankenstein* and another novel, *Valperga,* published in 1823. The two also enjoyed a close group of stimulating friends, notably Lord Byron and Leigh Hunt. The Shelleys were settled near Lenci, Italy, on the Gulf of Spezzia in 1822 when Percy drowned during a storm while sailing to meet Leigh and Marianne Hunt. After one mournful year in Italy, Mary returned permanently to England with her son.

After Percy died, Shelley struggled to support herself and her child. Sir Timothy Shelley offered her a meager stipend, but ordered that she keep the Shelley name out of print; all her works were thus published anonymously. In addition to producing four novels in the years after Percy's death, Mary contributed a series of biographical and critical sketches to *Chamber's Cabinet*

Reel Life

As early as 1908, Shelley's "hideous progeny" made its way into American movies. In 1931, playing a strangely sympathetic monster, Boris Karloff launched his brilliant career as a monster star and the movie became a gothic horror classic that would set the mold for monster movies to come.

Sequels to Frankenstein include *Bride of Frankenstein* (1935), *Son of Frankenstein* (1939), *Ghost of Frankenstein* (1943), *House of Frankenstein* (1945), *House of Dracula* (1945), *Abbott and Costello Meet Frankenstein* (1948), *The Curse of Frankenstein*, (1956) and *Frankenstein and the Monster from Hell* (1973). In 1974 Mel Brooks directed *Young Frankenstein*, and in 1994 Kenneth Branagh directed his version of *Frankenstein*, with Robert DeNiro playing the monster.

Cyclopedia, as well as occasional short stories—which she considered potboilers—to the literary annuals of the day. The Shelleys' financial situation improved when Sir Timothy increased Percy Florence's allowance with his coming-of-age in 1840, enabling mother and son to travel in Italy and Germany; their journeys are recounted in 1844's *Rambles in Germany and Italy in 1840, 1842, and 1843*. Too ill in her last few years to complete her most cherished project, a biography of her husband, Shelley died at the age of 54.

In the Shadow of the Monster

Although *Frankenstein* has consistently dominated critical discussions of Shelley's works, she composed several other novels as well as critical and biographical writings. Her five later novels attracted little notice, and critics generally agree that they suffer from wordiness and awkward plotting. After *Frankenstein*, *The Last Man*, published in 1826, is probably Shelley's best-known work. Critics consider this novel—in which Shelley describes the destruction of the human race in the twenty-first century—to be an inventive depiction of the future and an early prototype of science fiction. *Valperga* and 1830's *The Fortunes of Perkin Warbeck* are historical novels that have received little attention from literary critics, while *Lodore,* published in 1835, and *Falkner*—which appeared two years later and was thought by many to be autobiographical—have often been examined for clues to the lives of the Shelleys and their circle.

Shelley's stories were collected and published after her death, as was *Mathilda*, a novella that appeared for the first time in the 1950s. The story of a father and daughter's incestuous attraction, it has been viewed as a fictional treatment—or distortion—of Shelley's relationship with Godwin. Shelley composed the posthumously published verse dramas *Proserpine* and *Midas* to complement one of Percy Shelley's works; these garnered mild praise for their poetry after they were published in 1922. Critics also admire Shelley's nonfiction: the readable—though now dated—travel volumes; the essays for

Chamber's Cabinet Cyclopedia, which are considered vigorous and erudite; and her illuminating notes on her husband's poetry.

Since Shelley's death, critics have devoted nearly all of their attention to Frankenstein. The theme of *Frankenstein; or, The Modern Prometheus* is startling in its simplicity: A scientist rejects accepted theories, turns to his research, and patches together a human body from parts of corpses, in which he manages to instill life. The experiment goes wrong—bringing death and destruction to the scientist and his family. This theme has troubled or amused the world for over a century and a half, and the name of the scientist, Victor Frankenstein, has become synonymous with the irresponsible application of science and technology. It is this theme—its far sightedness and continued relevance—that qualifies *Frankenstein* as the first true work of science fiction, and Mary Shelley as its founding spirit.

Sources

Bloom, Harold, editor, *Mary Shelley: Modern Critical Views,* Chelsea House, 1985.

Gerson, Noel B., *Daughter of Earth and Water: A Biography of Mary Wollstonecraft Shelley,* Morrow, 1973. Harris, Janet, *The Woman Who Created Frankenstein: A Portrait of Mary Shelley,* Harper, 1979.

Levine, George, and U. C. Knoepflmacher, editors, *The Endurance of Frankenstein,* University of California Press, 1979.

Nuemann, Bonnie R., *The Lonely Muse: A Critical Biography of Mary Wollstonecraft Shelley,* Humanities, 1979.

Sunstein, Emily W., *Mary Shelley: Romance and Reality,* Little, Brown, 1989.

Robert Silverberg

Born: January 15, 1935, New York, New York

An award-winning sci-fi writer has a prolific nonfiction career.

Robert Silverberg is one of the best-known contemporary science fiction writers. He has won the field's Nebula and Hugo awards and has received more award nominations for his work than any other science fiction writer. He is also, according to Brian M. Stableford in *Masters of Science Fiction,* "the most prolific science fiction writer of the past two decades." What is perhaps most impressive is the fact that Silverstein is an even more prolific nonfiction writer: Writing in the *Magazine of Fantasy and Science Fiction,* Barry M. Malzberg claimed that Silverberg's science fiction work makes up, "at the most, fifteen percent of his output."

A Man with Many Names

Beginning his writing career while still a student at Columbia University in the 1950s, Silverberg decided to become a science fiction writer because of his own boyhood response to the genre. As he told Jeffrey M. Elliot in *Science Fiction Voices #2,* "When I was a boy, I read science fiction and it did wonderful things for me. It opened the universe to me. I feel a sense of obligation to science fiction to replace what I had taken from it, to add to the shelf, to put something there for someone else that would do for them what other writers had done for me."

Silverberg's first sales were to the science fiction magazines of the 1950s, and his first book was a juvenile science fiction novel. By the time he graduated from Columbia in 1956, his work was already so popular that the World

Science Fiction Convention, a gathering of the genre's devotees, voted him the Hugo Award as the best new writer of the year.

During the 1950s Silverberg produced hundreds of stories for science fiction magazines. In fact, he produced so much that he had to publish much of this work under an assortment of pseudonyms. Silverberg recalled that time to Charles Platt in *Dream Makers: The Uncommon People Who Write Science Fiction*: "I was courted by editors considerably back then, because I was so dependable; if they said, 'Give me a story by next Thursday,' I would." In 1959, however, a downturn in sales forced many science fiction magazines out of business. No longer able to support himself by writing for the genre, Silverberg began writing articles for popular magazines instead; continuing to produce a phenomenal volume of work, he churned out two pieces every working day.

A Prolific Popularizer of Science

Best Bets

1980 ***Lord Valentine's Castle***
A disinherited prince attempts to regain his throne.

1982 ***Majipoor Chronicles***
A young boy is able to "relive" historical events of the planet Majipoor thanks to an experience-record of history. Followed by a sequel, *Valentine Pontifex.*

1987 ***Project Pendulum***
Identical twins begin traveling in time—one into the future and the other into the past—as part of a secret U.S. government project.

1990 ***Letters from Atlantis***
Ray's body is in a deep sleep while his mind is sent back 180 centuries into the mind of Prince Ram, heir to the throne of the legendary Atlantis.

1994 ***Hot Sky at Midnight***
As ecological doom threatens the Earth, desperate researchers attempt to stave off the catastrophe while a Japanese megacorporation looks for ways to facilitate the population's flight from Earth.

In the early 1960s Silverberg turned from writing magazine articles to writing nonfiction books. During these early years Silverberg maintained a prolific writing pace, publishing nearly two million words per year—a feat he attributes to intense concentration: "I concentrated," the author recalled, "... and the words just came out right." Silverberg's reviewers are not so nonchalant: About the author's prodigious output, Malzberg said, "the man is prolific. Indeed, the man may be, in terms of accumulation of work per working year, the most prolific writer who ever lived."

Silverberg returned to the science fiction field after an absence of several years. Most observers agree that works from this period mark the beginning of Silverberg's first serious fiction in the genre. Malzberg summed up the turn in Silverberg's career, claiming that "in or around 1965 Silverberg put his toys away and began to write literature."

Richly Awarded but Poorly Understood

Silverberg began to experiment with technique and style, producing the award-winning novels *A Time of Changes* and *Nightwings,* several award-winning stories and novellas, and other novels that were nominated for major awards. Speaking of several books from this period in an article for the *New York Times Book Review,* Theodore Sturgeon found that Silverberg "changed into something quite new and different—his own man, saying his own things his own way, and doing it with richness and diversity."

He will tell a good story, he will fuse together content and form, and he will add to our perception of the human condition."

—Thomas D. Clareson, Magazine of Fantasy and Science Fiction

This new approach in his work put Silverberg in the forefront of the science fiction field. But the author was dissatisfied with the public's response to his work: Although his books won awards, they did not sell well and often met with uninformed critical comments from science fiction purists. "I was at first bewildered by the response I was getting from the audience," Silverberg told Platt. "There are passages in *Dying Inside* or in *Nightwings* which I think are sheer ecstatic song, but people would come up to me and say, 'Why do you write such depressing books?' Something was wrong." By 1975 all of Silverberg's more serious books—upon which he had placed such importance—were out of print. At that point he announced his retirement from science fiction.

One Last Book and the Dawn of a New Career

For the next four years Silverberg wrote no new science fiction, devoting his time instead to the garden outside his California home. "I had had my career," Silverberg explained. "Now I had my garden." But in 1978 he found himself back at his desk. In need of money, Silverberg decided to write one last book. The result was *Lord Valentine's Castle,* a massive novel that set a record when it was offered to publishers at auction; it fetched a whopping $127,500 from Harper & Row—the largest sum ever given for a science fiction novel at that time. Silverberg was a writer again.

In *Lord Valentine's Castle*—in which a disinherited prince attempts to regain his throne—Silverberg mixes elements from both science fiction and heroic fantasy. Jack Sullivan praised the clever combination of genre elements in the *New York Times Book Review,* calling *Lord Valentine's Castle* "an imaginative fusion of action, sorcery and science fiction, with visionary adventure scenes undergirded by scientific explanations." In his book *Robert Silverberg,* Thomas D. Clareson stated that "whatever else it does, *Lord Valentine's Castle* demands that its readers re-examine the relationship between science fiction and fantasy, for in this narrative Silverberg has fused the two together."

With *Lord Valentine's Castle* a rousing success, Silverberg began to write stories for *Omni* magazine, where several old friends were working. In 1982 he published *Majipoor Chronicles,* a novel fashioned from several short stories set on the planet introduced in *Lord Valentine's Castle.* Each story is an episode from Majipoor's history, which has been stored on an experience-record. By using a futuristic reading-machine, a young boy is able to "relive" these historical events. Finally, with *Valentine Pontifex,* Silver-

Insect creatures, the hjjks, threaten the peaceful existence of the People in *The New Springtime* (1990) by Robert Silverberg.

berg did what he had once vowed he would never do: He wrote a sequel to *Lord Valentine's Castle.* Lord Valentine, now restored to his position as ruler of Majipoor, faces opposition from the Piurivars—an aboriginal race dispossessed years before by Earthling colonists—who are releasing plagues and deadly bioengineered creatures upon the humans.

In his long career as a professional writer, Silverberg has produced an awe-inspiring body of work in several genres. As a writer of nonfiction, Silverberg has been more than a little successful; but as a writer of science fiction, he is among a handful of authors who have helped to shape the field into what it is today. In short, he is, in Elliot's words, "a titan in the science fiction field." "Few science fiction readers," Elliot continued, "have not been enriched and inspired by his contributions to the genre, contributions which reflect his love of the field and his deep respect for its readers."

Sources

Clareson, Thomas D., *Robert Silverberg,* Starmont House, 1983.

Elliot, Jeffrey M., *Science Fiction Voices #2,* Borgo Press, 1979.

Jonas, Gerald, review of *Hot Sky at Midnight, New York Times Book Review,* March 13, 1994, p. 30.

Jonas, Gerald, review of *The Positronic Man, New York Times Book Review,* November 14, 1993, p. 74.

Malzberg, Barry M., *Magazine of Fantasy and Science Fiction,* April 1971; April 1974.

New York Times Book Review, May 9, 1965; November 3, 1968; March 5, 1972; August 24, 1975; August 3, 1980; August 4, 1985; November 23, 1986.

Platt, Charles, *Dream Makers: The Uncommon People Who Write Science Fiction,* Berkley Publishing, 1980.

Review of *The Collected Stories of Robert Silverberg, Volume 1: Secret Sharers, Publishers Weekly,* August 24, 1992, p. 76.

Stableford, Brian M., *Masters of Science Fiction,* Borgo Press, 1981.

William Sleator

Born: February 13, 1945, Havre de Grace, Maryland

The recipient of numerous "best book" awards, William Sleator (pronounced "SLAY-tir") is a popular science fiction writer for both young readers and young adults. A mixture of fantasy and reality, his stories depict ordinary teenagers going about their daily lives. Their garden chores and vacations, however, are interrupted by fantastic incidents—involving aliens and clones, to name just a few—that suddenly disrupt these familiar routines.

A Musical Writer with a Penchant for Weirdness

From an early age, Sleator was interested in science. "Everybody in my family is a scientist except me," the author revealed. "I always liked science but was never good enough to be a real scientist." He also discovered that he enjoyed playing the piano, reading, and writing—hobbies that allowed him to express his penchant for things bizarre and supernatural. "Everything I did," he commented, "the stories I wrote, the music I played, had an element of weirdness to it. I suppose it came from the kind of stories, mostly science fiction, I read as a kid."

The Horn Book *Award-winning author of* Interstellar Pig *revels in weird science and psychological stories.*

For many years Sleator wavered between a writing career and a musical career. In 1963 he entered Harvard University, intent on pursuing a degree in music; later changing his mind, however, he graduated with a bachelor's degree in English. Sleator then moved to London, England, where he

Best Bets

resumed his study of musical composition and also worked as a pianist in ballet schools. He was drawn back into writing, though, after he helped a co-worker restore a run-down cottage and became curious about the building's bizarre history. "The place was interesting," he recalled, "way out in the middle of the woods, and eerie with graffiti from 1756 on the walls. There were burial mounds nearby where druids [members of an ancient priesthood] were buried and festivals were held. The whole thing was like a Gothic novel. So there was my first [book], *Blackbriar,* handed right to me." By 1974 Sleator had returned to the United States and joined the Boston Ballet Company as an accompanist. But after spending the next nine years juggling rehearsals, ballet tours, and writing, he finally quit the company to become a full-time author.

From ESP to Cosmic Debris

Among Sleator's more than 15 books for children and young adults are *House of Stairs* and *Into the Dream,* two stories that focus on the workings of the human mind. In *House of Stairs,* five young orphans find themselves imprisoned in an area with no walls, ceiling, or floors—only row upon row of stairs. Realizing that they are subjects in a bizarre psychological experiment, they struggle to prevent a large food-dispensing machine from completely controlling their responses. Sleator's *Into the Dream*—"a thriller of top-notch quality," according to a *Booklist* reviewer—introduces the reader to two classmates who possess extrasensory perception; they are able to see into the future. Foretelling danger, they work together to locate and warn the intended victim of a kidnapping, a young boy who has the extraordinary ability to move objects without touching them.

In *The Green Futures of Tycho* and *Interstellar Pig,* Sleator turns his sights to time travel and extraterrestrial beings. In the first story, a boy discovers a strange, egg-shaped object buried in his garden. Realizing it allows him to travel through time, he makes frequent trips to the future, where he meets his adult self. With each venture forward in time, however, he watches as his adult self becomes distorted and evil. In *Interstellar Pig,* 16-year-old Barney is on vacation at the beach when three neighbors move into a nearby cottage. Invited to join their game—called Interstellar Pig—Barney readily accepts, but soon finds that his neighbors are really aliens in disguise, and they're planning to kill him. About Barney's ordeal, Rosalie Byard commented in the *New York Times Book Review,* "Every menace penetrates the humdrum normality of the summer holiday scene in a convincing evolution from unsettling situation to waking nightmare."

In *Singularity,* Sleator explores the existence of other universes. Sixteen-year-old twins Barry and Harry discover that a playhouse on their uncle's property is built over a singularity—a hole that connects two separate galaxies. As strange cosmic debris keeps appearing through the hole, the twins discover that their uncle feared the arrival of a dangerous, intergalactic monster. Only Harry, it

Cover of *The Duplicate* by William Sleator.

seems, has the courage to venture inside and stand guard. "The details of Harry's year in the playhouse are fascinating," Ann A. Flowers declared in *Horn Book,* adding that the book is "an unusual, suspenseful yarn told by a master storyteller."

Exotic Places and Weird Science

These days, Sleator is a bit of a globe-trotter. "I now divide my time between Boston, Massachusetts, and Bangkok, Thailand," he explained. "I feel more at home in Thailand than in practically any other place I can think of. Partly this is because Thailand is so exotic that it feels almost like being on another planet. (Don't ask me why THAT should make me feel at home.)"

I prefer science fiction that has some basis in reality ... psychological stories, time-travel stories, but especially stories about people."

—William Sleator

Sleator still harbors an interest in music and would one day like to compose scores for films. He nevertheless continues to write books and takes his role as a science fiction author for young people seriously. "My goal is to entertain my audience and to get them to read," he once stated. "I want kids to find out that reading is the best entertainment there is. If, at the same time, I'm also imparting some scientific knowledge, then that's good, too. I'd like kids to see that science is not just boring formulas. Some of the facts to be learned about the universe are very weird."

Sources

Byard, Rosalie, review of *Interstellar Pig, New York Times Book Review,* September 23, 1984, p. 47.

Cart, Michael, review of *Oddballs, School Library Journal,* August 1993, p. 189.

Dunleavy, M. P., review of *Others See Us, New York Times Book Review,* April 24, 1994, p. 24.

Flowers, Ann A., review of *Singularity, Horn Book,* May 1985, pp. 320–321.

Review of *Into the Dream, Booklist,* February 15, 1979, p. 936.

Roback, Diane, review of *Strange Attractors, Publishers Weekly,* November 24, 1989, p. 72.

"William Sleator," *Authors and Artists for Young Adults,* Volume 5, Gale, 1991, pp. 207–215.

Robert Louis Stevenson

Born: November 13, 1850, Edinburgh, Scotland
Died: December 3, 1894, Apia, Samoa

Robert Louis Stevenson is best known as the author of the adventure classic *Treasure Island* and the adult horror story *The Strange Case of Dr. Jekyll and Mr. Hyde.* Both novels have a strange history: A map of an imaginary island gave Stevenson the idea for the first story while a nightmare inspired the premise of the second. And both tales share a theme common to most of Stevenson's stories: the impossibility of identifying and separating good and evil. While *Treasure Island*'s Long John Silver is at the same time a courageous friend and a treacherous cutthroat, Dr. Jekyll—who is not wholly good—is eventually ruled by Hyde because of his own moral weakness.

A Sickly Child with a Religious Upbringing

The only child of Thomas Stevenson and Margaret Balfour, Stevenson inherited his mother's weak lungs and was an invalid from birth. Before he was two years old, a young woman named Alison Cunningham joined the household to act as his nurse. Over 30 years later, Stevenson dedicated *A Child's Garden of Verses*—which reveals the sheltered, bedridden nature of his youth—to his childhood nurse.

Also known as Tusitala (the Teller of Tales), the agnostic author of Treasure Island *wrote children's verses and grown-up tales of horror.*

Not all of Stevenson's childhood was spent in the sickroom, though. He spent summers in the country at Colinton Manse, where he played outdoors with his many cousins. During these years, he wrote a number of composi-

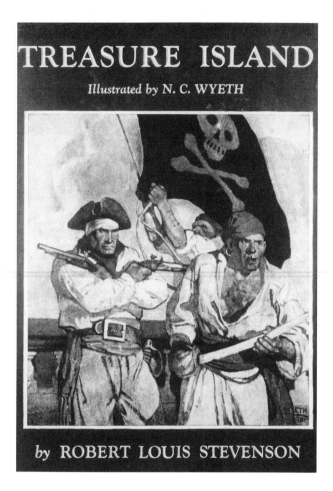

TREASURE ISLAND

Illustrated by N. C. WYETH

by ROBERT LOUIS STEVENSON

Cover of *Treasure Island,* by Robert Louis Stevenson. Illustrated by N. C. Wyeth.

tions—mostly on biblical themes—which reveal how much the young author was influenced by the strong religious convictions of his parents. During his college years, however, Stevenson's beliefs underwent a sharp reversal.

The Seamy Underside of City Life

Although Stevenson had attended school since he was seven, his attendance was irregular; his health was poor and his father doubted the value of formal education. Entering the University of Edinburgh when he was 16, Stevenson planned to become a lighthouse engineer like his father. Rather than apply himself to his studies, however, he became known for his outrageous dress and behavior. Sporting a wide-brimmed hat and a boy's velveteen coat, Stevenson—who was known as Velvet Jacket—explored the seamy side of Edinburgh; together with his cousin Bob, he smoked hashish and frequented brothels. At the wizened age of 22—with little to show for himself—he dealt his pious father a final blow: The young author declared himself an agnostic.

In order to appease his father, Stevenson studied law. Although he was called to the bar in 1875, he never practiced. Before and after he received his law degree, however, Stevenson's essays were published in several periodicals. Stevenson, it seems, had trained himself—while in school—to be a writer, imitating the styles of authors William Hazlitt and Daniel Defoe, among others. A constant traveler for most of his adult life, he based his first two books, 1878's *An Inland Voyage* and *Travels with a Donkey in the*

Cevennes, published the following year, on his excursions in France. Although the author took many trips in search of climates that would ease his poor health, he was—temperamentally speaking—a globe-trotter. His reasons for traveling to America in 1879, however, had nothing to do with poor health or wanderlust.

Love and Other American Adventures

Three years earlier, Stevenson had met Fanny Van de Grift Osbourne at an artist's colony near Paris. An American woman 11 years his senior, she was, at the time, separated from her husband and living abroad with her two children. Although Stevenson fell in love with her, Fanny returned to her husband and her California home in 1878. In August of the following year, Stevenson received a mysterious cable from Fanny, and he immediately left Scotland for America.

The journey almost killed him. On August 18, 1879, Stevenson landed in New York, having traveled across the Atlantic in steerage (where passengers pay the lowest fares and are given inferior accommodations). Already ill, his health became worse after he crossed the American plains on an immigrant train. Impoverished, sick, and starving, he lived in Monterey and then San Francisco—nearly dying in both places. His suffering was rewarded, however: Fanny obtained a divorce from her husband, and on May 19, 1880, she and Stevenson were married. For the honeymoon, the couple, Fanny's son Lloyd, and the family dog went to Mount Saint Helena and lived in a run-down shack at Silverado. All of Stevenson's American adventures became material for his writing. *Silverado Squatters* of 1883 chronicles his honeymoon experiences, while 1892's *Across the Plains, with Other Memories and Essays* and *The Amateur Emigrant from the Clyde to Sandy Hook,* published three years later, relate his trip to California. Only a year after he left Scotland, Stevenson returned to his homeland; in the summer of 1881, the author, Fanny, and Lloyd settled in the Braemar cottage where Stevenson began writing *Treasure Island.*

Best Bets

1883   ***Treasure Island***
Jim Hawkins discovers a treasure map, and an adventure classic is born.

1886   ***The Strange Case of Dr. Jekyll and Mr. Hyde***
Through his own experiments, scientist Dr. Jekyll releases the evil within himself.

1886   ***Kidnapped***
Kidnapped in the Scots uprising of 1775, young David Balfour must fight for his life and his honor. Followed by a sequel, *David Balfour.*

Reel Life

The Body Snatcher, 1945.

Grave robber supplies corpses to research scientists in nineteenth-century Edinburgh. One of horror-meister Boris Karloff's best efforts.

Kidnapped, 1938.

Child star Freddy (Little Lord Fauntleroy) Bartholomew brought tears to movie-goers' eyes as wee David Balfour—a role Roddy McDowall would also assume in the 1948 production.

The Master of Ballantrae, 1953.

Scottish heir rebels against the English crown, tries out the life of a pirate, and returns home—only to discover that his brother has designs on his title and on his sweetie.

The Strange Case of Dr. Jekyll and Mr. Hyde

In addition to several Hollywood versions, this book has been made into a made-for-cable show for Shelley Duvall's "Nightmare Classics" series (1989).

Treasure Island, 1934.

Featured a host of superstars over the years, including Lon Chaney, Jackie Cooper, and Lionel Barrymore.

The Wrong Box, 1966.

Anxious to collect a large inheritance, two elderly Victorian brothers try to kill each other.

A Pirate Tale That Told Itself

Stevenson recalled in his *Essays in the Art of Writing* how he once joined his stepson Lloyd—who was confined indoors because of rain—in passing the time by making colored drawings: "On one of these occasions, I made the map of an island; it was elaborately and (I thought) beautifully coloured; the shape of it took my fancy beyond expression; it contained harbours that pleased me like sonnets; and with the unconsciousness of the predestined, I ticketed my performance 'Treasure Island.'"

Filling in the map with names like "Spye-Glass Hill" and marking the location of hidden treasure with crosses, Stevenson decided to supplement the drawing with a pirate adventure story: "The future characters of the book began to appear there visibly among imaginary woods; and their brown faces and bright weapons peeped out upon me from unexpected quarters, as they passed to and fro, fighting and hunting treasure, on these few square inches of a flat projection. The next thing I knew I had some papers before me and was writing out a list of chapters." By the next morning, he had completed a draft of the first chapter.

On October 1, 1881, *Young Folks* magazine began publishing the tale in serial form under the pseudonym Captain George North. Stevenson's story received little notice. Although Fanny confessed that she didn't like the story and was against it ever appearing in book form, it was published as a book late in 1883. *Treasure Island* soon became a bestseller: In Stevenson's lifetime the number of copies sold reached the tens of thousands, and reviewers declared that this work of sheer entertainment had single-handedly liberated literature for young audiences from a narrow, moralistic rut.

Serials for *Young Folks*

In 1882 Stevenson and Fanny moved to Hyeres, in the south of France. There Stevenson suffered a hemorrhage that confined him to bed, prevented him from speaking, and rendered him incapable of writing prose. He was able, however, to write simple verse, and he wrote most of *A Child's Garden of Verses* while he recovered.

Stevenson had also followed *Treasure Island* with another boy's adventure story called *The Black Arrow,* which was published serially in *Young Folks* in 1883 and as a book in 1888. Although more popular with the readers of *Young Folks* than *Treasure Island* had been, *The Black Arrow* is hardly a classic. His next serial—*Kidnapped*—was a distinct improvement; appearing in *Young Folks* in 1886, it was published as a book the same year. Set in the Scottish Highlands in 1751, the story relates the wanderings of young David Balfour in the company of the reckless Alan Breck. *Kidnapped* was an achievement on a level with *Treasure Island,* and its characters are in many ways superior. While Jim Hawkins and Long John Silver of the earlier book are intriguing stereotypes, Balfour and Breck are personalities who have psychological depth. Seven years after *Kidnapped,* Stevenson wrote a sequel called *Catriona,* but it did not measure up to the original work.

Dr. Jekyll, Mr. Hyde, and Tusitala

Although *Kidnapped* earned Stevenson some recognition, its success in 1886 was overshadowed by another of his works published that same year, *The Strange Case of Dr. Jekyll and Mr. Hyde.* The story was sparked by a dream Stevenson had in which he visualized a man changing into a monster by means of a concoction made with white powder. Screaming in his sleep when Fanny woke him, he scolded his wife for interrupting the nightmare: "I was dreaming a fine bogey tale," he said. The next morning, he started writing furiously in bed, and in three days, had a completed draft of almost 40,000 words. When Fanny disapproved of the story, however, Stevenson threw the first manuscript into the fire and rewrote the tale as an allegory. Although the author later claimed that it was the worst thing he ever wrote, *Dr. Jekyll and Mr. Hyde* sold 40,000 copies in Britain during its first six months on bookstore shelves—making Stevenson somewhat of a celebrity.

After living temporarily at Saranac Lake, New York, in 1887, Stevenson, Fanny, Lloyd, and Stevenson's widowed mother began touring the South Pacific the following year. Eventually, the clan settled on the island of Upolu in Samoa in 1890, where, at the foot of Mount Vaea, Stevenson built a house called Vailima. Continuing to write, he became an advocate for the Samoans, who named him Tusitala, teller of tales. Tusitala's term in paradise, however, was short-lived: On December 3, 1894, at the age of 44, Stevenson died of a cerebral hemorrhage, leaving unfinished *Weir of Hermiston,* which promised to be his single greatest work. In a ceremony suitable for a king, nearly 60 Samoan men cleared a path to the summit of Mount Vaea, where Tusitala, the teller of tales, was laid to rest.

Sources

Daiches, David, *Robert Louis Stevenson and His World,* Thames & Hudson, 1973.

Dictionary of Literary Biography, Gale, Volume 18: *Victorian Novelists After 1885,* 1983; Volume 57: *Victorian Prose Writers After 1867,* 1987.

Hennessy, James Pope, *Robert Louis Stevenson,* Simon and Schuster, 1974.

Maixner, Paul. *Robert Louis Stevenson: The Critical Heritage,* Routledge & Kegan Paul, 1981.

Rankin, Nicholas, *Dead Man's Chest: Travels After Robert Louis Stevenson,* Faber & Faber, 1987.

Saposnik, Irving S., *Robert Louis Stevenson,* Twayne, 1974.

Stevenson, Robert Louis, "My First Book: 'Treasure Island,'" in his *Essays in the Art of Writing,* Chatto & Windus, 1905, pp. 111–131.

R. L. Stine

Born: October 8, 1943, Columbus, Ohio

Teens around the United States would agree that R. L. Stine is not funny, at least not often, in his young adult novels. They seem to like him that way, because they buy his books in astonishing numbers: Stine is one of the most-read authors of teen horror. But Stine didn't start out to write terror fiction for teens. He started out to be funny.

Once a humor writer, the author of the Fear Street series writes scary stories that appeal to kids, even those who don't like to read.

A Published Preteen

"I've had the most single minded life, I think, that anybody could have," Stine explained. "When I was nine years old I found an old typewriter up in the attic. I brought it downstairs and started typing stories and little joke books and magazines. I've been doing that ever since. I think I knew when I was nine that I wanted to be a writer."

Listening to his mother read Golden Books and storybooks, Stine was hooked at an early age. "I liked fantasy stories and fairy tales," he recalled. "I remember going into the school library, to the shelf of Grimm's fairy tales and Norse legends and reading every book." As he grew he began reading ghost stories, joke books, sports books, Matt Christopher books, and science fiction works, such as those by Ray Bradbury and Isaac Asimov. Although he wrote often, he didn't share his work with many people. "I was pretty shy at first," Stine remarked. "Mainly I loved writing and typing these stories."

Later, Stine began publishing little magazines and passing them out at school. "I was the kind of student who didn't have to work hard to get Bs. I

Best Bets

1986 _Blind Date_
A football player—who is kicked off the team after one of his teammates is injured in an accident—falls into a series of bizarre situations after he arranges a date with a girl he's never met.

1989 _The New Girl_
Corey tries to find out whether his new girlfriend, who lives on Fear Street, really exists. The first book of the Fear Street series.

1990 _Curtains_
When Rena, a Michelle Pfeiffer look-alike, wins a part in a summer camp play, she becomes the victim of a series of cruel and bizarre pranks.

1991 _The Secret Bedroom_
Having trouble adjusting to her new high school, Lea allows a ghost to possess her—a decision she regrets when the spirit causes the death of a girl in her class.

1992 _Prom Queen_
Prom Queen nominee realizes that a serial killer in the area has targeted Prom Queen nominees as his victims.

1994 _Deep Trouble_
A half-human, half-shark creature may be lurking in the coral. Part of the Goosebumps series, _Deep Trouble_ hit the top of _USA Today_'s best-seller list.

think every report card would say, 'Bob could do much better, he isn't really working up to the best of his ability.'" He was also the one who made jokes and broke the class up. "I remember being bored a lot in school, being more interested in things like radio shows, TV and writing." Stine enjoyed reading James Thurber and Max Shulman, a humorist from Minnesota who wrote the Dobie Gillis books. He was also an avid fan of such radio shows as _The Shadow, Suspense,_ and _Inner Sanctum._ "When I was a little kid I remember being real scared, lying in bed listening to these scary things on the radio. I loved that," Stine recalled.

Soft Drinks and Soap Stars

In college at Ohio State, Stine spent three years as editor of the campus humor magazine. "That's mainly what I did at Ohio State. I'd hang out at the magazine office in the Student Union and put out this magazine every month." After graduation, with a bachelor's degree in English, Stine taught social studies for one year in a junior high school, then headed for New York City. "I loved magazines and wanted to get some kind of magazine job," he said in an interview. "My ambition in life was to someday be editor of my own humor magazine."

Stine's first magazine job was with a publisher of fan and movie magazines. "The job was to make up interviews with celebrities, but we never met anyone," he recalled. "It was great training. In a way it was very creative work, because we had to make up everything. Sometimes we would do the same story two different ways. First as 'Those Whispers about Tom Jones, They're Not True,' then, 'Those Whispers about Tom Jones Are True.'" Stine's next job was with a trade magazine called _Soft Drink Industry._ "It was a horrible year, but the training helped me later as far as writing really fast," Stine remembered. "I would have to do twenty articles a day from stacks of news clippings on my desk. It taught me not to stop and think about it, just sit down and write."

The Author Goes *Bananas*

In 1968 Stine became an assistant editor for *Junior Scholastic* in New York City. On *Scholastic*'s payroll for 16 years, he worked on four magazines, two of which he created. After four years on *Junior Scholastic,* Stine was made editor of a new magazine, *Search*, a social studies magazine that did not read or look like a social studies magazine. Next came *Bananas,* a humor magazine for older kids. "My wife, Jane, was editing a magazine for kids called *Dynamite,* the biggest selling kids' magazine in the country," Stine explained. "It was selling over 1.25 million copies every month, and *Scholastic* decided to do a funny magazine, too, but for older readers. *Bananas* was the result, a humor magazine for kids twelve years old and up. I was doing what I had always wanted to do." He was 32 and had reached his life's ambition.

While editing *Bananas,* Stine received a call from Ellen Rudin, an editor of children's books at Dutton, a large and well-respected publisher. Having read *Bananas,* she asked him to consider writing a humorous book for younger readers. Although he had never considered writing children's books, the author agreed to work up an idea. *How To Be Funny*—Stine's first book—was published in 1982. "It was how to be funny in the cafeteria, at the breakfast table, in bed at night," Stine declared in his interview. "You know, a really offensive book for parents."

Jovial Bob Loses His Job

After that came many funny books, under the name Jovial Bob Stine, some of which he wrote with his wife, Jane. Also during those years, Stine published a number of "twist-a-plot" books, a form of "you choose the story line" book that was popular in the 1980s. Often based on licensed characters from television and movies—such as G.I. Joe and Indiana Jones—these stories had about 30 endings each, with countless plot twists; in short, they were great training for future novel writing.

At *Scholastic, Bananas* was beginning to lose readers; it was time to launch a different kind of humor magazine—*Maniac*—with a contemporary title and content geared toward kids 13 years and up. *Scholastic* was having financial troubles, however, and Stine was let go in a corporate reorganization. "I was fired!" he said, "but I was already doing all kinds of books for children for different publishers, so I came home and started writing more books." That was in 1985, and since then Stine has published over one hundred books for young readers.

A Novel Career

Stine was ready to try his hand at novels. When Jean Feiwel, editorial director at *Scholastic,* asked if he would try writing a scary novel for young adults, he accepted; she also suggested a title—*Blind Date*—and Stine went home to figure out a plot. After spending a lot of time working on that first novel, Stine was amazed that his story—which was published in the summer of 1986 and concerned a young man's memory lapse and involvement with a mysterious girl—was a big seller. After *Blind Date* Stine signed to do another book, *Twisted,* and then *The Baby-sitter.* Each novel, dealing in suspicious characters and life-threatening situations, promptly made the juvenile bestsellers lists. The teen-horror novel was in and Stine was becoming one of its most popular writers.

"It occurred to my wife and me that maybe a series with novels that came more often would sell," the author noted in an interview. Jane, who runs her own company called Parachute Press, suggested that Stine try to think of a series of scary books that would come out every other month or so. She would package the series and sell it, through her company, to a publisher. "So I sat down and thought. I needed a good title, then I could figure out a way to do a series of scary books," he recalled. "When the words 'Fear Street' sort of magically appeared, I wrote it down, then came up with the concept."

Jane and Parachute Press sold Fear Street—a place where terrible things always happen to its residents—to Archway, a division of Pocket Books. That first contract was for six books, and the series debuted with *The New Girl,* in which Corey's girl problems involve figuring out whether his new girlfriend, who lives on Fear Street, *really* exists. The Fear Street series took off like wildfire: There are now more than 30 books in the Fear Street and Fear Street: Super Chiller series. What's more, there are two miniseries of three books each—Fear Street: Cheerleaders, and Fear Street Saga. Since Stine writes all of the Fear Street novels, he keeps busy, writing about one book every month.

The Goosebumps series—aimed at 8- to 11-year-olds—has become very popular with younger readers. Kids seem to like the books for their unpredictability; "They like the fact that there is some kind of jolt at the end of every chapter," Stine commented. "They know that if they read to the end of the chapter they're going to have some kind of funny surprise, something scary, something that's going to happen right at the end of the chapter and force them to keep reading."

Real Teens and Reluctant Readers

Stine works hard at making the kids in his novels as real as possible: He uses "teen-speak," and the teens in his books dress like real teens. Because of this attention to realistic detail, readers identify with the teens in Stine's novels, which makes for a scarier read. Stine's philosophy of writing is that kids should have some books to read that are not just for learning or for instilling morals and social behavior. As the author remarked in an interview, "In these days, with so many distractions, and

Cover of R. L. Stine's *The Betrayal* from the Fear Street series.

so many reasons not to read, it's important that kids should be able to discover that they can turn to reading for entertainment, instead of television or Nintendo."

It's working. Letters from teens say, "I hate to read but I love your books," and "I never read any books because I don't like to read, but I buy every book you write." Teachers and librarians are telling about students who would never read books, but who now can't wait for the next Stine thriller. "It's rewarding for me," said Stine. "I feel so lucky that these books have become so popular."

Sources

Cronin, Alice, review of *Beach Party, School Library Journal,* January 1991, p. 97.

Cronin, Alice, review of *The Sleepwalker, School Library Journal,* September 1990, p. 258.

Devereaux, Elizabeth, and Kit Alderice, review of *Halloween Night, Publishers Weekly,* September 20, 1993, p. 31.

Fakih, Kimberly Olson, and Diane Roback, review of *The Babysitter, Publishers Weekly,* July 14, 1989, p. 79.

MacRae, Cathi Dunn, review of *Party Summer, Wilson Library Bulletin,* October 1991, p. 101.

Roback, Diane, and Richard Donahue, review of *Curtains, Publishers Weekly,* September 28, 1990, p. 104.

Roback, Diane, and Richard Donahue, review of *Fear Street: Ski Weekend, Publishers Weekly,* December 7, 1990, p. 142.

Stine, R. L., interview with Mary Lois Sanders for *Something about the Author,* Volume 76, Gale, 1994.

Bram Stoker

Born: November 8, 1847, Clontarf, Ireland
Died: April 20, 1912, London, England

Best known as the author of *Dracula,* one of the most famous horror novels of all time, Bram Stoker also wrote adventure and romance novels, several other horror novels, short stories, and a biography of his longtime friend and employer, the Shakespearean actor Sir Henry Irving. Despite his contributions to other genres, however, Stoker's renown rests on his creation of the Transylvanian count whose name has become synonymous with vampirism.

A Dramatic Career

Abraham Stoker was a sickly child, bedridden for much of his boyhood. As a student at Trinity College, however, he excelled in athletics as well as academics, and graduated with honors in mathematics in 1870. He worked for ten years in the Irish Civil Service, and during this time contributed drama criticism to the *Dublin Mail.* His glowing reviews of Henry Irving's performances encouraged the actor to seek him out. The two became friends, and in 1879 Stoker became Irving's manager; he also acted as manager, secretary, and even director at London's Lyceum Theatre. Despite his active personal and professional life, he began writing and publishing novels, beginning with *The Snake's Pass* in 1890; *Dracula* followed in 1897.

The majority of his works forgotten, the author of Dracula *made a lasting impression on horror literature and pop culture.*

After Irving died in 1905, Stoker was associated with the literary staff of the *London Telegraph* and wrote several more works of fiction, including the horror novels *The Lady of the Shroud,* published in 1909, and 1911's *The Lair*

Best Bets

of the White Worm (1911). Unlike the immortal Dracula, Stoker died in London on April 20, 1912.

Although most of Stoker's novels received favorable reviews when they appeared, they are dated by their stereotyped characters and romanticized Gothic plots, and are rarely read today. Although even the earliest reviews complained of the author's stiff characterization and penchant for melodrama, critics have universally praised his precise and beautiful place descriptions. Stoker's short stories, while sharing the faults of his novels, have fared better with modern readers. Anthologists frequently include the author's short stories in collections of horror fiction. Among these, "Dracula's Guest," originally intended as a prefatory chapter to *Dracula,* is one of the best known.

An Immortal Blood Drinker

Dracula is generally regarded as the culmination of the Gothic vampire story, preceded earlier in the nineteenth century by Dr. William Polidori's "The Vampyre," Thomas Prest's *Varney the Vampyre,* J. S. Le Fanu's *Carmilla,* and Guy de Maupassant's "Le Horla." A large part of the novel's initial success was due, however, not to its Gothicism but to the fact that, "to the Victorian reader," as Daniel Farson notes, "it must have seemed daringly modern." An early reviewer of *Dracula* in the *Spectator* commented that "the up-to-dateness of the book—the phonograph diaries, typewriters, and so on—hardly fits in with the medieval methods which ultimately secure the victory for Count Dracula's foes." Stoker utilized the epistolary style of narrative, presenting the story through a series of letters. The narrative, comprising journal entries, letters, newspaper clippings, a ship's log, and phonograph recordings, allowed Stoker to contrast his characters' actions with their own explanations of their acts.

Initially, *Dracula* was interpreted as a straightforward horror novel. Some early critics noted the "unnecessary number of hideous incidents" which could "shock and disgust" readers of *Dracula.* One critic even advised keeping the novel away from children and nervous adults. Dorothy Scarborough indicated the direction of future criticism in 1916 when she wrote that "Bram Stoker furnished us with several interesting specimens of supernatural life always tangled with other uncanny motives." In 1931 Ernest Jones, in his *On*

From the movie *Dracula,* starring Bela Lugosi.

Reel Life

In 1931 Bela Lugosi played his most famous role as the Transylvanian count who terrorizes the countryside in his search for human blood; in the blink of an eye, *Dracula* was a genre classic. The count later surfaced in *Dracula's Daughter* (1936), *Dracula Has Risen from the Grave* (1969), *Dracula Is Dead and Well and Living in London* (1973), *Dracula's Dog* (1978), and *Dracula's Last Rites* (1980), to name a few. Most recently, *Bram Stoker's Dracula*—better titled *Francis Ford Coppola's Dracula*—is a stunning version of the vampire tale starring Gary Oldman, Keanu Reeves, Winona Ryder, and Anthony Hopkins.

the Nightmare, drew attention to the theory that these "other uncanny motives" involve repressed sexuality. While many critics have since viewed *Dracula* from a Freudian standpoint, others have interpreted the novel from folkloric, political, feminist, medical, and religious points of view.

Today the name of Dracula is known to all—yet many have no idea who Bram Stoker was. What's more, the popularly held image of the vampire bears little resemblance to the demonic being that Stoker depicted: Adaptations of *Dracula* in plays and films have taken tremendous liberties with Stoker's characterization—and Stoker himself did not conform to established vampire legend. Yet *Dracula* has had a tremendous impact on readers—and subsequent horror literature—since it was published just before the turn of the century. Whether Stoker evoked a universal fear, or as some modern critics would have it, gave form to a universal fantasy, he created a powerful and lasting image that has made an indelible mark on popular culture.

Sources

Concise Dictionary of British Literary Biography, Volume 5: *Late Victorian and Edwardian Writers, 1890–1914,* Gale, 1991, pp. 310–316.

Farson, Daniel, *The Man Who Wrote Dracula: A Biography of Bram Stoker*, St. Martin's, 1976.

Leatherdale, Clive, *Dracula: The Novel and the Legend,* Aquarian Press, 1985.

Roth, Phyllis A., *Bram Stoker,* Twayne, 1982.

J. R. R. Tolkien

Born: January 3, 1892, Bloemfontein, South Africa
Died: September 2, 1973, Bournemouth, England

J. R. R. Tolkien is best known to most readers as the author of *The Hobbit* and *The Lord of the Rings,* widely regarded as the most important fantasy stories of the modern period. Tolkien drew on his familiarity with Northern and other ancient literatures and invented languages to create not just his own story, but his own world: Middle-earth, complete with its own history, myths, legends, epics, and heroes. Tolkien's works—especially *The Lord of the Rings*—have captivated countless readers and fascinated critics who recognize their literary depth.

A Young Man with a Talent for Languages

John Ronald Reuel Tolkien was born in Bloemfontein, South Africa, where his father, Arthur Reuel Tolkien, worked as a bank manager. Early in 1895, however—after young Tolkien's health began to fail—his mother, Mabel Suffield Tolkien, took her sons back to England. Unfortunately, Arthur, who had stayed behind in Africa, contracted rheumatic fever and died early in 1896; Mabel introduced her eldest son to two of his strongest passions—the Catholic church and the study of language—before she, too, died in November 1904. The orphaned sons were left under the guardianship of Mabel's close friend and confessor, Father Francis Xavier Morgan, who provided Tolkien with a father figure and

The author of The Lord of the Rings *created his own language and mythology in intricate and engaging tales about Middle-earth and its inhabitants.*

Best Bets

1937 ***The Hobbit; or, There and Back Again***
The story of hobbit Bilbo Baggins's travels and adventures in Middle-earth.

1954 ***The Fellowship of the Ring***
A story of good and evil in Middle-earth, filled with hobbits, dragons, and other mythical creatures. The first book of the Lord of the Rings trilogy, followed by *The Two Towers* and *The Return of the King.*

1977 ***Silmarillion***
A collection of tales and legends—published posthumously—that set the stage for Tolkien's other works and tell the story of the creation of the world and of the happenings of the First Age of Middle-earth.

helped finance his studies at King Edward's School in Birmingham and at Oxford University.

Tolkien's love of languages grew while he attended King Edward's School. Latin and Greek were important parts of the curriculum, and Tolkien excelled at both. Not satisfied with studying just these, he also taught himself some Welsh, Old and Middle English, Old Norse, and Gothic, with the encouragement and assistance of several of his teachers. Later he added Finnish to his list of beloved tongues; the Finnish epic *The Kalevala* had a great impact on his *Silmarillion,* and the language itself, said Tolkien biographer Humphrey Carpenter, formed the basis for "Quenya," the High-elven speech of his stories.

It was also while attending King Edward's that Tolkien met the third of his great loves: Edith Bratt. Like the Tolkiens, Edith was an orphan, and she was drawn toward the oldest brother, "with his serious face and perfect manners," wrote Carpenter. Their friendship gradually deepened into love. She was three years older than Tolkien, however, and was not a Catholic; when Tolkien's guardian Father Francis found out about the couple's relationship, he forbade Tolkien to see or write Edith again. Dutifully, Tolkien complied; but three years later, on the day he turned 21, he wrote to propose to Edith. Formally engaged the following year, they married in 1916.

Early Works and Imaginary Worlds

Tolkien began to create an imaginary world while still at Oxford, shortly before enlisting to fight in World War I. In 1914 the young author wrote a poem based on a line from the works of an Old English religious poet; titled "The Voyage of Earendel, the Evening Star," the poem tells of a mariner who sails across the heavens through the night, and was, according to Carpenter, "the beginning of Tolkien's own mythology." Nearly all of Tolkien's later fiction drew on his created languages and their related myths for their background. The scattered stories and documents that he wrote during these early years were edited by his son, Christopher Tolkien, and appeared after the author's death in the ongoing History of Middle-earth series and *The Silmarillion*. The poem about Earendel was joined by other stories, including "The Music of the Ainur," an account of the creation of the world; "The Silmarillion," the history of the return of the High-Elves to Middle-earth and their wars with Morgoth, the Great Enemy; "The Fall of Gondolin," the final assault of Morgoth on the last Elven fortress; and "The Tale of Beren and Luthien," a long poem describing the love of Beren, a mortal man, for Luthien, the immortal daughter of a king of Elves, who together penetrate the fortress of Morgoth and take back from him a Silmaril, one of the great Jewels of Light he stole before the first Rising of the Sun. In the process of bringing the jewel to her father, however, Beren is slain, and Luthien, for love of him, chooses to forsake her immortality to die as well.

Words and More Words

Tolkien was a philologist in the literal sense of the word: He was a lover of language. It was a passion he developed early and kept throughout his life, exploring tongues that were no longer spoken and creating languages of his own.

The Legendary Bilbo Baggins

In 1925—after holding a series of other positions—Tolkien was elected Rawlinson and Bosworth Professor of Anglo-Saxon at Oxford University, a post he held for 20 years. While teaching at Oxford, Tolkien began to compose *The Hobbit*. "Tolkien often recorded how he began the story," wrote Douglas A. Anderson in his introduction to *The Annotated Hobbit*. "One hot summer day he was sitting at his desk, correcting students' examination papers ... on English literature. He told an interviewer, 'One of the candidates had mercifully left one of the pages with no writing on it, which is the best thing that can possibly happen to an examiner, and I wrote on it, "In a hole in the ground there lived a hobbit." Names always generate a story in my mind: eventually I thought I'd better find out what hobbits were like.'" Around the end of the 1920s or beginning of the 1930s Tolkien began using the hobbit—now named Bilbo Baggins—as the basis for stories. "I had the habit while my children were still young of inventing and telling orally, sometimes of writing down, 'children's stories' for their private amusement," he stated in a 1964 letter. "*The Hobbit* was intended to be one of them."

Now regarded as a classic of literature for young readers, *The Hobbit* had at first no connection with Tolkien's legendary histories: It was simply the story of one hobbit's travels and adventures from his comfortable everyday

Artist Michael Whelan's depiction of Sam and Frodo's escape from Mount Doom from *The Return of the King,* the final book in The Lord of the Rings epic.

life into terrible danger—represented by a dragon—and back again into security. Tolkien's story owed its inspiration more to sources such as the Anglo-Saxon epic *Beowulf* and Victorian fairy tales such as George MacDonald's *The Princess and Curdie* and the collections of Andrew Lang. Gradually, however, Tolkien worked references to his own mythos into the story. In a letter to his publishers Allen & Unwin, Tolkien remarked that "Mr. Baggins began as a comic tale among conventional and inconsistent Grimm's fairy-tale dwarves, and got drawn into the edge of it—so that even Sauron the Terrible peeped over the edge."

Paperback Wars and a Magical Ring

The Hobbit was a great success when it was published in September 1937. Later that year Tolkien began work on a sequel; he had no clear idea, however, what the book would be about. For some time he toyed with a plot that told how Bilbo, having lost all his money, left home again in search of treasure. Dissatisfied with this story line, Tolkien developed another plot centered on the magic ring Bilbo found and on the references to the Necromancer in *The Hobbit*. By the end of August 1938, Tolkien had begun to call the new story *The Lord of the Rings*. He wrote to Allen & Unwin that the new book "is more grown up—but the audience for which *The Hobbit* was written has done that also. The readers young and old who clamoured for 'more about the Necromancer' are to blame, for the N[ecromancer] is not child's play."

It took Tolkien another 11 years to finish the story. Tolkien—burdened by a busy teaching schedule—was a perfectionist when it came to writing; seldom satisfied with his original ideas, he rewrote sections of the book many times. Although *The Lord of the Rings* was completed in 1949, due to disagreements Tolkien had with Allen & Unwin, it was not published until 1954, when the first two sections—*The Fellowship of the Ring* and *The Two Towers*—were released. The final volume, *The Return of the King*, was not published until late in 1955 because the indexes that Tolkien had promised were not finished. The work was a financial success, and over the next few years it was published in America and translated into many foreign languages.

Its greatest popularity, however, came in the mid-1960s when American university students discovered Tolkien's trilogy. Part of the work's renewed popularity was due to a dispute over publishing rights that attracted a great deal of attention. In 1965 the international copyright on the book had lapsed, and Ace Books, a prominent science fiction publisher, announced plans for a paperback edition of the work—an edition that would not pay the author any royalties. To prevent this, Tolkien revised the book, which was copyrighted as a second edition; the author's American publishers then produced their own "authorized" paperback, which soon sold more than one million copies. Ace

Reel Life

The Hobbit, 1978.

Hobbit Bilbo Baggins—brought to "live motion" animation by animator extraordinaire Ralph Bakshi—battles evil beings in Middle-earth with fellow furry-footed creatures. Features the voices of Orson Bean, John Huston, Otto Preminger, and Richard Boone.

The Lord of the Rings, 1978.

Hobbits, wizards, elves, and dwarves come to life in Ralph Bakshi's animated interpretation of Tolkien's classic trilogy. Live motion animation allows the Middle-earthlings to move with lifelike mobility.

Books later wrote to apologize to Tolkien, offering him a royalty on all the books they had sold and agreeing not to reprint the book after the stocks were exhausted. However, "Ace had unwittingly done a service to Tolkien," declared Carpenter, "for they had helped to lift his book from the 'respectable' hard-cover status in which it had languished for some years and had put it at the top of the popular best-sellers." By the end of 1968, three million copies of *The Lord of the Rings* had been sold around the world.

Luthien and Beren

Sales from revised editions of *The Lord of the Rings* and *The Hobbit* made Tolkien a moderately wealthy man. Having retired from teaching in 1959, he was better off financially than he had ever been before. Finally able to devote his time to finishing *The Silmarillion,* the author was at times overwhelmed by the sheer quantity of work that remained to be done in order to finish the book. What's more, Edith's health was failing; late in 1971 she died of complications from an inflamed gallbladder. Her headstone read simply, "Edith Mary Tolkien, Luthien, 1889-1971." Tolkien recalled in a letter to his son Christopher, "I never called Edith *Luthien*—but she was the source of the story that in time became the chief part of the *Silmarillion....* But the story has gone crooked, & I am left, and *I* cannot plead before the inexorable Mandos." Tolkien followed his wife less than two years later; the two were buried side by side, and to Edith's headstone was added the caption, "John Ronald Reuel Tolkien, Beren, 1892-1973."

In the last two years of his life, Tolkien received many honors; Oxford University awarded him an honorary Doctorate of Letters for his contributions to philology, and the British government made him a Commander of the Order of the British Empire. *The Silmarillion* was never published in the author's lifetime, but in 1977 Christopher completed the work and released it to great critical acclaim. Since then, many volumes of Tolkien's works—both fictional and philological—have been edited and published by family, friends, or former students. Looking back on his literary accomplishments, the author once recalled, "Having set myself a task, the arrogance of which I fully recognized and trembled at: being precisely to restore to the English an epic tradition and present them with a mythology of their own: it is a wonderful thing to be told that I have succeeded, at least with those who have still the undarkened heart and mind."

Sources

Carpenter, Humphrey, *J. R. R. Tolkien: A Biography,* Allen & Unwin, 1977, published as *Tolkien: A Biography,* Houghton, 1978.

Kolich, Augustus M., "J. R. R. Tolkien," *Dictionary of Literary Biography,* Volume 15: *British Novelists, 1930–1959,* Gale, 1983, pp. 520–530.

Tolkien, J. R. R., *The Annotated Hobbit,* Douglas A. Anderson wrote introduction and notes, Houghton, 1988.

Tolkien, J. R. R., *The Letters of J. R. R. Tolkien,* selected and edited by Humphrey Carpenter and Christopher Tolkien, Houghton, 1981.

Jules Verne

Born: February 8, 1828, Nantes, France
Died: March 24, 1905, Amiens, France

Well-versed in the scientific problems of his day, the author of Twenty Thousand Leagues Under the Sea *has been called* The Father of Science Fiction.

Jules Verne is widely recognized today as the masterful author of adventures for young readers, and many consider him to be the father of science fiction. Although he produced a large body of work, including short stories and plays, he is most celebrated for his "novels of anticipation" in which he combined high adventure with scientific predictions. His novels *Journey to the Center of the Earth, Twenty Thousand Leagues Under the Sea, The Mysterious Island, Around the World in Eighty Days,* and *From the Earth to the Moon* and its sequel *Around the Moon* rank as classics of literature for young readers.

A Poet Who Was Not Fond of the Law

The second child of four in a middle-class family, young Verne was born into a long line of lawyers—and his family, it seems, expected him to follow in his father's footsteps. Reasonably successful as a schoolboy, he was composing poetry by the age of 12. He loved to explore his surroundings, and he often made exploratory voyages with his brother Paul in a battered sailboat on the nearby Loire River.

In 1848 Verne went to Paris, where he studied law and began to write short stories and plays. Although he qualified for the bar, he chose instead to pursue a literary career, much to his father's chagrin. Nevertheless, the aspiring author had to support his wife—Honorine de Viane, a widow whom he married in 1857—and his son and two stepdaughters, so he worked as a stockbroker. Verne's business responsibilities were less demanding than the legal profession would have been, and, having settled with his family in a spacious three-story house in Amiens, he was free to pursue his literary interests.

A Lifetime Contract

Success as a novelist, however, was a long time in coming. Although he wrote several plays with the younger Alexandre Dumas, it was not until 1863 that he, then over 30, made his mark. An instant best-seller for children and adults alike, the adventure novel *Five Weeks in a Balloon* was the first in a series called Extraordinary Voyages: Worlds Known and Unknown. Now a marketable name, Verne was guaranteed an income under what became a lifetime contract with publisher Jules Hetzel, who also marketed the works of renowned French authors Honore de Balzac and George Sand.

Verne had discovered a successful formula: He immersed his hero in some currently intriguing scientific problem and predicted future technological advancements. As a result, he created a new genre—science fiction. Verne quickly developed work habits that allowed him to produce two books a year: Up at dawn every morning, he worked until noon, writing and rewriting. Always with several projects at different stages of completion, he wrote steadily for 43 years, mostly avoiding the social events that authors often use to help promote their works.

Extraordinary Voyages

Most of Verne's novels were first published in serialized form in periodicals, and the author often revised his works substantially before they were published in book form. *Journey to the Center of the Earth,* published in 1864, recounts the adventures of Professor Lidenbrock and his teenage nephew Axel, who descend deep into the earth through an extinct volcano in Iceland.

Best Bets

1869 ***From the Earth to the Moon***
Civil war veterans send a rocket ship to the moon. Followed by a sequel, *Around the Moon.*

1874 ***Journey to the Center of the Earth***
Professor Lidenbrock and his teenage nephew Axel descend deep into the earth through an extinct volcano.

1874 ***Around the World in Eighty Days***
Phileas Fogg and his servant, Passepartout, attempt to circle the world in 80 days.

1899 ***Twenty Thousand Leagues Under the Sea***
Captain Nemo wages war on the world from the *Nautilus,* a ship that sails under the sea.

From *Twenty Thousand Leagues Under the Sea,* by Jules Verne. Illustrated by Milo Winter.

Many of the debates that raged in Verne's time—concerning fossils and the origin of the earth and human beings—inspired the book's discoveries and adventures.

In *Twenty Thousand Leagues Under the Sea,* Verne also speculated about the future of submarines. He first came up with the idea for the tale about the submarine *Nautilus* and its cynical inventor, Captain Nemo, while sailing his boat, *Le Saint Michel,* on the English Channel. Professor Aronnax narrates the story, having been taken prisoner with his servant and a harpooner while attempting to solve the mystery of the creature that has been sinking ships in surprise attacks. Verne's characters discuss many issues—such as the killing off of whales and other sea creatures, the possibilities of underwater towns, and food resources—and overcome such obstacles as riding out a hurricane and freeing the submarine from a capsized iceberg.

During his lifetime, *Around the World in Eighty Days* was Verne's biggest success. One of the novels in the Extraordinary Voyages series, it employs very little science. Instead, it describes the fast-paced, often humorous journey of Phileas Fogg, an eccentric Englishman who has bet that he can circle the globe in 80 days. According to Jean Jules-Verne in his biography, *Jules Verne,* the author expressed his hopes for *Around the World* this way: "I have dreams about it! I hope our readers enjoy it as much as I. You know, I must be a bit crazy: I fall for all the extravagant things my heroes get up to. There's only one thing I regret: not to be able to get up to those things with them."

Everything that I invent, everything that I imagine, will always fall short of the truth, because there will come a time when the creations of science will outstrip those of the imagination."

—Jules Verne

Tourism, Pessimism, and the Passing of a Prophet

Verne began to enjoy a prosperous life, and, in 1876, bought a sailing yacht, the *Saint-Michel II*, which he replaced a year later with a steam yacht, christened the *Saint-Michel III*. But from 1875 until his death, Verne's novels changed dramatically. Instead of dealing with scientific developments, they focussed on tourism. More pessimistic in tone, they feature few machines, which are eventually destroyed; even agreeable characters meet with madness or death.

Not surprisingly, these novels did not enjoy the success of Verne's earlier works. By 1893 Verne began to suffer attacks of dizziness, eye problems, and leg pains that severely limited his activity. His declining health, however, did not prevent him from writing: "It won't stop me from slaving. What could I do without my work? What would become of me," Jules-Verne quoted the author as saying. To his biographers' dismay, Verne destroyed all of his personal files in 1898. In 1905, surrounded by his family, he died of diabetes at his home in Amiens.

Reel Life

Around the World in Eighty Days, 1956.

Victorian Englishman and his manservant set off on a spectacular journey to circumnavigate the world in 80 days.

Five Weeks in a Balloon, 1962.

Often-comic exploits of 19th-century expedition across Africa by way of balloon.

Journey to the Center of the Earth, 1959.

En route to the center of the earth, a scientist and a student find the long-lost mythic metropolis known as Atlantis.

The Mysterious Island, 1961.

Civil Was soldiers take off in a balloon and land on a Pacific island inhabited by humongous creatures.

20,000 Leagues Under the Sea, 1954.

Captain Nemo wages war on the surface society from a futuristic submarine. Meanwhile, a shipwrecked sailor and scientist attempt to save the world from the nefarious Nemo.

Sources

Costello, Peter, *Jules Verne: Inventor of Science Fiction,* Scribner, 1978.

Freedman, Russell, *Jules Verne: Portrait of a Prophet,* Holiday House, 1965.

Jules-Verne, Jean, *Jules Verne,* translated and adapted by Roger Greaves, Taplinger, 1976.

Martin, Andrew, *The Masked Prophet,* Oxford University Press, 1989.

Stewart, Ian, "The Rise and Fall of the Lunar M-Pire," *Scientific American,* April 1993, p. 120.

"Travelling Backwards," *The Economist,* August 19, 1989, p. 74.

Kurt Vonnegut, Jr.

Born: November 11, 1922, Indianapolis, Indiana

The author of Slaughterhouse-Five *writes tales that reflect his experiences as a witness to the horrors of Dresden.*

Best known as the author of *Slaughterhouse-Five; or, The Children's Crusade: A Duty-Dance with Death,* published in 1969, Kurt Vonnegut is a major voice in American literature. Readers applaud his pointed, satirical depictions of modern society. Emphasizing the comic absurdity of the human condition, he frequently depicts characters who search for meaning and order in an inherently meaningless and disorderly universe, and he focuses in particular on the futility of warfare, the destructive power of technology, and the human potential for both irrationality and evil. He also mocks institutions such as government and religion, which, in his opinion, offer harmful, bogus dogma as remedies for these problems. Finding no solutions to the problems that plague humanity, Vonnegut is ultimately a pessimistic author; nonetheless, he approaches his subjects with humor and compassion. As a result, his works—as Richard Giannone has noted—are "comic masks covering the tragic farce that is our contemporary life."

Fantasy, Satire, and Serious Literature

The son of a successful architect, Vonnegut attended Cornell University, where he majored in chemistry and biology. Later enlisting in the U.S. Army, he served in World War II and was eventually taken prisoner by the German army. Following the war, Vonnegut studied anthropology at the University of

Chicago and later moved to Schenectady, New York, to work as a publicist for the General Electric Corporation. During this period, he also began submitting short stories to various journals, and in 1951 he resigned his position at General Electric to devote his time solely to writing.

Beginning with *Player Piano,* Vonnegut published several novels throughout the 1950s and 1960s. However, since he frequently used elements of fantasy, he was classified as a writer of science fiction—a genre not widely accepted as "serious literature." His work did not attract significant popular or critical interest until the mid-1960s, when increasing disillusionment with American society led to widespread admiration for his forthright, irreverent satires. Vonnegut's reputation was greatly enhanced in 1969 with the publication of *Slaughterhouse-Five,* a vehemently antiwar novel that appeared during the peak of protest against American involvement in Vietnam. During the 1970s and 1980s Vonnegut continued to serve as an important commentator on American society, publishing a series of novels in which he focused on topics ranging from political corruption to environmental pollution. In recent years, Vonnegut has also become a prominent and vocal critic of censorship and militarism in the United States.

Although many critics attribute Vonnegut's classification as a science fiction writer to a complete misunderstanding of his aims, fantasy is nevertheless an important feature of his early works. *Player Piano* depicts a fictional city called Ilium in which the people have relinquished control of their lives to a computer humorously named EPICAC, a substance that induces vomiting. Vonnegut's protagonist, Dr. Paul Proteus, rebels against the emotional emptiness of a society in which—freed from the need to perform any meaningful work—the citizens have lost their sense of dignity and purpose. Vonnegut again examined themes of freedom and purpose in *The Sirens of Titan,* which takes place on several different planets, including a thoroughly militarized Mars where the inhabitants are electronically controlled. The fantastic settings of these works serve as a metaphor for modern society—which Vonnegut seems to view as absurd to the point of being surreal.

Best Bets

1959 *The Sirens of Titan*
Inhabitants are electronically controlled on the militarized planet of Mars.

1963 *Cat's Cradle*
The discovery of ice-nine—a form of ice that is capable of solidifying all water on Earth—threatens the planet.

1969 *Slaughterhouse-Five; or, The Children's Crusade: A Duty-Dance with Death*
After witnessing the bombing of Dresden, Billy Pilgrim suffers from a spiritual illness and becomes "unstuck in time."

1990 *Hocus Pocus*
Vietnam vet and college prof Eugene Debs Hartke starts to doubt his atheism when he discovers a strange coincidence in his life.

Reel Life

Slaughterhouse Five, 1972.

A suburban optometrist becomes "unstuck" in time and flits randomly through the experiences of his life, from the Dresden bombing to an extraterrestrial zoo.

Who Am I This Time?, 1982.

Two shy people are able to express their love for each other only through their roles in a local theater production of *A Streetcar Named Desire.* Directed by Jonathan Demme and stars Susan Sarandon and Christopher Walken.

A Bunch of X's and Pearls Before Swine

Vonnegut again focused on the role of technology in human society in *Cat's Cradle,* widely considered one of his best works. The novel recounts the discovery of a form of ice, called ice-nine, which is solid at a much lower temperature than normal ice and is capable of solidifying all water on Earth. Ice-nine serves as a symbol of the enormous destructive potential of technology, particularly when developed or used without regard for the welfare of humanity. In contrast to what he considers the harmful truths represented by scientific discoveries, Vonnegut presents a religion called Bokononism, based on the concept that there are no absolute truths, that human life is ultimately meaningless, and that the most helpful religion would therefore preach benign lies that encourage kindness, confer humanity with a sense of dignity, and allow people to view their absurd condition with humor. Vonnegut employs the motif of the cat's cradle—a children's game in which string is looped around the fingers to create elaborate patterns—to underline the absurdity of our lives. "No wonder kids grow up crazy," he wrote. "A cat's cradle is nothing but a bunch of X's between somebody's hands, and little kids look at all those X's ... no damn cat, and no damn cradle."

In *God Bless You, Mr. Rosewater; or, Pearls Before Swine,* Vonnegut presents one of his most endearing protagonists in the figure of Eliot Rosewater, a philanthropic but ineffectual man who attempts to use his inherited fortune for the betterment of humanity. Rosewater finds that his generosity, his genuine concern for human beings, and his attempts to establish loving relationships are viewed as madness in a society that values only money. Denunciating materialism and greed—as well as religions—in the modern world, the novel suggests that the wealthy and powerful invented the concept of divine ordination to justify and maintain their exploitation of others.

Life after Dresden

Vonnegut described *Slaughterhouse-Five* as a novel he was compelled to write: Based on one of the most extraordinary and significant events of his

The 1972 film *Slaughterhouse Five* starred Michael Sacks and was directed by George Roy Hill.

life, it recounts the author's experience as a prisoner of the German army, when he witnessed the Allied bombing that destroyed the city of Dresden and killed more than 135,000 people. One of the few to survive, Vonnegut was ordered by his captors to assist in the grisly task of digging bodies from the rubble and destroying them in huge bonfires.

Although the attack claimed many lives—and was directed at a target of no apparent military importance—it attracted little attention. *Slaughterhouse-Five* is Vonnegut's attempt to document and to denounce this event. Like Vonnegut, Billy Pilgrim, the protagonist of *Slaughterhouse-Five,* was present at the bombing of Dresden and has been profoundly affected by the experience. Suffering from a spiritual malaise that culminates in a nervous breakdown, he also suffers from a peculiar condition; "unstuck in time," he randomly experiences events from his past, present, and future. Vonnegut's novel is therefore a complex, nonchronological narrative in which images of suffering and loss prevail. "Ultimately," Charles B. Harris noted, "[*Slaughterhouse-Five*] is less about Dresden than it is about the impact of Dresden on one man's sensibilities. More specifically, it is the story of Vonnegut's story of Dresden, how he came to write it and, implicitly, why he wrote it as he did."

Having written *Slaughterhouse-Five,* Vonnegut began to focus directly on contemporary problems. *Breakfast of Champions; or, Goodbye Blue Monday* and *Slapstick; or, Lonesome No More,* for example, examine the widespread feelings of despair and loneliness that result from the loss of traditional culture in the United States. *Jailbird,* the story of a fictitious participant in the Watergate scandal of the Nixon administration, is a scathing indictment of the American political system; *Galapagos* predicts the dire consequences of environmental pollution; and *Hocus-Pocus; or, What's the Hurry, Son?* deals with the implications and aftermath of the war in Vietnam.

Although many of the above works are highly regarded, critics frequently argue that, in his later works, Vonnegut tends to repeat themes that he presented more compellingly in earlier works. Many also suggest that Vonnegut's narrative style—which includes the frequent repetition of distinctive phrases, the use of colloquialisms, and a digressive manner—becomes formulaic in some of his later works. Nevertheless, Vonnegut remains one of the most esteemed American satirists. Noted for their frank and insightful social criticism as well as their innovative style, his works present an idiosyncratic yet compelling vision of modern life.

Sources

Chernuchin, Michael, editor, *Vonnegut Talks!,* Pylon, 1977.

Current Biography, H. W. Wilson, March 1991, p. 52.

Giannone, Richard, *Vonnegut: A Preface to His Novels,* Kennikat, 1977.

Harris, Charles B., *Contemporary American Novelists of the Absurd,* College and University Press, 1971.

Kazin, Alfred, *Bright Book of Life: American Novelists and Storytellers from Hemingway to Mailer,* Little, Brown, 1973.

Kennard, Jean E., *Number and Nightmare: Forms of Fantasy in Contemporary Fiction,* Archon Books, 1975.

Klinkowitz, Jerome, *Kurt Vonnegut,* Methuen, 1982.

Klinkowitz, Jerome, and Donald L. Lawler, editors, *Vonnegut in America: An Introduction to the Life and Work of Kurt Vonnegut,* Delacorte, 1977.

Lundquist, James, *Kurt Vonnegut,* Ungar, 1977.

Mayo, Clark, *Kurt Vonnegut: The Gospel From Outer Space, or Yes, We Have No Nirvanas,* Borgo Press, 1973.

Schatt, Stanley, *Kurt Vonnegut,* Twayne, 1976.

H. G. Wells

Born: September 21, 1866, Bromley, England
Died: August 13, 1946, London, England

Herbert George Wells is best known as one of the forefathers of modern science fiction. His pioneering works in this genre foretold such developments as chemical warfare, atomic weapons, and world wars. *The Time Machine, The Island of Dr. Moreau, The Invisible Man,* and *The War of the Worlds*—all published before 1898—are classics that have profoundly influenced the course of twentieth-century science fiction. Wells's science fiction is driven by a pessimistic, apocalyptic vision. On the other hand, in his later works of speculative nonfiction—such as 1914's *The World Set Free, The Outline of History,* published from 1919 to 1920, *The Shape of Things to Come* in 1933, and 1941's *Guide to the New World*—he optimistically wrote of a future that holds the promise of utopia. As a social critic, Wells's advocacy of free love and socialism, as well as his attacks on what he considered the stifling moral constraints of Victorian society, contributed to the liberalization of modern Western culture.

The author of The Time Machine *wrote "scientific romances" that reflected his belief that man is a social animal caught up in an evolutionary pull toward the future.*

The Social Animal

Born to lower-middle-class parents—who were, in fact, servants to the gentry—Herbert George Wells escaped a similar life by winning a scholarship to the Normal School of Science at South Kensington, London, in 1884. Great Britain's first college to offer a science education for teachers, the Normal School of Science was founded by T. H. Huxley, who also served as its first dean. Wells regarded Huxley as the greatest man he ever met (although they never engaged in actual conversation).

Best Bets

Wells would later cite Huxley's influence as the single most influential aspect of his education. For Huxley, biology took in not only the study of man as an animal species but also as a social and cultural animal. What's more, it made a bid to replace the idea of man's unity under God with man's unity as a global species. For Wells, the goal of the growing international socialist movement was to unify and pacify the human race—still divided by competing nationalisms—thereby to reassert its essential oneness. According to Wells, when science proved theology a fiction, the God of the Above was replaced by the God of the Ahead, the evolutionary pull of the future toward a world socialist state.

As it happened, however, Wells lost his scholarship after his third year. Only Huxley, who taught Wells his first year, interested him. Thereafter he failed to keep up with his studies, preoccupied with activities such as debating and the college magazine, which he founded and edited. Wells had no intention of becoming a man of letters, though he showed an early interest in writing—as is revealed by *The Desert Daisy*, a narrative the author had penned as a 12-year-old. Beginning his professional career by writing journalistic sketches, Wells caught the attention of the editors of the English *Saturday Review,* who assigned him to review new fiction for their magazine; from 1895 to 1897, Wells passed judgment on almost every new novel published in English.

Chronic Argonauts and Time Machines

Wells would not limit himself to reviewing, however. All along he had been developing a promising idea, first introduced in a short story called "The Chronic Argonauts," which he had published in his college magazine two years after he dropped out of school. It was an idea that he hoped would establish him as a novelist in his own right. After many false starts, Wells's brainchild appeared in 1895 as *The Time Machine.* Hailed as a work of genius, it is regarded by modern critics as the one great Victorian epic dramatizing a Darwinian vision of cosmic time outside historical time. Wells continued on his way to winning fame with a series of similar novels—or scientific novels, as he called them—which have remained continuously in print since his death.

The best of them are *The Time Machine, The Island of Doctor Moreau, The Invisible Man, The War of the Worlds,* and *The First Men in the Moon.*

Wells's science fiction was profoundly influenced by his adaptation of Huxley's philosophical interpretation of Darwinian evolutionary theory: The course of life on Earth, like that of any organism, Huxley maintained, follows a pattern of quickening, maturation, and decadence. Writing at a time when the scientific community smugly believed that nothing remained to be discovered, Huxley's "cosmic pessimism" was deeply disturbing. In short, Huxley's philosophy implied that humankind faced inevitable decline. Although Wells did not pioneer fiction that speculated about technological advances, his early science fiction was among the first to explore such complex issues as the impact of technology on human affairs and the moral responsibility of scientists for their research and inventions.

The Strange Man's arrival ❧

From *The Invisible Man* by H. G. Wells. Illustrated by Charles Mozely.

The Father of Modern Science Fiction

To the end of his life, Wells regarded his scientific romances as inconsequential. So did the twentieth-century critical establishment until 1961, when Bernard Bergonzi, in his study *The Early H. G. Wells: A Study of the Scientific Romances,* persuasively argued that these works deserved to be ranked among the classics of the English language.

With the scientific romances, Wells defined a new area of twentieth-century literature, not only for science fiction authors but for a number of great mainstream writers who lent their talents to the genre. Notables who have acknowledged this debt include Evgeny Zamyatin, Aldous Huxley, C. S. Lewis, George Orwell, William Golding, Vladimir Nabokov, and Jorge Luis

Reel Life

Invisible Man, (multiple versions).

A scientist learns how to make himself invisible and terrorizes a British village.

The Magic Shop, 1986.

A boy and his grandfather visit a magic shop, where the shopkeeper performs fantastic tricks.

The Time Machine, (multiple versions).

A young man takes a trip to the future using a time machine.

War of the Worlds (multiple versions).

Martians invade a small southern California town.

Borges. Victorian critics accepted Wells's scientific romances as masterful works of art. But later critics took a different view. When his scientific romances were reprinted in the first issues of *Amazing Stories*—a magazine that, from 1926 onward, established science fiction as a unique genre among the many American publishers' categories that dominated the pulp magazine industry—Wells was proclaimed the "Father of Modern Science Fiction."

Wells is regarded as one of the most prominent champions of the early twentieth-century spirit of British liberal optimism. His works are ranked with those of socialist writer Bernard Shaw as examples of the era's exuberant sense of release from Victorian conventions and morals, and of unbridled confidence in the benefits that would derive from scientific progress. The continued popularity of his books, the tremendous body of criticism devoted to them, and the liberalizing effect that much of his work had on Western thought combine to make Wells a major figure of modern literature.

Sources

Batchelor, John, *H. G. Wells,* Cambridge University Press, 1985.

Bergonzi, Bernard, editor, *H. G. Wells: A Collection of Critical Essays,* Prentice-Hall, 1976.

Costa, Richard Hauer, *H. G. Wells,* Twayne, 1966, revised, 1985.

Ferrell, Keith, "The Challenges of Science Fiction," *Omni,* February 1992, p. 6.

Gill, Stephen, *The Scientific Romances of H. G. Wells,* Vesta, 1975.

Haining, Peter, *The H. G. Wells Scrapbook,* New English Library, 1978.

Huntington, John, *The Logic of Fantasy: H. G. Wells and Science Fiction,* Columbia University Press, 1982.

Pohl, Frederik, "Astounding Story: A Leading Science Fiction Writer Traces the Course of Sci-Fi in America," *American Heritage,* September-October 1989, p. 42.

Suvin, Darko, and Robert M. Philmus, editors, *H. G. Wells and Modern Science Fiction,* Bucknell University Press, 1977.

West, Geoffrey H. (formerly Geoffrey H. Wells), *H. G. Wells: A Sketch for a Portrait,* Howe, 1930.

Robert Westall

Born: October 7, 1929, Tynemouth, Northumberland, England
Died: April 15, 1993, London, England

When Robert Westall wrote his first novel, *The Machine Gunners,* he immediately became a prominent figure in contemporary young adult literature. Since the publication of *The Machine Gunners*—his careful recollection for his son of the tensions of a childhood spent in wartime England—Westall has written many well-received novels. The most notable of these include *Futuretrack Five, Urn Burial, The Scarecrows,* and *The Kingdom by the Sea.* While Westall's fiction ranges from historical drama to time-travel fantasy, the author's ability to create believable characters lends even the most fantastic tale an aspect of reality. Westall's adolescent characters often indulge in violence and profanity and are not always heroic; these features have inspired some controversy, but neither Westall's audience nor his critics have denied the emotional power of the author's best writing.

The author of The Scarecrows *writes everything from realistic fiction and time-travel fantasy to spooky and sinister tales.*

Stupendous Toys and the Oily Wizard

Westall's father, to whom he attributes the variety and vigor of his writing, was a foreman-fitter at the local gasworks. "But to me," the author recalled, "he was the Oily Wizard. When he came home from work, he smelt of strange and terrible magic—benzine and sulfur hung around his overalls and a cap, so filthy you could see no pattern on it. But his wizardry lay in more than that. I would watch him looking at an ailing engine, with his finger held lightly against it, feeling for vibration and his

Best Bets

1980   *The Scarecrows*
After Simon's father dies, the rage he feels rouses spirits that manifest themselves in the form of scarecrows.

1983   *Futuretrack Five*
A supercomputer named Laura monitors society in the twenty-first century.

1990   *The Promise*
After Bob's girlfriend dies, a promise he once made to her takes on a creepy new meaning.

1993   *Demons and Shadows*
A "Best of Westall" collection of 11 spooky stories, including "Graveyard Shift," in which a cemetery superintendent acts as a counselor to the newly buried. Followed by a companion volume, *Shades of Darkness*.

1993   *The Stones of Muncaster Cathedral*
Chosen to perform routine repairs on a cathedral, Joe Clarke discovers that diabolic forces reside in the old kirk.

head cocked on one side, listening for the one tiny sound that would mean trouble. I have never seen such concentration."

As a boy Westall eagerly looked forward to trips to the gasworks, an industrial otherworld that provided the perfect backdrop for his father's mechanical wizardry. After work, however, the perpetual grime of the gasworks clashed with his father's cultivated talents, which included drawing and toymaking. Westall's father taught his son to draw, and this early instruction put Westall on course to pursue an education, and later a career, in fine arts.

From Teenage Novels to *Homes and Gardens*

As an adolescent Westall began his first experiments as a writer. "I wrote my first novel in the summer holidays when I was twelve," he recalled. "In the loneliness of the four summer holidays that followed, I wrote four novels of increasing length and increasingly comprised of hopeless cliches borrowed from bad war movies and my parents' cowboy-novels.... I never dreamt of writing about my own life and times, as I regarded these as being so insufferably dull and boring that no one would want to read of them."

After entering high school, Westall began studying art; concentrating on sculpture, he was "too busy carving funny shapes in stone or plaster" to give much thought to writing for the next 14 years. There were, however, two memorable exceptions. As a first-year college student, Westall juxtaposed the peaceful memories of a bicycle trip and the hustle of his first college days into a short piece titled "Two Roads to Otterburn." The piece was published in the "Old Students Section" of Westall's high school magazine. After reading the piece, Westall's high school English teacher said, "You'll make a writer—if you go on writing honestly about what you *know*." Westall took the advice to heart, and seven years later, in 1956, while he was a graduate student at the University of London, he was again compelled to communicate his experiences in writing. The Soviet Union had just invaded Hungary, and Westall joined a student protest of Soviet aggression. There was a brief struggle between the students and the authorities, which left Westall so inspired that he wrote a 4,000-word editorial on the encounter. The piece was published in Westall's hometown newspaper, the *Newcastle Journal*.

Despite his success as a journalist, however, Westall still hadn't given a second thought to writing fiction. After completing graduate school, Westall took a series of jobs teaching art. But two years later, an opportunity to write fell in Westall's lap. After the author-artist wrote a well-received art review for a local newspaper, the editor in charge asked Westall to write a regular column. As a journalist, Westall learned to edit his own writing, to cut away excess, and to discuss abstract art in common terms without flaunting his critical vocabulary. As his reputation increased, Westall began to write for larger newspapers and magazines, eventually contributing antiques articles to *Homes and Gardens*. "As a journalist," Westall recalled, "I learnt to write crisply, interestingly, and even amusingly—I think as a journalist I became a real pro."

A Carnegie Medal-Winning War Story

It was around this time that Westall resumed his attempts at fiction. At first, the novels he began were as unsuccessful as those he had written as a teen. As his son, Christopher, approached his twelfth birthday, however, Westall was overcome by the desire to share his own childhood with the boy. A chapter at a time, he began to pen the story that would become his first published novel, *The Machine Gunners*.

The completed manuscript sat for two years before it was submitted for publication; when the novel was finally published, it won Great Britain's prestigious Carnegie Medal for excellence in children's literature. Set in England during World War II, *The Machine Gunners* tells the tale of five adolescent boys who struggle to survive the German Blitz. When a German plane crashes near the boys' town, the leader of the group, Chas McGill, scavenges a machine gun from the rear of the plane, which he then hides. In paramilitary fashion, he organizes the other boys around the weapon, secretly intending to use the gun to bring down other enemy planes. Throughout, Chas keeps the gang silent and loyal with a violent ferocity that eventually proves his undoing.

Cover of *The Promise* by Robert Westall.

As a tale of unsupervised youth, *The Machine Gunners* has often been compared to William Golding's *The Lord of the Flies* and has generated similar controversy. Some critics objected to Westall's graphic portrayal of the violence Chas employs to keep the gang loyal, and many also questioned the common use of profanity in the dialogue. Critics who favored the book praised Westall for its uncompromisingly realistic depiction of life during wartime. Margery Fisher, for example, wrote in *Growing Point,* "I can think of few writers who have put on paper as successfully as Robert Westall has done in *The Machine Gunners* the sheer muddle of [World War II] and the day-to-day difficulty, for civilians at least, of deciding what was important."

Scarecrows and Spooky Stories

"I write two kinds of books," Westall observed, "realistic, earthy, comical books; and spooky books. And they really have no relationship to each other." Westall's books since *The Machine Gunners* have dealt with a variety of topics, ranging from witch-hunting in the seventeenth century to ghosts that haunt other ghosts to a race of intelligent cats. John Webster, the cat-fancying, time-traveling hero of Westall's 1978 novel *The Devil on the Road,* is based on Westall's son Christopher—who was tragically killed in a motorcycle accident at the age of 18.

Westall's second Carnegie Medal winner, *The Scarecrows,* written in 1980, relates the tale of Simon Brown, a young teenage boy whose father has recently died. When his mother remarries, Simon is filled with an almost uncontrollable rage, directed primarily at his stepfather. In a supernatural twist, Simon's anger rouses the spirits of the past at an old mill near his home. These spirits are manifest in the forms of three lifelike scarecrows, which move daily through the fields toward the house. Sarah Hayes wrote in the *Times Literary Supplement* that—in spite of the frightening presence of the scarecrows—how "people talk and relate to each other, to their families and to themselves is what [Westall's] work is really about. And despite its earnest intent, his story is exciting, agonizing, tender and terrifying by turns, and never fails to grip."

An Optimistic Pessimist

Westall's vision of society is somewhat bleak. "I cannot say I like the way the world is going," he once remarked. "There have been advances; more prosperity in the West; a growth of conscience among the Western middle classes; the liberation, still incomplete, of women. But there has been a decay in the way people belonged together, looked after each other, and were proudly determined to stand on their own two feet."

Westall expresses this sentiment in literary fashion in his pessimistic novel about the future, *Futuretrack Five.* The novel is set in Great Britain in the early twenty-first century, where the entire social order is monitored and directed by Laura, a supercomputer with a deliberately disarming name. Society is sorted according to a nationally administered series of tests. Those who fail are sent to the ruined cities to scrape together a living in whatever manner possible, while those who receive higher test scores are rewarded with the privileges of the leisure class—such as video games, sex, and motorcycle racing. After Henry Kitson uncovers a government plan to reduce the population through genetic control, he and his companion Keri set out to undermine the government's sinister plot, which results in a chilling confrontation with Laura.

In a later work, *Kingdom by the Sea,* Westall returned to realistic depictions of life in Great Britain during World War II. The author recounts the fictional journey of Harry, who believes he is the sole member of his family to survive a bomb raid by the Germans. Determined to avoid being handed over to an insufferable relative, Harry sets out to make his own way in war-torn England. As his journey nears its end, Harry meets Mr. Murgatroyd—whose own son was lost at sea during the war—who takes Harry in as his adopted son. Harry finds his "kingdom by the sea" utterly blissful as new worlds of learning and adventure are revealed to him. In the end, however, Harry discovers that his family survived, and he must return to the small town of his childhood, a place far too small to contain the worldly young man he has become. "For the remainder of his adolescence, Harry will dream of his other life," explained Mary M. Burns in *Horn Book,* "biding time until he can once more journey to that country of the heart and mind which both sustained and changed him."

Following *Kingdom by the Sea,* Westall published nearly another dozen books before his death in 1993. In addition to his novels for young adults, he adapted *The Machine Gunners* into a play and edited what would become a well-received collection of memoirs, *Children of the Blitz: Memories of Wartime Childhood.* Westall's books remain popular, and *The Machine Gunners* is so widely read in Great Britain that it has become a standard text in British classrooms. Westall's highly charged, and sometimes controversial, writing will generate interest for a long time to come, particularly because his characters so clearly depict the struggles of adolescence. His insight into the lives and minds of the youth of both his own and his son's generation continues to startle readers by appealing to what Westall called "children's love of inevitable catastrophe."

Sources

Burns, Mary M., review of *The Kingdom by the Sea, Horn Book,* January/February 1992, p. 76.

Fisher, Margery, review of *Futuretrack Five, Growing Point,* January 1984, p. 4194.

Fisher, Margery, review of *The Machine Gunners, Growing Point,* October 1975, pp. 2707–2708.

Hayes, Sarah, "Threats from Within," *Times Literary Supplement,* March 27, 1981, p. 339.

Obituary, *Facts on File,* May 6, 1993, p. 344.

Westall, Robert, "Defence of—and by—Author Robert Westall," *Library Association Record,* January 1977, pp. 38–39.

Westall, Robert, "How Real Do You Want Your Realism?," *Signal,* January 1979, pp. 34–46.

Westall, Robert, *Something about the Author Autobiography Series,* Volume 2, Gale, 1986, pp. 305–323.

E. B. White

Born: July 11, 1899, Mount Vernon, New York
Died: October 1, 1985, North Brooklin, Maine

Few writers have achieved recognition in as many fields as did E. B. White. Regarded as one of the finest essayists of the twentieth century, he was the author of two classic stories for young readers—*Charlotte's Web* and *Stuart Little*—and his extensive contributions to the *New Yorker* were instrumental in making that magazine a success.

Of Mouselike Creatures and a Man's Instincts

Of his various achievements, White's books for young readers—of which he wrote only three—probably attracted the most popular acclaim. Inspired by a vivid dream, White began in 1939 to write a story about a small, mouselike character. Whenever one of his 18 nieces and nephews wanted to hear a story, he improvised new adventures for his hero, Stuart Little. In 1945, gathering these adventures together, he sent a book-length manuscript to Harper & Row for consideration. Editor Ursula Nordstrom found it "marvelously well-written, and funny, and touching," she recalled in an article for the *New York Times Book Review,* and accepted *Stuart Little* for publication.

Considered to be the best living personal essayist during his lifetime, the author of Charlotte's Web *was best known for his stories for young readers.*

Not everyone, however, was as enthusiastic as Nordstrom about White's mouse tale. Anne Carroll Moore—then head of children's literature at the New York Public Library and the most influential person in juvenile publishing at the time—found the book to be "nonaffirmative, inconclusive, unfit [for young readers]," Nordstrom related. Harper nevertheless went ahead with publication, convinced that *Stuart Little* showed merit. "It is unnerving," Nordstrom quoted White as saying, "to be told you're bad [for young readers]; but I detected in Miss Moore's letter an assumption that there are rules governing the writing of juvenile literature.... And this I was not sure of. I had followed my instincts in writing about Stuart, and following one's instincts seemed to be the way a writer should operate." Speaking of the book in his *Letters of E. B. White,* White revealed that "in a way, Stuart's journey symbolizes the continuing journey that everybody takes—in search of what is perfect and unattainable. This is perhaps too elusive an idea to put into a book for [young readers], but I put it in anyway."

Several reviewers believed that *Stuart Little* has the same wide appeal as do the classics of literature for young readers. Writing in the *Saturday Review of Literature,* R. C. Benet believed that readers of all ages would enjoy the book. "The exact number of years of the reader," he stated, "won't matter here any more than it does with 'Alice [in Wonderland],' 'The Wind in the Willows,' some of [A. A.] Milne, or indeed the work of Walt Disney, who created that other popular mouse." White, in any case, found an enthusiastic audience: *Stuart Little* has sold more than two million copies in English and has been translated into 20 other languages.

A Pig, a Spider, and a Trumpet-Playing Swan

White's next youth-oriented book, *Charlotte's Web,* was published in 1952. Without fanfare—or even a previous mention that he was working on another book for a young audience—White dropped by his publisher's office with the manuscript. The author took Nordstrom by surprise: "He gave me the only copy in existence of 'Charlotte's Web,'" she remembered, "got back on the elevator and left." Nordstrom read only a few chapters before deciding to publish the book; recalling her impressions of White's manuscript, she later commented, "I couldn't believe that it was so good!"

Charlotte's Web is set on a farm much like the one White owned in Maine. The story "seems to have developed," Peter M. Neumeyer observed in the *Dictionary of Literary Biography,* "directly and exclusively out of

White's joy in his own rural existence." White explained to Lee Bennett Hopkins in *More Books by More People*, "I like animals and my barn is a very pleasant place to be.... One day when I was on my way to feed the pig, I began feeling sorry for the pig because, like most pigs, he was doomed to die. This made me sad. So I started thinking of ways to save a pig's life. I had been watching a big, gray spider at her work and was impressed by how clever she was at weaving. Gradually I worked the spider into the story,... a story of friendship and salvation on a farm." And in *Fairy Tales and After: From Snow White to E. B. White,* Roger Sale noted that White has referred to *Charlotte's Web* as a "hymn to the barn." "It is the word 'hymn,'" Sale wrote, "and the sense of celebration and praise, that is important here.... The essential celebration is of the beautiful things change brings or can bring." Since its initial publication in 1952, *Charlotte's Web* has sold well over three million copies, quickly becoming an American classic for young readers.

Illustration from *Charlotte's Web* by E. B. White. Illustrated by Garth Williams.

As a piece of work, [Charlotte's Web] *is just about perfect, and just about magical in the way it is done."*

—*Eudora Welty writing in the* New York Times

It wasn't until 1970 that White published his next book for young readers, *The Trumpet of the Swan.* As in *Stuart Little* and *Charlotte's Web,* the characters in *The Trumpet of the Swan* are animals who participate in the human world and overcome great obstacles to achieve their goals. Like the

Reel Life

Charlotte's Web, 1973.

When Charlotte the spider saves Wilbur the pig from being butchered, the two become fast friends. Animated story features the voices of Debbie Reynolds, Henry Gibson, Charles Nelson Reilly, and Paul Lynde.

previous two books, *Trumpet of the Swan* grew out of an experience in the author's own life: White's fascination with the trumpeter swans at the Philadelphia Zoo, initiated by a story in the *New York Times,* led him to tell the story of Louis, a voiceless trumpeter swan. Because he cannot speak, his human friend Sam Beaver takes Louis to school with him to learn to read and write. Thereafter, Louis carries a chalkboard and chalk with him to write out his messages. His father, who wants him to be able to communicate with other swans as well, steals a trumpet for him to play. Soon Louis's trumpet playing leads to nightclub work and to a meeting with Serena, a female swan with whom he falls in love.

The year after White published his final tale, he was awarded the National Medal for Literature. In an article for *Publishers Weekly,* he thanked the National Institute of Arts and Letters for the award. Defining the role of the writer in this article, he wrote, "I have always felt that the first duty of a writer was to ascend—to make flights, carrying others along if he could manage it. To do this takes courage.... Today, with so much of earth damaged and endangered, with so much of life dispiriting or joyless, a writer's courage can easily fail him. I feel this daily.... But despair is not good—for the writer, for anyone. Only hope can carry us aloft.... Only hope, and a certain faith.... This faith is a writer's faith, for writing itself is an act of faith, nothing else. And it must be the writer, above all others, who keeps it alive—choked with laughter, or with pain."

White continued to write poetry, sketches, articles—and coauthored *The Elements of Style,* a classic book on English grammar—before he died in 1985, after suffering from Alzheimer's disease.

Sources

Benet, R. C., article in *Saturday Review of Literature,* January 30, 1954.

Davis, Linda H., "The Man on the Swing," *New Yorker,* December 27, 1993, p. 90.

Hopkins, Lee Bennett, *More Books by More People,* Citation, 1974.

Neumeyer, Peter M., "E. B. White," *Dictionary of Literary Biography,* Volume 22: *American Writers for Children, 1900-1960,* Gale, 1983, pp. 333–350.

Nordstrom, Ursula, article in *New York Times Book Review,* May 12, 1974, pp. 8, 10.

Sale, Roger, *Fairy Tales and After: From Snow White to E. B. White,* Harvard University Press, 1978.

White, E. B., "The Faith of a Writer: Remarks by E. B. White Upon Receiving the 1971 National Medal for Literature," *Publishers Weekly,* December 6, 1971.

White, E. B., *Letters of E. B. White,* edited by Dorothy Lobrano Guth, Harper, 1976.

T. H. White

Born: May 29, 1906, Bombay, India
Died: January 17, 1964, at sea on board the S.S. *Exeter*

The author of The Once and Future King *turned from a miserable childhood to tales of King Arthur.*

Although T. H. White first became popular for his nonfiction works about the countryside of the United Kingdom, he is best known today for his fantastic fiction. In his four-part *The Once and Future King*—dubbed "one of the most brilliant fantasy novels in literature," by Lin Carter in *Imaginary Worlds*—he made the legends of King Arthur accessible for the twentieth century. A critic for the *Chicago Sunday Tribune* said of White, "He has the priceless gift of being able suddenly to look at something upside down and make you see it in the same way."

Psychopathic Parents and a Sadistic Schoolmaster

White did not have a happy childhood. His parents—a quarrelsome couple who divorced when he was 14—had married hastily, and soon found that they were completely incompatible. "There was a great deal of shooting in the air in those days," Sylvia Townsend Warner quoted White as saying in her biography *T. H. White*. "I am told that my father and mother were to be found wrestling with a pistol, one on either side of my cot, each claiming that he or she was going to shoot the other, and himself or herself, but in any case, beginning with me."

Around 1912 White was sent to his maternal grandparents' home, where he lived happily for six years. In 1920, however, his parents divorced. "This meant that my home and education collapsed about my ears," White explained in Warner's book; "and ever since I have been arming myself against disaster." In September of that year he was sent to Cheltenham College, a boys' school intended in part to train army officers, where more misery awaited him. The school enforced a military discipline, carried out by certain upperclass students called prefects; and White described his housemaster—a teacher residing in the boys' boardinghouse—as "sadistic."

Learning to Fly

The trauma of these childhood years left White with a sense of inferiority that compelled him to excel. "This is why I learn," he explained years later in Warner's biography. "Compensating for my sense of inferiority, my sense of danger, my sense of disaster ... I had to excel with my head as well as with my body and hands."

After leaving Cheltenham, White entered Queens' College, Cambridge, where life proved much happier. A favorite of his professors, he became a lifelong friend and correspondent of his tutor, L. J. Potts. When White was stricken with tuberculosis in his second year, the professors formed a convalescent fund to send him to Italy to recuperate—while there, he composed his first novel, *They Winter Abroad*. After White graduated, they helped him win an appointment as head of the Department of English at Stowe School. "It was a position of authority under an enlightened headmaster who allowed him ample rope," Warner wrote in her introduction to *The Book of Merlyn*. "He learned to fly, in order to come to terms with a fear of falling from high places, and to think rather better of the human race by meeting farm laborers at the local inn."

King Arthur and a Young Boy's Wishes Fulfilled

Soon, however, White tired of the teaching and looked for a way to leave the profession. In 1936 he compiled *England Have My Bones,* a book made up of bits and pieces of his fishing, hunting, and flying experiences; the book became a national best-seller, and provided him with enough income to abandon teaching permanently. It was while living in a gamekeeper's cottage near Stowe that White rediscovered Thomas Malory's *Morte d'Arthur,* the

Best Bets

1938 ***The Sword in the Stone***
The story—based on the medieval *Morte d'Arthur*—of Arthur's youth and training to be the future king of England. Followed by *The Witch in the Wood, The Ill-Made Knight, The Once and Future King,* and *The Candle in the Wind.*

1977 ***The Book of Merlyn: The Unpublished Conclusion to the Once and Future King***
The author returns to the story of Arthur, bringing the royal Brit back to the animals.

Arthur's Less Popular Relatives

In the years between the publication of The Ill-Made Knight *and* The Once and Future King *White completed several other books for young readers, including* Mistress Masham's Repose *and* The Master. *Although these are respected works, they never attracted the same popularity or critical attention as did* The Once and Future King.

fifteenth-century account of the legends and tales surrounding the figure of King Arthur. "Do you remember I once wrote a thesis on the *Morte d'Arthur?*" White wrote in a letter that is cited in Warner's book. "Naturally I did not read Malory when writing the thesis on him, but one night last autumn I got desperate among my books and picked him up in lack of anything else.... Anyway, I somehow started writing a book. It is not a satire. Indeed, I am afraid it is rather warm-hearted—mainly about birds and beasts. It seems impossible to determine whether it is for grown-ups or children. It is more or less a kind of wish-fulfillment of the things I should like to have happened to me when I was a boy."

White described the book to his friend as "a preface to Malory"; published in England and in America (where it was chosen as a Book-of-the-Month Club selection), *The Sword in the Stone* recounts Arthur's youth and the training he received for his future role as king.

White immediately began work on the sequel, *The Witch in the Wood* (later published as *The Queen of Air and Darkness*), which sets the stage for the tragedy of Arthur's life and death; it shows Arthur beginning to put the teachings of Merlyn, the magician, to use, as he introduces England to the rule of Law instead of oppression.

After *The Queen of Air and Darkness* came *The Ill-Made Knight,* which describes the search for the Holy Grail and how it caused Arthur's knights to scatter. While Arthur is less prominent in this story than he had been in the first two, Sir Lancelot takes center stage. Finally, *The Candle in the Wind* forms the fourth volume of *The Once and Future King.* Never published separately, it traces the years of Arthur's long defeat, ending with Arthur facing Mordred's army across Salisbury plain, stripped of everything except the hope that his dream might live on.

Merlyn, World War II, and an Overtalkative Hedgehog

Although *The Candle in the Wind* was the last book he based on Malory's work, White realized that it was not the end of his own version of the story.

As Warner cites in her introduction, on November 14, 1940, he wrote, "Pendragon can still be saved, and elevated into a superb success, by altering the last part of Book 4, and taking Arthur back to his animals." This final volume, which would feature the reappearance of Arthur's teacher, would be called *The Book of Merlyn*. "I shall have the marvelous opportunity of bringing the wheel full circle," White concluded, "and ending on an animal note like the one I began on. This will turn my completed epic into a perfect fruit, 'rounded off and bright and done.'"

But World War II played havoc with White's plan. By the time he completed *The Candle in the Wind* and *The Book of Merlyn,* England was embroiled in war and suffered from paper shortages. White's English publisher balked at the idea of producing such a long, expensive work. *The Book of Merlyn* was not published with the other four books in 1957, and did not appear until 1977—15 years after White's death—when the University of Texas Press discovered the manuscript among some of White's papers. *Merlyn,* however, disappointed some readers

Illustration from *The Sword in the Stone* by T. H. White. Illustrated by Robert Lawson.

because of the author's determination to prove his thesis. "The book," declared Warner in her introduction, "clatters on like a factory with analysis, proof and counterproof, exhortation, demonstration, explanation, historical examples, parables from nature—even the hedgehog talks too much."

The Road Back from Camelot

By the time the war ended, White was suffering from personal problems; although he had lived in Ireland for nearly six years, the locals regarded him

Reel Life

Camelot, 1967.

Academy Award-winning musical production of *The Once and Future King* stars Vanessa Redgrave, Franco Nero, and Richard Harris.

The Sword in the Stone, 1963.

Animated Disney version of the first volume of *The Once and Future King,* in which Merlin and Archimedes the Owl teach young Arthur about the ways of the world.

as a foreigner and a possible spy. Asked to leave in 1946, he settled in the Channel Islands and continued to write. The author's greatest popularity came years later, with the 1960 opening of the Broadway musical *Camelot,* starring Julie Andrews and Richard Burton. He wrote, in a passage quoted in Warner's biography, "The reviews of the musical have been mixed, but it will survive under its own power. I have pretended to everybody that I am perfectly satisfied with this new version of my book, as it is a corporate effort which involves many people, some of whom I love, and it is up to me to put a shoulder to the wheel." After *Camelot* came a U.S. lecture tour that ended tragically; on the return trip, White died at sea from an acute coronary. In tribute to the official historian of Camelot, White's epitaph calls him an author "who from a troubled heart delighted others loving and praising this life."

Sources

Canham, Erwin D., "'A Yankee's Odyssey'—Far Frontiers—'The Once and Future King': Arthur and the 'Matter of Britain,'" *Christian Science Monitor,* August 28, 1958, p. 11.

Carter, Lin, *Imaginary Worlds: The Art of Fantasy,* Ballantine Books, 1973.

Chicago Sunday Tribune, July 5, 1959.

Crane, John K. *T. H. White,* Twayne, 1974.

Obituary, *Newsweek,* January 27, 1964.

Warner, Sylvia Townsend, *T. H. White: A Biography,* Viking, 1967.

White, T. H., *The Book of Merlyn,* introduction by Sylvia Townsend Warner, University of Texas Press, 1977.

Patricia C. Wrede

Born: March 27, 1953, Chicago, Illinois

P atricia C. Wrede is one of the most innovative authors writing fantasy today. Her novels and stories, ranging from modern versions of traditional fairy tales to comic fantasy, break new ground in the genre. Much of her fantasy is set in a vaguely medieval, Celtic setting. While Wrede occasionally makes use of these settings, she expands the boundaries of fantasy to include Renaissance and Regency-era England in *Snow White and Rose Red, Sorcery and Cecelia,* and *Mairelon the Magician.* Wrede is also the author of several volumes of related works, including the Lyra cycle of novels (which take place on her own created world of the same name) and the Enchanted Forest books, which are comic variations on fairy-tale motifs.

The author of the Lyra books writes magic-filled stories set in unusual lands and alternate earths.

The Business of Writing

Wrede attended Carleton College in Minnesota, where, placing out of English classes, she never got around to taking any others. "I'd pick something that I didn't know anything at all about," the author recalled, "and I'd take a class in it to see if it turned out to be interesting. That seems to be kind of a characteristic of writers. They'll find a subject that they don't know anything about and deliberately choose to write a book about it. I know a number of writers who work that way."

Graduating in 1974, Wrede took a year off to figure out what to do next. "In some ways I have a very tidy mind," she explained. "I like to set things in order, and accounting and finance is something that appeals to that aspect of

Best Bets

1982 ***Shadow Magic***
The story of Alethia, the daughter of a noble house in the world of Lyra, an alternate earth shaped by magic and the threat of the Shadowborn, spirits who inhabit men's bodies and destroy their minds. The first book of the Lyra series, followed by *Daughter of Witches*.

1984 ***The Seven Towers***
The adventures of Amberglas, a powerful sorceress and Carachel, a wizard-king.

1990 ***Dealing with Dragons***
The first book in the Enchanted Forest series, followed by *Searching for Dragons, Calling on Dragons,* and *Talking to Dragons*.

1991 ***Mairelon the Magician***
Street waif Kim is hired to burgle a magician in an alternate England in the early 19th century.

1993 ***Talking to Dragons***
The fourth (and supposedly final) entry of Wrede's Enchanted Forest series takes place 16 years after the conclusion of *Calling on Dragons*. After 16-old Daystar ventures into the forest, old friends of Cimorene's join forces with him to rescue King Mendanbar and drive the wizards from the forest.

me. I also find money infinitely fascinating, even if it belongs to other people." Wrede obtained her M.B.A. in 1977 and, although she no longer works in finance, has continued to apply her business knowledge in her writing. "An awful lot of writers seem to overlook the fact that [writing] is a business," she explained. "It needs to be handled and treated like a business."

The Many Faces of Lyra

After college, Wrede began work on her first novel, *Shadow Magic;* it would be five years before she finished it. Published by Ace Books in 1982, *Shadow Magic* tells the story of Alethia, daughter of a noble house of the nation of Alkyra. The novel introduces the world of Lyra—an alternate earth literally shaped by magic and by the threat of the Shadowborn, spirits who inhabit men's bodies and slowly destroy their minds. Wrede's imaginary world grew out of stories she had told her siblings. "I told bedtime stories to my sisters when I was at home. I told myself bedtime stories, too, and over time I built up this world in which to tell stories." The history of Lyra dates from the end of the Wars of Binding, the conflict in which the Shadowborn were finally restrained by the power of the gifts of Alkyra. While the events of *Shadow Magic* take place more than 3,000 years after the Wars of Binding, other Lyra novels examine other eras in the world's history.

Wrede followed *Shadow Magic* with 1983's *Daughter of Witches,* another Lyra book that follows the sentencing of bondservant Ranira on suspicion of sorcery and her subsequent escape from the prison city of Drinn. "I had an extremely elaborate background world worked out for my first book," Wrede explained, "and it seemed very natural to me to continue using that background rather than try and make up another one. But I didn't want to use the same country; I wanted to explore some different aspects of this world.

One of my complaints about a great deal of fantasy and science fiction is that a planet is generally a very large place, and you don't often get a sense of that. It tends to be much more like a country than a planet; frequently there's not a lot of diversity in terms of culture and history. I wanted to make it very clear that although I'm going to write a number of books about this planet, it's big."

The Seven Towers, Wrede's third book, was published in 1984. Although not part of the Lyra cycle, the book introduces several of Wrede's most memorable characters: Among these are Amberglas, a powerful sorceress who speaks in a sort of stream-of-consciousness pattern; and Carachel, the wizard-king of Tar-Alem, whose struggle against the magic-devouring Matholych has led him to practice black magic.

Everything You Always Wanted to Know About Dragons

In 1985 *Talking to Dragons,* Wrede's fourth book, was published by Tempo Books under their Magic Quest imprint. Mixing elements of traditional fairy tales with modern wit, it tells the story of Daystar, a young man of 16 who has lived his entire life on the outskirts of the Enchanted Forest with his mother, Cimorene. One day a wizard appears, and the consequences of that wizard's arrival send Daystar into the Enchanted Forest alone with a magic sword and no idea what he's supposed to be doing.

Although *Talking to Dragons* was supposed to be just one book, Wrede found herself returning to the Enchanted Forest. "Well, one thing led to another," she recalled, "so I wrote *Dealing with Dragons.*" Wrede's sequel tells how Cimorene—refused the right to pursue her own interests (such as fencing, Latin lessons, and the like), and forced into a marriage not to her liking—flees to the lair of the dragon Kazul and becomes its princess. Eventually Cimorene becomes instrumental in securing Kazul's succession as King of the Dragons and helps defeat the Society of Wizards. When Jane Yolen—an editor at Harcourt Brace Jovanovich—read Wrede's book, she loved it; so much, in fact, that she asked Wrede to write a book to link *Dealing with Dragons* with the earlier Dragon story.

Searching for Dragons, published in 1991, came next, and prompted yet another Enchanted Forest book, *Calling on Dragons,* published in 1993. In

Cover of *Mairelon the Magician,* by Patricia Wrede.

this third book evil wizards have stolen King Mendanbar's sword, endangering the forest. Among those who set to retrieve the sword are Morwen and her two cats. "Cats are traditionally associated with witches and magic," Wrede explained. "It's something about the way those eyes sort of glow in dim light.... But if you stop and think about it, practically every animal is associated with magic. Horses are associated with magic in many ways and birds, hawks in particular, fish—the salmon of knowledge in Celtic mythology. But cats do seem to have a certain special something."

A Different History

Wrede started a very different type of fantasy writing with *Sorcery and Cecelia,* her seventh book. Written with Caroline Stevermer, a friend, *Sorcery and Cecelia* is set in an alternate England in which magic is systematized and taught in the public schools just after the Napoleonic Wars. The book consists of a series of letters written between two cousins who have become entangled in a power struggle between wizards. Her next book, *Snow White and Rose Red,* is also set in an alternate England—this time during Tudor times. A retelling of one of the stories collected in *Grimm's Fairy Tales,* it mixes in historical characters such as Dr. John Dee, mathematician and astrologer to the court of Queen Elizabeth. The title characters Blanche and Rosamund, daughters of the widow Arden, live on the edges of a forest near the river Thames that marks the boundary of the magical realm of Faerie. Because of their isolation and occasional odd behavior the widow and her daughters are suspected of using magic—a serious crime in Elizabethan England and punishable by death.

Next, Wrede set *Mairelon the Magician* in an alternate England—sometime around 1816–1817, shortly after the Napoleonic Wars ended. The main character, Kim, a street waif who has grown up in the slums, is hired to burgle the wagon of a performing magician. He turns out to be a real magician, however, and she gets caught. Since he's an eccentric fellow, though, he decides to take her under his wing rather than turn her in.

The Power of Magic

Magic, Wrede explained, is at the core of fantasy fiction. "When you're writing fantasy you're writing about magic, and magic is not something that exists in the real world, like rocks. Essentially magic is a metaphor for something else, and I've had a lot of fun sitting down with other writers and discussing what magic is a metaphor for in their books. It varies from writer to writer and frequently from book to book. Some writers consciously adapt the metaphor of magic in their books, but for me, magic tends to be a metaphor for power. Magic for me is the essence of the ability to make things happen, to get things done. When you're the C.E.O. [Chief Executive Officer] of a corporation you can say, 'I want this to happen' and people will go out and make it happen. You have the power to make it happen. And in my books the fundamental question is, if you can do anything, what do you do? If you've got the power to make stuff happen, good stuff or bad stuff, what do you do with it?"

Sources

Collings, Michael, "Pleasant Fantasy on Serious Themes" (review of *The Seven Towers*), *Fantasy Review,* September 1984, pp. 35–36.

Margolis, Sally T., review of *Dealing with Dragons, School Library Journal,* December 1990, p. 25.

Review of *Daughter of Witches, English Journal,* December 1981, p. 67.

Wrede, Patricia C., interview with Kenneth R. Shepherd for *Authors and Artists for Young Adults,* Volume 8, Gale, 1992.

Laurence Yep

Born: June 14, 1948, San Francisco, California

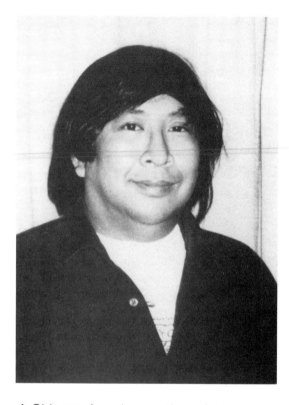

A Chinese American author whose stories about life as an outsider have garnered a Boston Globe-Horn Book Award.

Best known for his books about young people from multicultural backgrounds, Laurence Michael Yep claims that writing has aided him in his search for cultural identity. "In a sense I have no one culture to call my own," he explained, "since I exist peripherally in several. However, in my writing I can create my own."

Aliens, Identity, and the Planet Harmony

As a Chinese American boy growing up in an African American neighborhood in San Francisco, Yep found the issue of identity a difficult one. To friends in the neighborhood, Yep stated in *Literature for Today's Young Adults,* "I was the all-purpose Asian. When we played war, I was the Japanese who got killed; then, when the Korean war came along, I was a North Korean Communist." Yep attended school in San Francisco's Chinatown, but, since he did not speak Chinese like many of his peers, he felt like an outsider. And his sense of social identity became even more complicated when he began attending a predominantly white high school.

While still in high school, Yep discovered—and began writing—science fiction, publishing his first story when he was 18 years old. Five years and many stories later, he published *Sweetwater,* a science fiction novel about Tyree, a young man who belongs to a minority group of transplanted aliens on the planet Harmony. The group's struggle for survival in what is often a hostile environment evokes themes of family bonds, individual freedom, cultural traditions, and racism. Critics praised Yep's early work, commending, in particular, his beautiful writing.

Dragonwings, Bachelors, and Fung Joe's Flying Machine

Yep's second work, *Dragonwings,* was the product of six years' research into Chinese American history. Although he uncovered plenty of factual information, he found little that discussed the human experience of the Chinese immigrants in the United States. He discovered that from the 1850s to the 1930s, men from economically distressed areas of southern China came to work in the United States. Earning money to send back to their impoverished families, these men formed a bachelor society. They generally returned to China when circumstances allowed, but, in later years, Chinese women began to join their husbands to raise families in the United States.

Best Bets

1973 **Sweetwater**
The Earth-born colonists of the star Harmony face an invasion of hydras and sea dragons, and 13-year-old Tyree's blind sister has the special power to save her family's life.

1982 **Dragon of the Lost Sea**
The exiled dragon princess and her young human companion Thorn strive to restore the princess's clan to its ancestral home. Followed by *Dragon's Steel, Dragon Cauldron,* and *Dragon War.*

1991 **Dragon Cauldron**
Dragon princess Shimmer and her entourage attempt to return the Inland Sea to Shimmer's people; a sequel to *Dragon Steel.*

1992 **Dragon War**
Shimmer's quest concludes in this sequel to *Dragon Cauldron* as she calls on her scattered dragons to unite against her brother Pomfret and the Boneless King.

*P*robably the reason that much of my writing has found its way to a teenage audience is that I'm always pursuing the theme of being an outsider—an alien—and many teenagers feel they're aliens."

—Laurence Yep

The new Chinese American family society, although often set apart from white society, strove to adapt to American customs. Many, such as Yep's own family, lost touch with the rich cultural traditions of their homeland and the history of the founding Chinese bachelor society. For a third-generation Chinese American like Yep, it took a great deal of research—and a powerful imagination—to understand his ancestors' experience.

Yep came across the story of Fung Joe Guey, a Chinese American man who built and flew his own flying machine in 1909, around the same time the

Wright brothers received international attention for their early flights. Hoping to base a novel on Fung Joe Guey, Yep found only two short newspaper articles about the man and his flight; he then decided to embellish the specifics with his own idea of the *human* story behind the facts.

In order to envision Chinatown and its bachelor society of the early 1900s, Yep went through a unique process of imaginative discovery—one he compares to growing up. "I would have to project myself back into the past and see how I myself would react to others in that same situation," Yep related in *Reading Teacher*. "I had grown up as a child in the 1950s so that my sense of reality was an American one. Now I had to grow up again, but this time in the 1900s, developing a Chinese sense of reality.... I would also have to discover what relationships would be like within that bachelor society—that lonely group of men who spent most of their adult years apart from family and home."

> *There are scenes in* Child of the Owl *that will make every Chinese American child gasp with recognition. 'Hey! That happened to me. I did that. I saw that,' the young reader will say, and be glad that a writer set it down, and feel comforted, less eccentric, less alone."*
>
> —*Maxine Hong Kingston writing in* Washington Post Book World

Dragonwings is the story of eight-year-old Moon Shadow, who leaves his mother in China's Middle Kingdom to join his father in the bachelor society of turn-of-the-century San Francisco. "The story is narrated with humor and detail," Joe Stines summarized in *Dictionary of Literary Biography*, "blending Chinese folklore, myths, and legends with historical facts, such as the great San Francisco earthquake, the Chinese bachelor community of Chinatown, and the daring biplane flight of Fung Joe Guey." Other critics applauded Yep's ability to create complex characters and his sensitive portrayal of the prejudice they faced in the United States.

Life in Chinatown and Autobiography as Fiction

Yep's 1977 young people's novel, *Child of the Owl*, is set in San Francisco's Chinatown of the 1960s. In this story Casey, a young girl brought up by a gambling father and then a suburban uncle, is confused by her dual American and Chinese heritage. Having been exposed only to American ways—and therefore having no means of identifying with her Chinese background—

Casey discovers new worlds when she is sent to live with her grandmother, Paw-Paw, in Chinatown. A winner of the Boston Globe-Horn Book Award, *Child of the Owl* has been praised by critics for its vivid depiction of Chinatown and for its skillful interweaving of myth with everyday reality.

Yep's 1979 semiautobiographical novel *Sea Glass* is the story of Craig Chin, a boy whose feelings of rejection by both white and Chinese American cultures pervade his search for identity. Uprooted from San Francisco's Chinatown to the small town of Concepcion, Craig is caught between cultures. Meanwhile, Craig's father, a former athlete, pushes him to be an "All-American" boy. Nevertheless, with the help of an eccentric uncle, Craig learns to accept himself as he is. Critics commended the fully developed characters in *Sea Glass,* as well as Yep's successful portrayal of the "outsider" position.

Yep, who believes that good writing is based on what an author knows, acknowledged that *Sea Glass* hit "close to home." Writing about himself and his Chinese heritage, he said in *Literature for Today's Young Adults,* "requires me to take a razor blade and cut through my defenses. I'm bleeding when I finish and I have to take time off by writing fantasy or something only marginally related to my Chinese heritage."

Cover of *The Star Fisher,* a novel about a Chinese American girl learning how to follow her dreams, by Laurence Yep.

A Man of Many Genres

Yep has made significant contributions to several genres of fiction for young readers. During the 1980s he wrote three mysteries; of these, *The Mark Twain Murders* and *The Tom Sawyer Fires* feature as their main character nineteenth-century American writer Mark Twain as a young reporter in San Francisco. Yep also wrote a series of fantasy novels—including *Dragon of the Lost Sea, Dragon Steel, Dragon Cauldron,* and *Dragon War*—about Shimmer, a dragon princess who sets out with a young human boy to save her undersea world from the witch Civet. Reviewers applauded the characterizations, the high adventure, and the integration of Chinese myth into the structure of these fantasy novels. The early 1980s also saw the publication of Yep's *Shadow Lord,* a "Star Trek" novel, and *Kind Hearts and Gentle Monsters,* a well-received psychological novel about a romance between a very logical teenage boy and a very emotional teenage girl.

Yep's 1984 book *The Serpent's Children* is a historical novel set in nineteenth-century China. It concerns Cassia, a young girl who, along with her family, becomes part of a revolutionary brotherhood that seeks to rid China of corrupt influence in order to establish an enlightened peace. Although Cassia's family suffers greatly, she manages to fight the ruling clans of her village and to keep peace within her own family. In the book's sequel, *Mountain Light,* Cassia and her father return from a revolutionary quest in China's Middle Kingdom, meeting Squeaky Lau, the book's narrator, on their journey. Although some reviewers faulted Yep's narrative in these two historical novels, many praised Yep's insight into Chinese history and culture, his strong characterizations, and his ability to debunk stereotypes. Yep continued his cultural musings in later collections. In *The Rainbow People,* published in 1980, the author retells Chinese American folktales from the 1930s. *Tongues of Jade,* published in 1991, adds 17 folktales about spirits, farmers, sages, and fools.

Yep—who also writes for adult readers—is an avid proponent of the power of literature for young readers. "To write for [young people], he wrote in *Reading Teacher,* "one must try to see things as they do; and trying to look at the world with ... fresh, inexperienced eyes ... enables the writer to approach the world with a sense of wonder."

Sources

Burnson, Patrick, "In the Studio With Laurence Yep," *Publishers Weekly,* May 16, 1994, p. 25.

Kingston, Maxine Hong, "Middle Kingdom to Middle America," *Washington Post Book World,* May 1, 1977, pp. E1, E8.

Yep, Laurence Michael, essay in *Literature for Today's Young Adults,* edited by Alleen Pace Nilsen and Kenneth L. Donelson, 2nd edition, Scott, Foresman, 1985, pp. 426-427.

Yep, Laurence Michael, "Writing *Dragonwings,*" *Reading Teacher,* January 1977, pp. 359–363.

Jane Yolen

Born: February 11, 1939, New York, New York

Jane Yolen is a writer of fiction, poetry, and plays for young adults and children, as well as a folksinger, critic, essayist, and editor. Best known for her literary folk and fairy tales, Yolen uses elements of old stories to illustrate modern themes. Her creations range from ABC books to texts on kite flying and stories about vampires. The recipient of many awards, she has spoken all over the United States to groups of young readers at schools, libraries, and conferences.

An Economical Carrot

Although Yolen was born in New York City, she spent her childhood in a number of places. After a brief period in California, her family moved to Virginia; there, they lived with her grandparents while her father worked in England for the government during World War II. Following the war, her family returned to New York City. Yolen's father, who wrote books and radio scripts, came from a line of Russian storytellers; her mother wrote short stories and created crossword puzzles. Both parents read to Yolen as soon as she

This well-traveled author of folk and fairy tales says she transforms her own joys and sadness into "tales for the people."

was old enough to listen, and she learned to read before starting to school. In first grade she finished the semester's reading overnight and was skipped to the second grade, where teachers encouraged her in reading and writing. Writing the school musical (both lyrics and music), Yolen—who was the "lead carrot" among a cast of vegetable-children—wrote a stirring finale in which the vegetables join together to form a salad.

Best Bets

1982 ***Dragon's Blood***
Jakkin, who works as a keeper in a dragon nursery on Austar IV, secretly trains a fighting pit dragon in the hopes of winning his freedom. Followed by *Heart's Blood* and *A Sending of Dragons.*

1988 ***Werewolves: A Collection of Original Stories***
Fifteen stories about those creatures with hairy palms and fingers all the same length.

1990 ***The Dragon's Boy***
A retelling of the Arthurian legend in which Merlin disguises himself as a fire-breathing dragon.

1991 ***Vampires***
Vampires lurk where you least expect them—a good-looking teen at the mall; Aunt Hortense on her yearly visit; even the piano teacher.

1993 ***Xanadu***
A collection of fantasy stories from established genre writers as well as from contributors not normally identified with fantasy. Followed by *Xanadu 2.*

Yolen served as class secretary for three years and can still remember the names in the roll call. She also studied ballet for eight years, played fantasy games in Central Park, and loved music, especially folk songs. While in the sixth grade she scored well on a test and was accepted at Hunter, a school for gifted girls. While at Hunter she completed her eighth-grade social studies exam in rhyme, and also wrote her first two books—a nonfiction story of pirates and a 17-page novel about the pioneer west, which she calls "a masterpiece of economy."

Quaker Camps and Literary Schooling

When she was 12 and 13, Yolen attended a Quaker summer camp in Vermont, where she became interested in pacifism and storytelling. Later, between high school and college, she spent a summer working in an American Friends Service Committee work camp in Yellow Springs, Ohio. Her experiences at both camps sparked her interest in Quaker beliefs, and she eventually wrote a biography called *Friend: The Story of George Fox and the Quakers.* Introduced to Catholicism by a friend, she again broadened her religious outlook, as is reflected in many of the rituals in her fairy tales.

When Yolen was 13 her family moved to Westport, Connecticut, where she attended Staples High School. There, she was captain of the girl's basketball team, served on the newspaper staff, was a member of the jazz, Spanish, and Latin clubs, won the school's English prize, and toured and performed with the choir. She took piano lessons and learned to ride the famous Lipizzaner show horses, although her instructor, she recalls, was a man "who spoke only loud and unintelligible German."

While Yolen attended Smith College, she developed her writing skills, earning tuition money by singing folk songs and writing poetry. With stories published in magazines and newspapers, she hoped to become a journalist, but soon found that she was too emotional to conduct interviews. Nevertheless, she won the journalism award at Smith—in addition to all of the poetry prizes. After graduation, anxious to see if she could be a successful writer, Yolen worked for various publishers in New York City. In 1963 she joined Alfred A. Knopf, where she met many successful authors, and—encouraged by her peers—wrote books of her own.

Kite Stories and Faery Flags

Yolen's inspiration comes from any number of sources. The daughter of a kite enthusiast, she researched, wrote, and published a book called *World on a String: The Story of Kites* for her father. In 1962, in the garden of her parents' home, Yolen married David Stemple, a photographer and professor of computer science. Her fairy tale *The Girl Who Loved the Wind* is dedicated to him and celebrates their meeting. After ordering a Volkswagen camper, the couple sailed for Europe, where they toured for several

Cover of *Dragon's Blood* by Jane Yolen.

months. While in Scotland she saw a plaque on a castle wall that declared, "This is the Faery Flag"; intrigued, she wrote a story of the same name. Yolen and Stemple shared a number of adventures during this time: They climbed a mountain in Greece, worked in an orange grove in Israel, "mushed" on a dogsled in Alaska, and went rafting down the Colorado River.

Yolen and her husband have three children and live in a 14-room house in Hatfield, Massachusetts, with a crafts center in their large barn. As her children grew older, Yolen's writings changed, progressing from children's books to young adult and adult fiction; she resists attempts to classify her work, however. Advising young people to read and write every day, she also conducts workshops across the country for aspiring authors.

I would like to believe that there is that of faerie in each of us, a little trickle or stream that, if we could but tap it, would lead us back to the great wellspring of magic we share with every human being, every creature—and the world."

—Jane Yolen

Yolen's popularity continues to grow: Her first book for adults, *Cards of Grief,* was selected by the Science Fiction Book Club, and her series books, featuring Piggins and Commander Toad, are favorites with children. "I consider myself a poet and a storyteller," she said. "I just want to go on writing and discovering my stories for the rest of my life because I know that in my tales I make public what is private, transforming my own joy and sadness into tales for the people." Further, she said, "Knowing that ... magic has consequences, whether it is the magic of wonder, the magic of language, or the magic of challenging a waiting mind, ... it is up to the artist, the writer, the storyteller to reach out and touch that awesome magic. Touch magic—and pass it on."

Sources

Bradburn, Frances, review of *A Letter From Phoenix Farm, Wilson Library Bulletin,* May 1993, p. 94.

Norris, Sue, review of *Animal Fare, School Library Journal,* April 1994, p. 123.

Perrin, Noel, review of *Letting Swift River Go, New York Times Book Review,* November 8, 1992, p. 54.

Review of *Grandad Bill's Song, Publishers Weekly,* May 23, 1994, p. 87.

Rogers, Susan L., review of *Here There Be Dragons, School Library Journal,* January 1994, p. 117.

Roggenkamp, Karen S. H., review of *Briar Rose, English Journal,* March 1994, p. 96.

Sutton, Roger, review of *All Those Secrets of the World, New York Times Book Review,* May 19, 1991, p. 30.

Yolen, Jane, essay in *Something about the Author Autobiography Series,* Volume 4, Gale, 1987, pp. 327-346.

Yolen, Jane, interview with Jean W. Ross for *Contemporary Authors New Revision Series,* Volume 29, Gale, 1990, pp. 463-469.

Hugo Award Winners

Established in 1953, the Science Fiction Achievement Awards (Hugo Awards) honor Hugo S. Gernsback, who founded *Astounding,* the first science fiction magazine, and invented the term science fiction. Members of each years World Science Fiction Convention select winners in the following categories: novel; novella; novelette; short story; non-fiction book; dramatic presentation; professional artist; professional editor; semiprozine; fanzine; fan writer; fan artist; and original artwork. Awarded annually, the Hugo Award is a metal rocket ship, designed by Jack McKnight and Ben Jason, mounted on a base.

Best Novel

1993 *Green Mars* by Kim Stanley Robinson
1992 (tie) *Doomsday Book* by Connie Willis
         A Fire upon the Deep
            by Vernor Vinge
1991 *Barrayar* by Lois McMaster Bujold
1990 *The Vor Game* by Lois McMaster Bujold
1989 *Cyteen* by C. J. Cerryh
1987 *The Uplift War* by David Brin
1986 *Speaker for the Dead*
            by Orson Scott Card
1985 *Neuromancer* by William Gibson
1984 *Startide Rising* by David Brin
1983 *Foundation's Edge* by Isaac Asimov
1982 *Downbelow Station* by C. J. Cherryh
1981 *The Snow Queen* by Joan D. Vinge
1980 *The Fountains of Paradise*
            by Arthur C. Clarke
1979 *Dreamsnake* by Vonda McIntyre
1978 *Gateway* by Frederick Pohl
1977 *Where Late the Sweet Birds Sang*
            by Kate Wilhelm
1976 *The Forever War* by Joe Haldeman
1975 *The Dispossessed* by Ursula K. Le Guin
1974 *Rendezvous with Rama*
            by Arthur C. Clarke
1973 *The Gods Themselves* by Isaac Asimov

1972 *To Your Scattered Bodies Go*
            by Philip Jose Farmer
1971 *Ringworld* by Larry Niven
1970 *The Left Hand of Darkness*
            by Ursula K. Le Guin
1969 *Stand on Zanzibar* by John Brunner
1968 *Lord of Light* by Robert Zelazny
1967 *The Moon is a Harsh Mistress*
            by Robert Heinlein
1966 (tie) *...And Call Me Conrad*
                by Roger Zelazny
            Dune by Frank Herbert
1965 *The Wanderer* by Fritz Leiber
1964 *Way Station* by Clifford D. Simak
1963 *The Man in the High Castle*
            by Philip K. Dick
1962 *Stranger in a Strange Land*
            by Robert A. Heinlein
1961 *A Canticle for Leibowitz*
            by Walter M. Miller, Jr.
1960 *Starship Troopers* by Robert Heinlein
1959 *A Case of Conscience* by James Blish
1958 *The Big Time* by Fritz Leiber
1956 *Double Star* by Robert A. Heinlein
1955 *They'd Rather Be Right*
            by Mark Clifton and Frank Riley
1953 *The Demolished Man* by Alfred Bester

Best Novella

1993	*Down in the Bottomlands* by Harry Turtledove
1992	*Barnacle Bill the Spacer* by Lucius Shepard
1991	*Beggars in Spain* by Nancy Kress
1990	*The Hemingway Hoax* by Joe Haldeman
1989	*The Last of the Winnebagos* by Connie Willis
1988	*Eye for Eye* by Orson Scott Card
1987	*Gilgamesh in the Outback* by Robert Silverberg
1986	*Twenty-four Views of Mount Fuji, by Hokusai* by Roger Zelazny
1985	*Press Enter* by John Varley
1984	*Cascade Point* by Timothy Zahn
1983	*Souls* by Joanna Russ
1982	*The Saturn Game* by Poul Anderson
1981	*Lost Dorsai* by Gordon R. Dickson
1980	*Enemy Mine* by Barry B. Longyear
1979	*The Persistence of Vision* by John Varley
1978	*Stardance* by Spider Robinson and Jeanne Robinson
1977	(tie) *By Any Other Name* by Spider Robinson
Houston, Houston, Do You Read by James Tiptree, Jr.
1976	*Home is the Hangman* by Roger Zelazny
1975	*A Song for Lya* by George R. R. Martin
1974	*The Girl Who Was Plugged In* by James Tiptree, Jr.
1973	*The Word for World is Forest* by Ursula K. Le Guin
1972	*The Queen of Air and Darkness* by Poul Anderson
1971	*Ill Met in Lankhmar* by Fritz Leiber
1970	*Ship of Shadows* by Fritz Leiber
1969	*Nightwings* by Robert Silverberg
1968	(tie) *Riders of the Purple Wage* by Philip Jose Farmer
Weyr Search by Anne McCaffrey

Best Novelette

1993	*Georgia on My Mind* by Charles Sheffield
1992	*The Nutcracker Coup* by Janet Kagan
1991	*Gold* by Isaac Asimov
1990	*The Manamouki* by Mike Resnick
1989	*Schrodinger's Kitten* by George Alec Effinger

1988	*Buffalo Gals, Won't You Come Home Tonight* by Ursula K. Le Guin
1987	*Permafrost* by Roger Zelazny
1986	*Paladin of the Lost Hour* by Harlan Ellison
1985	*Bloodchild* by Octavia Butler
1984	*Blood Music* by Greg Bear
1983	*Fire Watch* by Connie Willis
1982	*Unicorn Variation* by Roger Zelazny
1981	*The Cloak and the Staff* by Gordon R. Dickson
1980	*Sandkings* by George R. R. Martin
1979	*Hunter's Moon* by Poul Anderson
1978	*Eyes of Amber* by Joan D. Vinge
1977	*The Bicentennial Man* by Isaac Asimov
1976	*The Borderland of Sol* by Larry Niven
1975	*Adrift Just off the Islets of Langerhans* by Harlan Ellison
1974	*The Deathbird* by Harlan Ellison
1973	*Goat Song* by Poul Anderson
1969	*The Sharing of Flesh* by Poul Anderson
1968	*Gonna Roll Them Bones* by Franz Leiber
1967	*The Last Castle* by Jack Vance
1959	*The Big Front Yard* by Clifford D. Simak
1956	*Exploration Team* by Murray Leinster
1955	*The Darfsteller* by Walter M. Miller, Jr.

Best Short Story

1993	"Death on the Nile" by Connie Willis
1992	"Even the Queen" by Connie Willis
1991	"A Walk in the Sun" by Geoffrey A. Landis
1990	"Bears Discover Fire" by Terry Bisson
1989	"Kirinyaga" by Mike Resnick
1988	"Why I Left Harry's All-Night Hamburgers" by Lawrence Watt-Evans
1987	"Tangents" by Greg Bear
1986	"Fermi and Frost" by Frederik Pohl
1985	"The Crystal Spheres" by David Brin
1984	"Speech Sounds" by Octavia Butler
1983	"Melancholy Elephants" by Spider Robinson
1982	"The Pusher" by John Varley
1981	"Grotto of the Dancing Deer" by Clifford Simak
1980	"The Way of Cross and Dragon" by George R. R. Martin
1979	"Cassandra" by C. J. Cherryh
1978	"Jeffty Is Five" by Harlan Ellison
1977	"Tricentennial" by Joe Haldeman

1976 "Catch That Zeppelin!" by Fritz Leiber
1975 "The Hole Man" by Larry Niven
1974 "The Ones Who Walk Away from Ome-
     las" by Ursula K. Le Guin
1973 (tie) "Eurema's Dam" by R. A. Lafferty
          "The Meeting" by Frederik Pohl
          and C. M. Kornbluth
1972 "Inconstant Moon" by Larry Niven
1971 "Slow Sculpture" by Theodore Sturgeon
1970 "Time Considered as a Helix of Semi-
     Precious Stones"
     by Samuel R. Delany
1969 "The Beast That Shouted Love at the
     Heart of the World"
     by Harlan Ellison
1968 "I Have No Mouth, and I Must Scream"
     by Harlan Ellison
1967 "Neutron Star" by Larry Niven
1966 "'Repent, Harlequin!' Said the Ticktock-
     man" by Harlan Ellison
1965 "Soldier, Ask Not"
     by Gordon R. Dickson
1964 "No Truce with Kings"
     by Poul Anderson
1963 "The Dragon Masters" by Jack Vance
1962 "The Hothouse series"
     by Brian W. Aldiss
1961 "The Longest Voyage"
     by Poul Anderson
1960 "Flowers for Algernon" by Daniel Keyes
1959 "Kirinyaga" by Mike Resnick
1958 "Or All the Seas With Oysters"
     by Avram Davidson
1956 "The Star" by Arthur C. Clarke
1955 "Allamagoosa" by Eric Frank Russell

Gandalf Award
(Grand Master)

1980 Ray Bradbury
1979 Ursula Le Guin
1978 Poul Anderson
1977 André Norton
1976 L. Sprague de Camp
1975 Fritz Leiber
1974 J. R. R. Tolkien

Best Dramatic Presentation

1993 *Jurassic Park*
1992 "The Inner Light," *Star Trek: The Next
     Generation*
1991 *Terminator 2*
1990 *Edward Scissorhands*
1989 *Who Framed Roger Rabbit*
1988 *The Princess Bride*
1987 *Aliens*
1986 *Back to the Future*
1985 *2010*
1984 *Return of the Jedi*
1983 *Blade Runner*
1982 *Raiders of the Lost Ark*
1981 *The Empire Strikes Back*
1980 *Alien*
1979 *Superman*
1978 *Star Wars*
1976 *A Boy and His Dog*
1975 *Young Frankenstein*
1974 *Sleeper*
1973 *Slaughterhouse-Five*
1972 *A Clockwork Orange*
1970 News coverage of Apollo XI
1969 *2001: A Space Odyssey*
1968 City on the Edge of Forever (*Star Trek*)
1967 The Menagerie (*Star Trek*)
1965 *Dr. Strangelove*
1962 *The Twilight Zone*
1961 *The Twilight Zone*
1960 *The Twilight Zone*

Nebula Award Winners

Established in 1966, the Nebula Awards recognize excellence in science fiction and fantasy writing. The Science Fiction Writers of America, which was established in 1965 by Damon Knight, select the best novel, novella, novelette, and short story published during the previous calendar year. The committee also presents the Grand Master Nebula Award to a living author in recognition of lifetime contributions to the field of science fiction. Presented no more than six times in a decade, the award is unique: Made of a block of lucite containing a rock crystal and a spiral nebula made of metallic glitter, the Nebula is handmade, and no two are alike.

Best Novel

1994 *Red Mars* by Kim Stanley Robinson
1993 *Doomsday Book* by Connie Willis
1992 *Stations of the Tide*
    by Michael Swanwick
1991 *Tehanu: The Last Book of Earthsea*
    by Ursula K. Le Guin
1990 *The Healer's War*
    by Elizabeth Ann Scarborough
1989 *Falling Free* by Lois McMaster Bujold
1988 *The Falling Woman* by Pat Murphy
1987 *Speaker for the Dead*
    by Orson Scott Card
1986 *Ender's Game* by Orson Scott Card
1985 *Neuromancer* by William Gibson
1984 *Startide Rising* by David Brin
1983 *No Enemy But Time* by Michael Bishop
1982 *The Claw of the Conciliator*
    by Gene Wolfe
1981 *Timescape* by Gregory Benford
1980 *The Fountains of Paradise*
    by Arthur C. Clarke
1979 *Dreamsnake* by Vonda N. McIntyre
1978 *Gateway* by Frederik Pohl
1977 *Man Plus* by Frederik Pohl
1976 *The Forever War* by Joe Haldeman
1975 *The Dispossessed* by Ursula K. Le Guin
1974 *Rendezvous with Rama*
    by Arthur C. Clarke
1973 *The Gods Themselves* by Isaac Asimov
1972 *A Time of Changes* by Robert Silverberg
1971 *Ringworld* by Larry Niven
1970 *The Left Hand of Darkness*
    by Ursula K. Le Guin
1969 *Rite of Passage* by Alexei Panshin
1968 *The Einstein Intersection*
    by Samuel R. Delany
1967 (tie) *Flowers for Algernon*
     by Daniel Keys
     Babel-17 by Samuel R. Delany
1966 *Dune* by Frank Herbert

Best Novella

1994 *The Night We Buried Road Dog*
    by Jack Cady
1993 *City of Truth* by James Morrow
1992 *Beggars in Spain* by Nancy Kress
1991 *The Hemingway Hoax* by Joe Haldeman
1990 *The Mountains of Mourning*
    by Lois McMaster Bujold
1989 *The Last of the Winnebagos*
    by Connie Willis
1988 *The Blind Geometer*
    by Kim Stanley Robinson
1987 *R & R* by Lucius Shepard
1986 *Sailing to Byzantium*
    by Robert Silverberg
1985 *PRESS ENTER* by John Varley

1984	*Hardfought* by Greg Bear
1983	*Another Orphan* by John Kessel
1982	*The Saturn Game* by Poul Anderson
1981	*The Unicorn Tapestry* by Suzy McKee Charnas
1980	*Enemy Mine* by Barry Longyear
1979	*The Persistence of Vision* by John Varley
1978	*Stardance* by Spider and Jeanne Robinson
1977	*Houston, Houston, Do You Read?* by James Tiptree, Jr.
1976	*Home Is the Hangman* by Roger Zelazny
1975	*Born with the Dead* by Robert Silverberg
1974	*The Death of Doctor Island* by Gene Wolfe
1973	*A Meeting with Medusa* by Arthur C. Clarke
1972	*The Missing Man* by Katherine MacLean
1971	*Ill Met in Lankhmar* by Fritz Leiber
1970	*A Boy and His Dog* by Harlan Ellison
1969	*Dragonrider* by Anne McCaffrey
1968	*Behold the Man* by Michael Moorcock
1967	*The Last Castle* by Jack Vance
1966	(tie) *The Saliva Tree* by Brian W. Aldiss
	He Who Shapes by Roger Zelazny

Best Novelette

1994	*Georgia on My Mind* by Charles Sheffield
1993	*Danny Goes to Mars* by Pamela Sargent
1992	*Guide Dog* by Mike Conner
1991	*Tower of Babylon* by Ted Chiang
1990	*At the Rialto* by Connie Willis
1989	*Schrodinger's Kitten* by George Alec Effinger
1988	*Rachel in Love* by Pat Murphy
1987	*The Girl Who Fell into the Sky* by Kate Wilhelm
1986	*Portraits of His Children* by George R. R. Martin
1985	*Bloodchild* by Octavia E. Butler
1984	*Blood Music* by Greg Bear
1983	*Fire Watch* by Connie Willis
1982	*The Quickening* by Michael Bishop
1981	*The Ugly Chickens* by Howard Waldrop
1980	*Sandkings* by George R. R. Martin
1979	*A Glow of Candles, a Unicorn's Eye* by Charles L. Grant

1978	*The Screwfly Solution* by Raccoona Sheldon
1977	*The Bicentennial Man* by Isaac Asimov
1976	*San Diego Lightfoot Sue* by Tom Reamy
1975	*If the Stars Are Gods* by Gordon Eklund and Gregory Benford
1974	*Of Mist, and Grass, and Sand* by Vonda N. McIntyre
1973	*Goat Song* by Poul Anderson
1972	*The Queen of Air and Darkness* by Poul Anderson
1971	*Slow Sculpture* by Theodore Sturgeon
1970	*Time Considered as a Helix of Semi-Precious Stones* by Samuel R. Delany
1969	*Mother to the World* by Richard Wilson
1968	*Gonna Roll the Bones* by Fritz Leiber
1967	*Call Him Lord* by Gordon R. Dickson
1966	*The Doors of His Face, the Lamps of His Mouth* by Roger Zelazny

Best Short Story

1994	"Graves" by Joe Haldeman
1993	"Even the Queen" by Connie Willis
1992	"Ma Qui" by Alan Brennert
1991	"Bears Discover Fire" by Terry Bisson
1990	"Ripples in the Dirac Sea" by Geoffrey Landis
1989	"Bible Stories for Adults, No. 17: The Deluge" by James Morrow
1988	"Forever Yours, Anna" by Kate Wilhelm
1987	"Tangents" by Greg Bear
1986	"Out of All Them Bright Stars" by Nancy Kress
1985	"Morning Child" by Gardner Dozois
1984	"The Peacemaker" by Gardner Dozois
1983	"A Letter from the Clearys" by Connie Willis
1982	"The Bone Flute" by Lisa Tuttle*
1981	"Grotto of Dancing Deer" by Clifford D. Simak
1980	"giANTS" by Edward Bryant
1979	"Stone" by Edward Bryant
1978	"Jeffty Is Five" by Harlan Ellison
1977	"A Crowd of Shadows" by Charles L. Grant
1976	"Catch the Zeppelin!" by Fritz Leiber
1975	"The Day Before the Revolution" by Ursula K. Le Guin
1974	"Love Is the Plan, the Plan Is Death" by James Tiptree, Jr.
1973	"When It Changed" by Joanna Russ

1972 "Good News from the Vatican"
      by Robert Silverberg
1971 No Award
1970 "Passengers" by Robert Silverberg
1969 "The Planners" by Kate Wilhelm
1968 "Aye, and Gomorrah"
      by Samuel R. Delany
1967 "The Secret Place"
      by Richard McKenna

Grand Master

1993 Frederik Pohl
1991 Lester del Rey
1990 No Award
1989 Ray Bradbury
1988 Alfred Bester
1987 Isaac Asimov
1986 Arthur C. Clarke
1984 André Norton
1982 Fritz Leiber
1979 L. Sprague de Camp
1977 Clifford D. Simak
1976 Jack Williamson
1975 Robert A. Heinlein

*Did not accept the award

Index

C

G

M

X

Y

Z